SCHOOL CRISIS PREVENTION AND INTERVENTION

Mary Margaret Kerr
University of Pittsburgh

Merrill
is an imprint of

PEARSON

Upper Saddle River, New Jersey
Columbus, Ohio

Library of Congress Cataloging-in-Publication Data

Kerr, Mary Margaret.
   School crisis prevention and intervention / Mary Margaret Kerr.
      p. cm.
   Includes bibliographical references and index.
   ISBN-13: 978-0-13-172176-0 (pbk.)
   ISBN-10: 0-13-172176-3 (pbk.)
   1. School crisis management—United States.   2. School violence—United States—Prevention.
   3. Schools—United States—Security measures.   I. Title.
   LB2866.5.K47 2009
   363.11'9371–dc22

                                   2007045860

Vice President and Executive Publisher: Jeffery W. Johnston
Publisher: Kevin M. Davis
Editor: Meredith D. Fossel
Editorial Assistant: Maren Vigilante
Senior Project Manager: Linda Hillis Bayma
Production Coordination: GGS Book Services/India
Design Coordinator: Diane C. Lorenzo
Cover Designer: Ali Mohrman
Cover image: SuperStock
Operations Specialist: Susan Hannahs
Director of Marketing: Quinn Perkson
Marketing Coordinator: Brian Mounts

Pearson Education Ltd.
Pearson Education Singapore Pte. Ltd.
Pearson Education Canada, Ltd.
Pearson Education—Japan

Pearson Education Australia Pty. Limited
Pearson Education North Asia Ltd.
Pearson Educación de Mexico, S.A. de C.V.
Pearson Education Malaysia Pte. Ltd.

Merrill
is an imprint of

ISBN-13: 978-0-13-172176-0
ISBN-10:   0-13-172176-3

This book is dedicated to those who respond to crises in schools.

May your darkest hours find you in the company of colleagues as courageous, compassionate, and capable as those with whom I have worked.

ABOUT THE AUTHOR

 Ken Kerr

Mary Margaret Kerr directs outreach services for the University of Pittsburgh's youth suicide and violence prevention center, STAR-Center. This state-funded center has provided crisis response services, training, and consultation to school agencies, districts and communities across Pennsylvania for over two decades. Dr. Kerr has responded to over 1,000 school-related crises, including the TWA 800 crash and school shootings. She designed the Pittsburgh Schools crisis response team model, one of the first in the country, and has consulted with many schools on crisis responding and school safety. Her team's *Postvention Standards Manual: A Guide for a School's Response in the Aftermath of a Sudden Death* is widely recognized as a model. Dr. Kerr also served as an expert panelist for the U.S. government report, *A Guide for Intermediate and Long-term Mental Health Services after School-related Violent Events.*

Certified as a school superintendent, Dr. Kerr served Pittsburgh Schools as Director of Pupil Services, before working for many years in the Los Angeles Unified School District as a federal consent decree administrator. An Associate Professor at the University of Pittsburgh, Dr. Kerr now leads the School-Based Behavioral Health training program in the Psychology in Education Department, and serves as a faculty member in Administrative and Policy Studies and Psychiatry.

Dr. Kerr holds two degrees from Duke University and completed her doctorate at American University before joining the faculty at Vanderbilt University. She is also the author (with C. Michael Nelson) of *Strategies for Addressing Behavior Problems in the Classroom*, a Pearson/Merrill textbook.

PREFACE

"It is only in our decisions that we are important."

JEAN-PAUL SARTRE

DIFFICULT DECISIONS

I decided to write this book late one night after working with a school where hit lists had surfaced three times in a couple of weeks. The latest list, found by a night custodian, named teachers as potential victims. The staff's apprehension was palpable as they tried to decide what to do next. Driving home, I recalled the conversation earlier that evening.

"This is crazy. I never expected to be dealing with death threats. So much for being a principal. I should have gone to the police academy," began the principal.

"I know what you mean. They taught us to do press releases, but I never thought they'd be about this," added the district PR specialist.

"Well, we talked about kids who didn't like science, but no one ever warned me that they might kill me over it," joked a teacher, trying to lighten the mood.

"Hey, I think I found something . . . no, never mind. It's a book, and we don't have time to order it," offered another teacher searching the Internet for advice on threat assessment.

A young counselor directed her comment to me. "Hey, you're the professor. So, tell us," she continued in an angry tone, "if we're supposed to make all these decisions, then why on earth don't they teach us this stuff in graduate school?"

"Yeah, and how about putting the information in one place?" muttered the teacher at the computer.

"There has to be a better way," I had thought to myself.

As both a professor and a crisis responder, I have watched as schools struggle to make good decisions in scary situations. Decisions are at the heart of crisis responding. In fact, the origin of the word *crisis* is the Greek word *krisis,* which means "a decision that brings correction." Yet making correct choices in a school crisis is not easy.

Several factors contribute to this dilemma. First, the number of books and articles to consider has grown exponentially. Yet few who work in schools have the time to study these texts, and fewer preparation programs even ask them to. The Internet also has inundated school personnel with information. Although many of these sources are outstanding, others dispense advice that is incorrect, inappropriate, or outdated. Some of the highly marketed resources are cost-prohibitive, while obscure but excellent government sources may remain undiscovered. Deciding what advice to follow is not so easy. School personnel, their desks littered with Internet printouts, have trouble making meaning out of so much information.

A second factor contributing to our difficult decisions is the scarcity of research in school crisis prevention and intervention. As you can imagine, researchers don't find conducive conditions immediately following a school's critical incident. Therefore, evidence-based guidance is not readily available. Fortunately, we do have excellent research from related fields to guide us. For example, mental health researchers have studied topics such as child trauma, the role of resilience in preventing posttraumatic stress disorder, and adolescent suicide contagion. However, most school personnel have limited access to such clinical publications. Moreover, clinical research may not take into consideration the real-world context—a *school* in crisis. As one school counselor lamented after reading a paper on crisis responding, "This is all great if you are running a mental health clinic, but I am in a school here."

Fourth, within the school crisis literature one finds different conceptual frameworks, depending on the backgrounds of the authors and the goals of their work. Some writers focus primarily on school safety and security, while others attend solely to the psychological needs of victims. School personnel find their questions unanswered by a single approach but lack the time to read broadly across several disciplines.

Finally, crisis responding is largely an experiential expertise, accumulated after multiple opportunities to "learn by doing." Yet schools do not experience crises regularly, so even veteran school professionals can't accumulate vast crisis experience like their counterparts in emergency response agencies do. Complicating the lack of experience is the fact that no two crises are identical. Even if school staff members had once experienced a death at school, their subsequent experiences with fatalities would require different responses. Every crisis leaves its own autograph.

In conclusion, school personnel—like those who confronted me years ago—face a myriad of resources but often possess limited personal experience, time, or expertise. Therefore, they must rely on the best practices of expert practitioners, who in turn draw their guidelines from supporting research in fields such as psychology, counseling, medicine, safety and security, and communications.

In response to these concerns, I combed through thousands of resources to assemble the best examples of expertise in one handbook. I selected content not only for one employee group but for *all* school personnel. To make the information more accessible, I have explained technical terms, illustrated unfamiliar concepts, and unpacked big ideas so you might feel comfortable exploring ideas outside your own background. To deepen experiential knowledge, real-life case studies and vignettes fill these pages. Now let's take a look at how the information is organized.

HOW THIS BOOK IS ORGANIZED

The introductory chapter outlines a definition and four-phase conceptual framework for school crisis prevention and intervention. Acronyms and graphic designs to facilitate recall of important concepts appear throughout the text. Illustrations based on actual crises help you relate new information to your previous experiences and knowledge.

Chapters 2 through 4 address the first two phases, *prevention/mitigation* and *preparation*, offering guidance on crisis policies and procedures, crisis team training, and crisis communications. Beginning with Chapter 5, you'll find a crisis-specific focus: accidents and illnesses, violence and suicide, and disasters, respectively. Within each topic, you will learn about prevention, mitigation, response, and recovery steps.

The final chapters deal with the *recovery* phase of a crisis as we turn our attention toward supporting students after traumatic events, including death. The final chapter focuses on crisis responders, teaching how to identify and prevent burnout and compassion fatigue.

FEATURES OF THE TEXT

Chapters 2 through 10 each begin with a school crisis unfolding. Each of these cases uses vivid dialogue based on an actual event to engage you. (Specific details, including the names of individuals and schools, have been changed to protect the privacy of those who were involved.) At the end of each chapter, the case concludes, allowing you to experience a simulated crisis response, from the perspective of a responder or participant. Shorter case vignettes appear throughout all chapters. Taken together, these real-life depictions allow you to experience crises vicariously and to build your own repertoire of experiences.

"Let's reflect" features in each chapter invite you to pause and consider suggestions, concepts, or questions. At the end of each chapter, discussion and application ideas provoke conversations and serve as a review.

Throughout the book, we have used forms, checklists, tables, and sample communications to enhance the text. Technical terms are boldfaced and defined in the text so you do not have to consult other sources.

School crisis prevention and intervention is a field of changes and ever-growing information. To ensure that you are aware of the very latest resources, you can go to the book's Companion Website at www.prenhall.com/kerr for links to reports, advisories, handbooks, forms, and examples.

ACKNOWLEDGMENTS

Crisis prevention and intervention is a team effort. Similarly, each of the chapters here reflects wisdom and experience from colleagues who generously taught me about school crisis prevention and intervention. I wrote this book to share their lessons with a wider audience.

Nicholas Long launched my career in crisis intervention when he took me on as a doctoral student at American University. His weekly supervision shed light on my early mistakes with youth in crisis and built my confidence in precarious situations.

I am especially indebted to my Pittsburgh Public Schools colleagues, who many years ago volunteered for our first crisis teams. Setting high standards for themselves, they were pioneering partners in an uncharted and highly stressful mission. Throughout these years, early enlightening conversations with Jake Milliones, Janet Yuhasz, Stanley Rideout, Helen Faison, Richard C. Wallace, Jr., and Bernie Manning have remained with me.

My colleagues at Services for Teens at Risk (the STAR-Center) have made themselves available to schools and our patients 24 hours a day for over 21 years. Many have sacrificed holidays and weekends to guide individuals and institutions through tragedy. Bringing calm to countless crises, they continue to strengthen and enlighten me. Highlighted in the chapter on postvention (Chapter 9) are many lessons learned from Star-Center's Director, David Brent, and our colleagues Paula McCommons, Brian McKain, Kim Poling, and Sue Wesner.

Mark Lepore, a well-respected disaster mental health specialist, answered the call with characteristic cheerfulness and competence and authored the chapter on disasters. Brian Coder, Amanda Hetrick, Marilyn Ingoldsby, Angela Mills, and Lisa Musgrave assisted Dr. Lepore in writing one of the chapter cases.

I am indebted to my colleagues who enriched this book with their stories. Jan Garda, Paula McCommons, Denise Sedlacek, Blair Stoehr, and Janet Yuhasz revisited tough memories to bring these pages to life. To protect the identities of the schools and individuals in crises, we do not cite the authors individually.

The following reviewers read and reread manuscripts, raising thoughtful questions and offering advice for which I am deeply grateful: Terry Diamanduros, Georgia Southern University; Chris McCarthy, University of Texas; P. Laurice Sommers, Los Angeles Unified School District; Susan M. Staples, Oklahoma City Public Schools; Sherry Ward, University of Central Oklahoma; and Pamela Wilson, Portland Public School District. I hope that you recognize your considerable influence on this work.

A highly skilled editorial team shepherded the process from prospectus to publication. Kevin Davis, the first editor to endorse this project, brought creativity and sensibility to the project. Without his advocacy, these words would still be in my head. Meredith Sarver Fossel, who took over the editorship, moved in and out of my inbox and voice mail with impeccable timing, cheerfully answering questions and offering savvy advice. Linda Bayma and Kathy Burk, with whom I have had the pleasure of working for several years, encouraged me with their optimism and practical suggestions. Maren Vigilante joined the project in its final stages but responded to my questions as a veteran. Completing an arduous process, sharp-eyed Babitha Balan and Anne Lesser inspected every line of the manuscript and made many fine suggestions. Jamey Joy Covaleski patiently tracked down permissions, edited text and tables, and corrected mistakes. This marks our seventh book together, and I continue to marvel at her organizational and editing skills.

For two years, my loyal friends have asked, "How's the book?" They have put up with forgotten birthdays, absentminded tennis games, petulant phone calls, and late-night e-mails about subject matter that never interested them in the first place. I wish that I could name all of you here. Please know that I am in your debt.

My family has played a major role in my development as a crisis specialist. Despite extraordinary tragedies, my mother, Alexa Kerr, has moved forward always, illustrating remarkable resilience. Tommy Kerr, my brother, followed in my mother's footsteps as a writer and artist. Tommy's creative and kind communications always have reassured me. Kenneth Kerr, my brother, followed in my father's footsteps as an emergency medical responder. Years ago, Kenneth introduced me to emergency response protocols; he has helped me think through many emergencies ever since.

My husband, Bruce Perrone, learned early from his parents to put his needs second to those whose medical crises intruded on their family life. Bruce has been unquestioning in his support of my career, despite its interruptions of his own business and of our life together. I can do this work because of him.

Our children, Rob and Cristina Perrone, have had it rough. They have endured countless personal safety lectures, complied with unpopular precautions, and read more first-aid brochures than any child should have to. For their entire lives, they have shared me with conference calls, pagers, cell phones, and crises. Now young adults, they continue to astonish me with their compassion, gratitude, and many talents.

Finally, I want to thank you, the readers. I sincerely hope this book helps you with your decisions. Nothing could be a more fitting tribute to all who have helped me.

Discover the Companion Website Accompanying This Book

THE MERRILL COMPANION WEBSITE: A VIRTUAL LEARNING ENVIRONMENT

Technology is a constantly growing and changing aspect of our field that is creating a need for content and resources. To address this emerging need, Merrill has developed an online learning environment for students and professors alike—Companion Websites—to support our textbooks.

In creating a Companion Website, our goal is to build on and enhance what the textbook already offers. For this reason, the content for each user-friendly website is organized by chapter and provides the professor and student with a variety of meaningful resources.

Common Companion Website features for students include:

- **Chapter Objectives**—outline key concepts from the text.
- **Interactive Self-quizzes**—complete with hints and automatic grading that provide immediate feedback for students. After students submit their answers for the interactive self-quizzes, the Companion Website **Results Reporter** computes a percentage grade, provides a graphic representation of how many questions were answered correctly and incorrectly, and gives a question-by-question analysis of the quiz. Students are given the option to send their quiz to up to four email addresses (professor, teaching assistant, study partner, etc.).
- **Essay Questions**—these questions allow students to respond to themes and objectives of each chapter by applying what they have learned to real classroom situations.
- **Web Destinations**—links to www sites that relate to chapter content.

To take advantage of the many available resources, please visit the *School Crisis Prevention and Intervention* Companion Website at

www.prenhall.com/kerr

BRIEF CONTENTS

CONTENTS

CHAPTER 1

An Overview of Crisis Prevention and Intervention

If you are reading this, you have a role in school crisis prevention and intervention. Whether you are a student preparing to go into the field, or a crisis specialist, school employee, student, parent, or community member, you make a difference in how your local school will prevent or respond to its next crisis. As a member of a school community, you bring a perspective to the crisis—a perspective born out of your prior experience, your professional expertise, and your talents. In fact, the individuals in a school community often determine whether a situation becomes a crisis or merely a manageable emergency.

To guide your thinking about school crises, let's begin with a definition of school crisis. Then we'll use a model for crisis prevention and intervention to frame your reading through the remaining chapters. A conceptual framework is important because it delineates the planning assumptions on which your crisis work is based. As one frustrated school psychologist observed:

> I've worked in four different schools, and each one had a different view on what constitutes a crisis or a crisis response. In my first school, the principal refused to call in a team unless the Federal Emergency Management Agency ordered it! Her mantra was "Nothing is going to interfere with instruction in my school." Then I worked in a school where we called crisis codes for everything—I couldn't get any work done. That school was constantly disrupted. My third school embraced crisis responding, but we did nothing to prevent the crises in the first place—our whole emphasis was on counseling *after* the event. Now get this—this year I'm in a school where the principal disdains "that touchy-feely psychological stuff" and focuses solely on security. He actually assigned me to metal detector duty. Give me a break!

Although our field has no generally accepted definition for a school crisis, we can draw from work in related disciplines. Several authors have defined crises in general and school crises in particular (Johnson & Stephens, 2002; Slaikeu, 1990). Three key features of their definitions typically overlap: (1) an unexpected disruption to a school's normal routines, (2) resulting psychological upset, and (3) the need for actions that exceed a school's customary responses.

Some catastrophes would create a crisis in *any* school because the impact would overwhelm even the most capable staffs. Yet, other incidents might never even take place because of skillful prevention. Still other potential tragedies might be mitigated by collaboration between skilled professionals and community members. Recognizing that the factors constituting a crisis will differ among schools, we nevertheless offer the following definition for use in this text:

> A school crisis is a temporary event or condition that affects a school, causing individuals to experience fear, helplessness, shock, and/or horror. A school crisis requires extraordinary actions to restore a sense of psychological and physical security. The origin of the crisis need not be school-based; outside incidents and conditions also can create a crisis for a school.

This definition includes the term *condition* to highlight the possibility that a crisis may extend over time (such as in the case of unresolved, repeated bomb threats or a natural disaster with long-term effects). We emphasize the continuing nature of an initial incident because the needs of individuals within a school often extend beyond the initial response to crisis (Dreshman, Crabb, & Tarasevich, 2001; Herman, 1997). As if a rip in the fabric of one's school's culture, these damages require time and attention to mend. We incorporate *individual reactions*—fear, helplessness, shock, and/or horror—to capture the essential elements of a traumatic event as defined in the mental health literature (Bryant & Harvey, 2000) and to serve as a reminder of the personal toll on children, adolescents, and adults. In addition, we distinguish the *additional efforts* required to address a schoolwide crisis. These endeavors include the development of policies, procedures, and communication plans, and team preparation—each a subject of subsequent chapters, and each an important element of a model of crisis prevention and intervention. Finally, we include events in the *community* because they can have a devastating impact on a school.

Let's reflect . . .

Consider the definition for school crisis. Based on your experience, how do you think schools vary in their "normal routines," in their "customary responses," and in their readiness for unexpected events in the community? What variables influence a school's customary response and readiness?

A MODEL FOR SCHOOL CRISIS PREVENTION AND INTERVENTION

Leaders in the school crisis field recognize the need for conceptual frameworks that cross disciplinary and geographical boundaries (Jimerson, Brock, & Pletcher, 2005). In response, the U.S. Department of Education convened a panel of experts who identified four interconnected phases:

1. **Mitigation/Prevention** addresses what schools and districts can do to reduce or eliminate risk to life and property.
2. **Preparedness** focuses on the process of planning for the worst-case scenario.
3. **Response** is devoted to the steps to take during a crisis, including the communications we convey.
4. **Recovery** deals with restoring the learning and teaching environment after a crisis. (U.S. Department of Education, 2003, pp. 1-6 and 1-7)

We concur that these are the essential phases identified in the school crisis literature. Moreover, to facilitate your understanding of each phase, we have "unpacked" these four big ideas into smaller practical segments. Figure 1.1 displays a model that incorporates the federal model's four phases with annotations to help you understand the essential steps in implementation.

In the following pages, we delineate the general steps within each of the four major phases identified by the federal government. As we explain each phase, we suggest questions to be answered, sources of help and information, challenges, and illustrations.

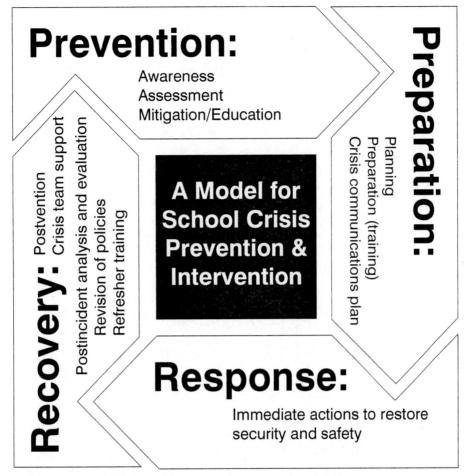

Figure 1.1
A Model for School Crisis Prevention and Intervention.

MITIGATION/PREVENTION

Recall that the goal of this phase is to reduce or eliminate the risk to life and property. This phase begins with some inkling that there could be a problem. *Awareness* is a perpetual and multidimensional phase that may be characterized as an initial gathering and filtering of information by many individuals in the school community. As we take the sometime small first steps toward crisis mitigation and prevention, we ask these questions:

1. What are we hearing and seeing?
2. What is missing? What are we not hearing and seeing?
3. What do we know?
4. Where can we get more information?

Good assessment never stops. Rather, essential data emerge as the result of (1) information and (2) intelligence garnered through (3) supervision and (4) surveillance. As Figure 1.2 depicts, we use the acronym **ISIS** to remember these four cornerstones of safety: **IS It Safe?**

Information is the knowledge we have about our school, community, students, and visitors. We gain this information through the routine *supervision* we do during the school day. Hallway chats with students as well as formal student advisory council meetings are two examples of information gathering. As you will learn in Chapter 7, good supervision is a major predictor of school safety. *Intelligence* refers to secretive information that others do not want us to learn. Through surveillance, we gather intelligence about school safety risks. Surveillance may include seeing, hearing, or even smelling: We overhear conversations in

ISIS: Is It Safe ?

Information	**Intelligence**
Information through supervision	Intelligence through surveillance
Supervision	**Surveillance**

Figure 1.2
Is It Safe? Acronym.

the corridors, study students' messages posted on popular websites, smell smoke in a rest room, or spot graffiti.

Information and intelligence gathering extends from the "micro" local school level to the "macro" level. For example, a bus driver might overhear kids talking about an incident involving weekend violence and plans for retribution, while a school psychologist may attend a national conference and return with information about a new choking game that youth are playing. Even hearsay can be important as the beginning of a path to fully understanding an emerging problem.

Not all of the information or intelligence will be accurate or useful, so the challenge is to filter and use the information responsibly. This phase requires many skills. We must be able to avoid biases, listen to diverse voices and points of view, remain open minded, sift through information in a timely way, identify which sources are credible, summarize findings, and communicate information so others might use it. Interagency councils at the district level and school-based safety committees are two vehicles for implementing these steps. In addition, professional associations and district consortia often have confidential e-mail exchanges where members can post questions for colleagues to answer.

Assessment of risk begins as soon as we have reliable information about a potential risk. At this stage we ask,

1. Who or what is at risk?
2. What are the risk factors and warning signs?
3. How much time do we have?
4. Is the risk immediate?
5. How extensive or serious is the risk/danger?

During this phase, we rely on an individual or a group to follow through with an assessment of the risk. The nature of the assessment depends on the problem and the time available. It might be very straightforward and quick (e.g., a phone call to verify an impending flood), an annual assessment (e.g., an annual facilities inspection), or an ongoing process of surveillance to follow up on "leads" (e.g., rumors of a problem at the prom). Information to inform this process may come from national, regional, or state sources. The data may be collected locally through checklists, screenings, audits, walk-throughs, observations, and analyses of past incidents.

The challenges at this phase include the need to be thorough and accurate while being timely. Research on workplace violence tells us that it is important to empower employees in this process so they feel they are part of the solution (National Institute for Occupational Safety and Health, 2002). Yet confidentiality and discretion are important if we do not want to violate individuals' rights, to raise undue anxiety, or to cause alarm in the school community.

Continuing the earlier example, let's say that the bus driver's information about neighborhood violence is confirmed by the local police later that morning. Following up, the assistant principal asks all staff to listen for conversations about the incident as they supervise transitions, lunch, arrival, and dismissal in the school. In other words, the staff is using surveillance to gather more intelligence. Counselors also meet with students from the affected neighborhood to get a sense of what they experienced. The attendance office checks to see if any students from the neighborhood are absent. By early afternoon, a lunch aide reports that three students were talking about the incident and hinted that something was going to happen the next day. Counselors also confirm from their conversations that the two absent students have been threatened. The crisis is imminent, so you must simultaneously try to mediate the dispute while readying your school for the possibility of a fight. As is often the case, you simultaneously try crisis mitigation/prevention strategies (such as mediation and involvement of community leaders and parents) while readying yourself for the worst-case scenario.

Sometimes the awareness and assessment data do not indicate an immediate problem but suggest that *mitigation/prevention/education* should take place. The questions we answer at this phase are:

1. What can we do to keep this from happening here?
2. How can we reduce the harm or disruption to our school and community?

Let's revisit the example of the psychologist who returned from a conference with information about a choking game. Conversations with students, local medical experts, and police might indicate that the game is not well known locally, thereby giving the school community time to engage in prevention/education with parents and students. (See Chapter 6 for a case study about this lethal pastime.)

Like awareness and assessment, mitigation/prevention and education take place at both "macro" and "micro" levels. Media attention often spotlights major prevention efforts, but changes in minor daily routines can be just as beneficial. For example, a school district in collaboration with other agencies may host community-wide forums on violence and injury prevention but also engage in small but meaningful actions such as inspecting incoming packages (for anthrax) or sending e-mails advising cafeteria staff not to allow students to move foldable tables (see Chapter 6).

To inform our mitigation/prevention/education efforts, we turn to lessons learned from past experiences, experts and their research, government agencies, and best practices in various fields. The challenges of this phase are to find credible information sources, to locate or create user-friendly awareness materials for several audiences, and to do so while balancing other responsibilities.

Chapter 2 aids your general awareness, assessment, and mitigation/prevention/education efforts, beginning with an examination of your school's history of critical incidents. Chapters 6 through 8 offer specific strategies for the assessment and prevention of accidents and injuries, of school violence, and of community-level crises and disasters.

CRISIS PREPARATION

The goal of crisis preparation as espoused by the U.S. Department of Education model is to prepare for the "worst-case" scenario. The "what if" questions we ask at this phase are:

1. Do we have the authority to respond to this crisis?
2. What are we allowed or directed to do?
3. How would we mobilize internal and external resources?
4. How would we work with emergency responders, including the police?
5. How would we respond to restore safety and security?
6. What would we communicate internally within the school district and externally to others?
7. What would our students, parents, and employees need from us?

Preparation:

Planning
Preparation (training)
Crisis communications plan

We break this phase into three segments: *crisis planning, crisis preparation,* and *crisis communications planning.* Crisis planning must be linked back to prevention. As new risks are verified, we need revisions in policies and procedures as well as in crisis preparation (team refreshers and school drills) and in crisis communications (such as sample letters, school site plans, contact information lists, and handouts).

To illustrate this phase, we have selected an excerpt from a 2003 memorandum from the U.S. Department of Homeland Security reported in a North Dakota Department of Health Alert. Notice in reading these recommendations that some are at the macro level, whereas others involve small changes in normal routines. Ask yourself how the information might have come to the attention of a school district and how the district might have revised its policies and/or procedures (crisis planning), prepared its personnel and crisis team (crisis preparation), and drafted its crisis communications plan.

Examples of soft targets with uncontrolled access include hospitals, malls, restaurants and schools. All available antiterrorism measures should be rigorously reexamined—to include: physical security perimeters, personnel awareness and reporting methods. The following are the recommended general protective measures that apply:

- Encourage personnel to take notice and report unattended packages, devices, briefcases or other unusual materials immediately; inform them not to handle or attempt to move any such object, especially near air intakes.
- Encourage personnel to know emergency exits and stairwells and the locations of rally points to ensure the safe egress of all employees.
- Increase the number of visible security personnel wherever possible.
- Institute/increase vehicle, foot, and roving security patrols varying in size, timing, and routes.
- Enclosed spaces, such as rest rooms, should be inspected.
- Delivery to concessions in stadiums, arenas, and conference centers should be inspected prior to scheduled events.
- Implement random security guard shift changes.
- Limit the number of access points and strictly enforce access control procedures.
- Deploy visible security cameras and motion sensors.
- Arrange for law enforcement vehicles to be parked randomly near entrances and exits.
- Review current contingency plans and, if not already in place, develop and implement procedures for receiving and acting on threat information; alert notification procedures; terrorist incident response procedures; evacuation procedures; bomb threat

procedures; hostage and barricade procedures; chemical, biological, radiological, and nuclear (CBRN) procedures; consequence and crisis management procedures; accountability procedures; and media procedures.

- Conduct internal training exercises and invite local emergency responders (fire, rescue, medical, and bomb squads) to participate in joint exercises. (North Dakota Department of Health Alert Network, 2003)

Obstacles to crisis preparation include being unaware of the risk, denial, or refusal to act on information we receive. For example, a school may not be on a distribution list for such alerts, leaders may not have taken the threat seriously, or they may have lacked the collaborative infrastructure to prepare personnel and plans. Perhaps the greatest challenge of crisis preparation is finding the time to engage in such collaborative planning, training, and documentation.

In summary, crisis preparation depends on thoughtful leadership, identification of district and community expertise, interagency coordination, good policies and procedures, well-rehearsed protocols, and an effective crisis communications plan (CCP). Districts must address the concerns of the media in their local communities as well. The next three chapters focus on crisis planning, preparation, and communications, respectively. These elements are fundamental to an effective crisis response, the third major phase.

CRISIS RESPONSE

Crisis response answers the dreaded question, "Now what?"

Response:
Immediate actions to restore security and safety

The goals of crisis response are to restore physical and psychological safety to those affected. For schools, this also necessitates the rapid and safe reunification of children with their parents or guardians. We rely in this phase on emergency response protocols that use specific communications (such as codes) to direct our actions and whereabouts. Because we draw on medical emergency responders for much of what we do during school crisis response, you may encounter terms that are unfamiliar. For example, many people use the term **triage** to refer to setting priorities in a crisis. This term originates from the French word for "sort" and is used in medical settings to describe a process by which patients are classified according to their injuries, likelihood of survival, and priority for treatment. We may also rely on mnemonic devices to help us remember what to do, as illustrated in Figure 1.3.

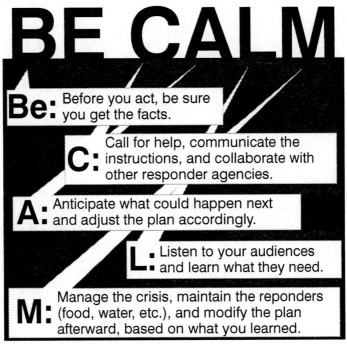

Figure 1.3
Be CALM Acronym.

In Chapter 2 we expand on the acronym **Be CALM**, but as a general reminder:

- **B**efore you act, **be** sure you get the facts.
- **C**all for help, **c**ommunicate the instructions, and **c**ollaborate with other responder agencies.
- **A**nticipate what could happen next and **a**djust the plan accordingly.
- **L**isten to your audiences and **l**earn what they need. Working with the media is essential.
- **M**anage the crisis, **m**aintain the responders (food, water, etc.), and **m**odify the plan afterward, based on what you learned.

In addition to learning some new terminology and protocols, the challenges of this phase, often unique to each crisis, are many. Making simultaneous rapid decisions under highly stressful conditions with others you may not know is never ideal. Therefore, schools rely on standardized decision-making and communications protocols and checklists to "take the guesswork" out of our decisions to the extent possible. These systems also hasten decisions and communications by eliminating interpretations and discussions.

To illustrate this crisis response phase, we have selected a protocol for lockdown, evacuation, or relocation decisions, shown in Figure 1.4. (When used in the field, the diamond-shaped boxes that indicate critical decisions are printed in red to speed one's review of the steps.) Ask yourself some questions as you study the flowchart. In what ways might this

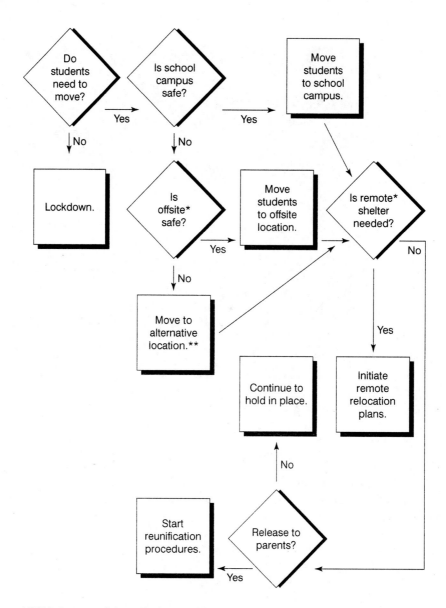

*"Offsite" means off the school campus but in vicinity.
 "Remote" means a location further from the school than offsite location.
**Be sure to prepare primary and secondary evacuation routes in advance.

Adapted from the San Diego School District.

Figure 1.4
Lockdown, Evacuation, or Relocation Decisions.

Source: From *Practical Information on Crisis Planning: A Guide for Schools and Communities*, 2003,
Washington, DC: U.S. Department of Education, Office of Safe and Drug-Free Schools.

visual representation help us in a crisis? Do you agree with the key decisions? What policies, procedures, and interagency agreements would underlie the successful implementation of this process? How would you prepare a crisis team to lead this process? How would you prepare students and staff?

Including all of the crisis response protocols one might need is not practical in a textbook, but we have provided you with examples and good sources for response plans in Chapters 6 through 9. After all, each school needs to think about how it should adapt recommended protocols because every school has its own school and community characteristics, culture, traditions, individuals, and community resources to consider.

RECOVERY

In comparison with crisis response, *recovery* is a more reflective time, as we address the psychological and other long-term needs of those who have survived the crisis. When a death has occurred, we may refer to this phase as *postvention*. We should ask ourselves the following questions during the first phase of recovery:

1. How can we restore the school facility (if damaged)?
2. How can we help people recover a sense of psychological safety while respecting their need to grieve?
3. How do we address reminders and anniversaries of the crisis?

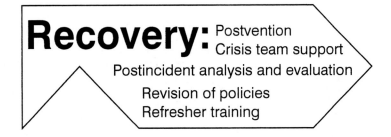

During this phase, teachers, school psychologists, counselors, social workers, nurses, and other mental health professionals play a key role in reassuring the members of the school community. Families are essential in helping children recover from a traumatic experience, but they often need our guidance. Parent meetings sometimes take place during this phase as families struggle with their feelings of fear, anger, loss, anxiety, and sadness.

Memorials are planned during the recovery phase as individuals seek ways to remember those lost. Once again we find value in large-scale macro responses as well as small heartfelt gestures. For example, a community may remember those lost in a school disaster through memorial services with hundreds in attendance, while a local yearbook photographer may spend quiet hours alone, retrieving and printing photographs of the deceased to share with their families. Recovery is an inclusive phase, where many lay individuals will make important and long-lasting contributions to the healing of their school community. As a popular saying goes, "No one can do everything, but everyone can do something."

To illustrate this phase, we have selected a letter to a school from a crisis specialist, following a tragedy in which a young child was killed in a fire. The letter guides the teachers of his surviving sibling, as they consider reminders of the fire and seek ways to support Latif through his grief.

> Enclosed are copies of my school work review pages for Latif this week. Please feel free to share them with the faculty. The only sensitive topic I noticed was the spelling list of holidays. His little brother Kosey's death was on New Year's Eve, so perhaps you could remove *New Year's Day* from the list.
>
> Latif will meet with his therapist today at 4 P.M. His baseball home opener is Saturday, and they will make a plan about how he can handle the parade with the fire trucks.
>
> Just so you know the local amusement park is a sensitive subject, as the family had a great time there last summer with Kosey. I have noticed that the posters are out in the schools now. Latif may be startled by these. Perhaps someone could talk with him and ask him what would help.
>
> I drove to the Dardanes' home with the most wonderful confidence in the school, after our meeting. You all have really touched me with your concern and care for this dear boy and his family. Thank you so very much for your leadership.

As you read through these suggestions, ask yourself these questions. What might be the reminders of a death by fire? By flooding? By violence? How could a school support teachers who are caring for a child in mourning? These questions are addressed in Chapters 5 and 9.

When time allows, crisis teams must face some hard questions and try to find honest answers to them:

1. What happened?
2. How and why did it happen?
3. Was the incident preventable?
4. Was the response effective?
5. How can we improve?
6. What lessons can we share?

These deliberations comprise the *evaluation* phase of recovery, a phase often overlooked in our haste to return to our normal duties after the disruption of a crisis. Here's one approach to evaluation:

> [T]o assign a team member to the role of evaluator, whose main responsibilities include conducting drills and readiness checks, designing questionnaires and structured interviews, and collecting data on crisis team performance and outcome. They advise that the evaluator should have a budget and be familiar with program and practice evaluation methods. Other options would be to partner with a local university or social services agency that could provide consultants for research projects. The evaluator can also be responsible for the demobilization and debriefing with crisis team members after a crisis response.[1]

---

[1]From *Preparing for Crises in the Schools: A Manual for Building School Crisis Response Teams* by S. E. Brock, J. Sandoval, and S. Lewis, 2001, New York: Wiley, described in "Crisis Intervention and Crisis Team Models in Schools," by K. S. Knox and A. R. Roberts, 2005, *Children and Schools, 27* (2), p. 96. Copyright 2005 by the National Association of Social Workers, Inc. Reprinted with permission.

Throughout the recovery phase, we must be attentive to *crisis team support* to reduce the risk of secondary stress reactions, all too common consequences of serving on a crisis team. Team members do not have to experience directly a crisis to suffer its psychological consequences. Chapter 10 describes the risk factors and warning signs for what we call vicarious traumatization. This chapter also offers suggestions for helping crisis responders to be resilient. After all, to serve schools during their darkest moments can be transformational. As one colleague put it, "A candle shines brightest in the darkness."

SUMMARY

To help you understand the vast body of information available here and in other texts, we have elaborated on the four-stage school crisis model proffered by the U.S. Department of Education. This model emphasizes prevention and preparation. Ongoing assessment begins when we have information and intelligence gathered through supervision and surveillance (ISIS). Beginning with often subtle clues that something could go wrong, schools must then assess risk using formal measures such as threat assessment, interviews, facilities checklists, or observations. These data contribute to the development of crisis policies and procedures, incorporating the step by step within a crisis plan and a crisis communications plan. Teams learn about these procedures in the preparation phase. All of the aforementioned activities should precede a crisis response.

The crisis response phase requires a team to problem-solve based on its grasp of the situation. We help teams recall what to do through the acronym Be CALM. This acronym captures the general functions that support the more specific "in the moment" protocol. Once the initial crisis period has passed, we move to the recovery phases, in which we provide supports to the witnesses and victims to prevent long-term psychological impairment and to restore school routines. Finally, we evaluate the incident and the response, using this analysis to modify our original assessment and plan in an interconnected flow of actions.

DISCUSSION AND APPLICATION IDEAS

1. Do an Internet search for definitions of crisis and then develop your own definition.
2. Make a list of questions that you'd like to answer as you read this textbook. If you have trouble finding the answer, feel free to e-mail the author at mmkerr@pitt.edu.
3. Get a copy of the school crisis plan for your school or district and analyze whether it accounts for all of the phases described in this chapter.
4. Using articles in local or online newspapers, gather illustrations for these crisis model phases: preparation (including information that suggests a potential problem), planning, response, and recovery.

   • How well did the schools prepare, in your estimation?
   • What types of responses did they implement?
   • How did they support schools and families during recovery?

REFERENCES

Brock, S. E., Sandoval, J., & Lewis, S. (2001). *Preparing for crises in the schools: A manual for building school crisis response teams.* New York: Wiley.

Bryant, R. A., & Harvey, A. G. (2000). *Acute stress disorder: A handbook of theory, assessment, and treatment.* Washington, DC: American Psychological Association.

Dreshman, J. L., Crabb, C. L., & Tarasevich, S. (2001). *Caring in times of crisis: A crisis management/postvention manual for administrators, student assistance teams, and other school personnel.* Chapin, SC: YouthLight.

Herman, J. L. (1997). *Trauma and recovery.* New York: Basic Books.

Jimerson, S., Brock, S., & Pletcher, S. (2005). An integrated model of school crisis preparedness and intervention: A shared foundation to facilitate international crisis intervention. *School Psychology International, 26* (3), 275–296.

Johnson, K., & Stephens, R. D. (2002). *School crisis management: A hands-on-guide to training crisis response teams.* Alameda, CA: Hunter House.

Knox, K. S., & Roberts, A. R. (2005). Crisis intervention and crisis team models in schools. *Children and Schools, 27* (2), 93–100.

National Institute for Occupational Safety and Health. (2002). *Working with stress* (DHHS [NIOSH] publication No. 2003–114d). Washington, DC: U.S. Department of Health and Human Services.

North Dakota Department of Health Alert Network. (2003, September 22). *Health update: Homeland security chemical threat information.* Retrieved December 28, 2006, from http://www.keystosaferschools.com/Reports/HealthAlertAdvisory20030922.pdf

Slaikeu, K. A. (1990). *Crisis intervention: A handbook for practice and research* (2nd ed.). Boston, MA: Allyn & Bacon.

U.S. Department of Education, Office of Safe and Drug-Free Schools. (2003). *Practical information on crisis planning: A guide for schools and communities.* Retrieved June 25, 2006, from http://www.ed.gov/admins/lead/safety/crisisplanning.pdf

CRISIS PLANNING

CASE STUDY

As principal of an elementary school, I often work for a few hours after the students leave. That day, however, I had made plans to leave school at 3 P.M. to prepare for my daughter's birthday party. At home, 45 minutes' drive from school, I was setting the table when the phone rang. The head of transportation for our district was shouting over the phone.

"Connie, it's Dave from transportation. Look, there has been a shooting! And the kids on your school bus witnessed it. They were at a stoplight on the corner of Foxworth and Senesta. The police are on the way. We don't know if the guy is alive. The shooter got away but he saw the kids. How soon can you get here? The bus driver is trying to remain calm, but she's scared. The kids are hysterical. Wait! The driver is radioing in. I have to take that call. Call me back."

My thoughts raced chaotically. I couldn't think. We have a district crisis policy and lots of procedures, but they didn't cover this situation.

"Now calm down, Connie. Just CALM DOWN," I repeated over and over, trying to pull myself together to make a plan. I grabbed my keys and dashed for the car, before I realized that during rush hour it would take me over an hour to reach the school. Then it hit me that I didn't even know which bus was involved or where it was.

"What streets did he say? Foxworth? Which bus goes by that corner?" As I tried to picture the location of the incident, I ran back into the house to find the bus lists I had brought home. At least that would tell me which kids were on the bus. I sorted through the papers on my desk. With the other hand, I grabbed the phone and called the school. No answer.

Let's reflect . . .

Imagine you are the principal. What information do you need now? What's your immediate goal? What are the children's needs? Are they in immediate danger? What about the bus driver? Consider the parents whose kids are not arriving home on time. What do they need from you?

THE GOALS OF CRISIS PLANNING

In this chapter we explore how to develop effective policies and plans for preventing and responding to crises. This is the paperwork aspect of school crisis preparation. The specific goals of crisis planning are to create policies and procedures that:

- **Reestablish the safety and welfare of employees, students, and others affected by the incident.** An effective plan includes strategies to address short- and long-term health needs of students, faculty, and families (School Violence Resource Center [SVRC] Fact Sheet, 2004).

- **Reunite students with their families as soon as it is safe and appropriate to do so.** Because of their strong emotions and sense of urgency, parents panicked about their children's welfare can complicate a crisis. On the morning of September 11, 2001, for example, many schools faced throngs of parents who insisted on going directly into classrooms to get their children. Other parents jammed the telephone lines, preventing crucial calls from coming into the school office. This behavior is understandable and predictable, so a plan must address how schools should communicate with parents and facilitate their safe reunification with their children.
- **Keep the school and community reasonably well informed.** People in crisis become more upset when they feel they are not getting the facts. The community at large will seek its information about the crisis through any means, including school contacts, radio, television, and print media, and the grapevine. A key component of the crisis plan is to outline how, when, and by whom information will be communicated within and outside the school. The plan should establish what information would be shared with staff, students, families, and the community and who would be responsible for conveying this information (U.S. Department of Education, 2003).
- **Return the school to its normal routines.** One of the primary goals of a crisis plan is to help those affected by a crisis to return to precrisis functioning (Lerner, Lindell, & Volpe, 1999). The timetable for this goal will depend on the extent and severity of the crisis. Sometimes in a crisis, we are lured into "premature closure" of the situation, convincing ourselves and others that things are back to normal when they are not.
- **Provide psychological and physical supports for those affected by the crisis.** Throughout this text, we offer advice on how to support those in crisis.
- **Identify and refer those at risk for unhealthy behaviors and reactions.** Screening those affected by the event is essential if we want to provide them support. This process requires us to develop policies and procedures that enable collaborations with providers in the community.
- **Eliminate, reduce, or address the ongoing threat to individuals at school.** Effective crisis response strategies have been shown to reduce inappropriate behaviors in the school setting (Montana Healthy Schools Network, 2005). In many ways, crisis response is crisis prevention—prevention of a "spinoff" crisis or identification of the factors that initially allowed the crisis to happen. For example, what you learn from a crisis interview with a victim of bullying can help you prevent future incidents.
- **Maintain a healthy crisis response team.** The crisis plan must incorporate strategies to prepare and sustain team members because stress reactions and burnout are commonplace for crisis responders. One effective strategy to prevent burnout is to provide alternative crisis team members who can serve as backup or on a rotating basis (Knox & Roberts, 2005).
- **Use research and postincident analyses to improve future responses.** Learning from our mistakes and from the reports of others is essential for effective policies and plans. Too often, districts expend great initial efforts, only to have their plans become stagnant and ineffective.

With these goals in mind, school district administrators must set aside time, budget, and personnel to develop and refine policies and procedures. Fortunately, we have many free government resources to aid schools in their crisis planning, including the U.S. Department of Education's Emergency Response and Crisis Management (ERCM) Technical Assistance Center Crisis planning is a considerable undertaking that cannot be relegated to one or two school employees or a small subcommittee that meets episodically without any resources. The work of school crisis planning begins at the top of the district hierarchy, with the school board. Let's first examine how to develop effective policies and procedures.

DEVELOPING CRISIS POLICIES

Crisis plans are most effective when aligned with crisis policies adopted by the school board (Vermont School Crisis Planning Team, 2004). Such policies authorize actions in a crisis. Nevertheless, many school boards overlook this essential foundation. Without a written policy, individuals are forced to make "best guesses" about the position of their school districts. As one principal observed, "We have no policy to guide us, so instead of site-based management, we have site-based blame. I never know when I am going out on a limb only to have the central office chop it off."

What is the difference between crisis procedures and policies? A **policy** is a brief written expression of guiding ideas, derived from regulations, mandates, or an organization's philosophy. A crisis policy sets forth the position of the board, provides guidance to those responding to crises, and authorizes a general course of action. **Procedures**, in contrast, provide detailed implementation protocols or step-by-step crisis plans. Table 2.1 illustrates crisis policies and procedures. As you review this table, you will discover how the wording of a policy can alter significantly not only the decisions but also the timetable available to those in a crisis.

A policy must comply with local and state laws, ordinances, and procedures. You do not want to find out during a crisis that your district's policies are unsupported by federal, state, and local mandates (i.e., laws, standards, codes, regulations). Because these regulations are binding on a school district, it's a good idea to start with them. Here are some steps to follow.

First, examine federal, state, and local policies and procedures. You may find these in agency directives and memoranda, in bulletins from the district's central office, in community agency files (police, protective services, emergency management agency, courts, mental health agencies, hospitals, and health-care agencies), and in individual school building guidebooks.

Second, try to have a policy for each of these potential crisis situations:

- Facilities problems (electrical outage, heating, plumbing)
- "Unrest," protests, strikes
- Natural disasters or events (weather)
- Transportation delays, problems, and accidents
- Individual accidents and illnesses
- Medical problems affecting many (e.g., avian flu, meningitis)
- Behavioral health crises (overdose, suicidality, trauma)
- Intentional acts against persons (abuse; assault; rape; assaults with chemical, syringe, mace; bomb threats; sexual harassment; bullying)
- Hostage situations
- Kidnapping or missing person
- Intentional acts against property (theft, vandalism, graffiti)
- Events outside school that affect the school community (students/staff witnessing a crime or accident, airline crash)

Table 2.1
Examples of Crisis Policies and Their Impact on Procedures

Crisis	Policy Examples	Impact on Procedure
A 16-year-old student has shared her plan for taking her own life. She is so intent on suicide that she refuses to see the staff in the school-based mental health clinic. Her school has been unable to secure her family's cooperation.	"Our district takes whatever steps are permissible under state law to safeguard the life of a suicidal student. We work closely with mental health and law enforcement agencies to secure appropriate mental health assistance, even in situations where parents are unavailable or unwilling to seek such help."	This district's policy would allow a school employee to petition the mental health delegate of the court to order an involuntary mental health assessment. The court delegate would consider the petition and could authorize the local police to transport the student to a local mental health clinic or hospital emergency room.
	"As an educational institution, our district believes that parents are the best decision-makers in matters pertaining to their children's health. We defer to parents in making all decisions regarding their children's mental health needs."	This school's employees do not have the district's authorization to proceed with a petition to the court. Employees face a dilemma during this crisis.
A sudden blizzard has affected a large elementary school located in a hilly area of the city. Students are awaiting their transportation home.	"All decisions regarding transportation of students to and from school will be made by the Chief of Transportation. No other employees have the authority to make such decisions."	The principal may not hold the students until the roads are safer. This decision remains with the chief of transportation. Getting this approval could take valuable time and increase parental anxiety.
	"We recognize that road-conditions in a district of this size should not be made unilaterally by an individual who is not present to assess the conditions. We encourage local principals to consult with local law enforcement officials and with district transportation employees, including drivers, in making decisions."	The principal has the authority to assess local conditions, consult with those near the school, and make a timely decision based on these observations.

Table 2.1 *(continued)*

Crisis	Policy Examples	Impact on Procedure
A middle school has an evening open house planned for parents. At 2 P.M., the principal learns of rumors that two feuding families plan to fight at the school.	"We believe that parents are the children's first and best teachers. Our district embraces parental involvement and will remove all barriers to their participation."	Should the district staff choose to use metal detectors at the open house, they may face questions and complaints. If a parent refuses to go through the metal detectors, the school principal may not know what steps she can take.
	"We believe that parents play an integral role in their children's education. We also believe that we have a responsibility to parents, their children, and our staff to maintain safe schools. Therefore, all visitors to our schools may be asked to show identification, go through a metal detector, or comply with other safety measures as allowed by law."	The local principal has the authority to implement additional safety measures. Parents who refuse to comply may be asked to leave, in keeping with the district's policy.

Few districts have had the opportunity to prepare for *all* potential events. Here are some ideas for setting priorities for drafting policies that address crises likely to happen in your school or district. First, review last year's data on critical incidents, discipline referrals, weather-related emergencies, facilities problems, community incidents, and violence. In one example, Canevit, Lovell, and Pope (2005) evaluated the Milwaukee Public Schools Division of Security and Safety. They utilized data such as juvenile arrests, selected adult offenses, student incidents, administrative actions, suspensions, expulsions, and anecdotal accounts from school officials. These data could inform crisis policy development. In Chapters 6 through 8, we explain how to use government data to support your planning for illnesses, accidents, school violence, and natural disasters.

Next, ask local agencies and other stakeholders for their assessment of priorities. Consider your "public(s)." What is important to them? For example, the local merchants may be upset about truant students engaging in vandalism, while parents of young children may be concerned about the threat of kidnapping or a bus accident. Parents of teens may be anxious to prevent suicide and underage drinking. The juvenile court staff may want to monitor serious habitual offenders who transfer into your district. Not all of these priorities constitute school crises. Yet other agencies' appraisal of school safety risks can help you prevent minor problems from escalating into crises.

As you poll community stakeholders, consider the cultural needs of your school community. Crisis policies and plans should consider cultural perspectives. Overlooking the views of groups can alienate those groups just when you need them during a difficult time.

One practical example is crisis communications that convey important messages in accessible text in primary languages. Finally, consider the special needs of your students and staff who might require different support or communications in a crisis situation.

Once you have identified likely crises, collaborate with other agencies on policies. Swap policies and procedures with other youth-serving agencies in your community. Request policies from comparable institutions as well as your local emergency responders and police departments. Newgass and Schonfeld (2000) argue that when creating effective crisis plans, schools should increase collaboration with other schools as well as community mental health and social service providers. If you do not have a solid relationship with the other schools, law enforcement, and youth-serving agencies in your community, this policy-and-procedure discussion may be a good place to begin an ongoing dialogue. Although it is important to collaborate with outside sources, schools should be careful to consider how these policies and procedures would work (or not work) in their own school. After evaluating numerous crisis plans, Trump (2002) found that many schools borrowed from outside sources without adapting guidelines to their own schools.

To facilitate crisis preparation, districts should form an interagency advisory group that meets on a regular basis. This group should include all government agencies in your municipality and county that serve students and their families (i.e., child protective services, disability advocates, community mental health/mental retardation/ drug and alcohol programs, police, fire, and emergency agencies, juvenile justice and probation offices, the local and/or county health department) as well as community leaders and businesses (e.g., NAACP, religious leaders, mayor, utility companies, Chamber of Commerce). School social workers can facilitate many of these partnerships. These local partners are essential for the success of your crisis prevention and response efforts, checking to ensure that policies are current, supported by local leadership, and consistent with any changes in regulations.

Set a schedule for developing policies. To keep the task from being burdensome, ask for help from your state agencies or school boards association, hire a writer to pull together notes from meetings, or tailor a ready-made template to your own needs. Your district's policies will require accompanying procedures that direct employees on what they do, keeping in mind contractual language and union agreements. The next section offers a general overview of what constitutes these procedures, forming a comprehensive crisis plan.

ELEMENTS OF A COMPREHENSIVE CRISIS PLAN

A comprehensive crisis plan addresses many crisis situations and includes the four elements we introduced in Chapter 1. Let's review these four elements and see how they frame a crisis plan.

Prevention guidelines tell us how to prevent a problem. Research shows that a crisis plan with prevention guidelines is more likely to result in a response that reduces the short- and long-term consequences of a crisis on an individual (Lerner et al., 1999). *Mitigation guidelines* should tell people how to know if a problem is about to happen and how to reduce risk. For example, in the event of a telephoned bomb threat, does the school secretary know to record specific information about the threat and identifying information about the caller? Do students know what to do if there is a fire alarm?

Crisis response guidelines tell us how to get help and specific steps to take and those to avoid. For example, you may recall the steps in cardiopulmonary resuscitation as A (airways), B (breathing), and C (compressions). When crisis members experience stress, they may forget essential guidelines. In Chapter 1 we introduced a simple mnemonic device to help crisis team members recall the essential steps in any crisis: **Be C-A-L-M**. Let's examine those steps in more detail now, as a mental checklist for the steps you need to outline in a crisis plan. *Be* stands for "**Be**fore you act, **be** sure you have the facts, especially if you are leaving your classroom or office." For example, responders need to know where the incident has occurred, where the students are, if anyone requires medical attention, who have been notified, etc. These steps should be included in a protocol, as first communications either from the scene to the coordinator or from the coordinator to those who are going to the scene. "**Be sure you ask for help.**" Always let others know where and why you are responding, so that you will have backup support if needed. This step reminds planners to direct first responders or witnesses to call for help immediately rather than trying to resolve a crisis alone.

> # Be:
> Before you act, be sure you get the facts.

C stands for several important pieces of a crisis plan, beginning with **callout procedures.** These are the steps we take to reach essential crisis responders, such as school staff, law enforcement, emergency management agencies, social services, and health providers. Some person(s) in the district should carry a pager so that the coordinator immediately can convene the crisis response team in the event of an emergency. C also stands for **collaboration with other agencies,** including social service agencies, law enforcement, juvenile court and probation staff, transportation providers, and local print and electronic media representatives. **Coordination of staff** includes "jobs" each staff member will fulfill in a crisis. The crisis plan should spell out specific duties for each person or role. **Communication procedures** keep crisis responders and your publics abreast of new developments. Without these, people will rely on the inevitable rumors. The Crisis Communications Plan is a supplementary plan focusing specifically on how information is gathered and disseminated.

> # C:
> Call for help, communicate the instructions, and collaborate with other responder agencies.

"**A**" reminds us not to **avoid** being overly focused on the present but also to **anticipate** what could happen next. Crisis coordination requires the ability to anticipate and plan for the "what ifs." The A also symbolizes the need to **activate** the crisis plan; we cue responders to use their protocols instead of inventing individual responses. However, there is usually a need to **adjust** the plan accordingly. No two crises are identical, so we must be prepared to tailor the response to the immediate situation. Even the most comprehensive plans cannot anticipate all the possible scenarios and effects of crisis in schools (Knox & Roberts, 2005).

> **A:** Anticipate what could happen next and adjust the plan accordingly.

Letter **L** suggests that we **look for signs** of things getting worse or better, of new crises, or of the restoration of routines. This information allows us to adjust our plans. **Listen to your audiences** refers to the need to reach out to community sources to find out what's really happening.

> **L:** Listen to your audiences and learn what they need.

Finally, "M" stands for "**Maintain the crisis team's mental and physical health.**" For example, crisis team members should carry water, personal hygiene items, and medications in their crisis kits. Crisis responders should take turns, to avoid burnout and fatigue. "**M**" also stands for "**Meet and modify.**" Meet with the crisis team after the crisis to modify and improve the crisis plan. These BE CALM steps comprise crisis intervention, what we do at the time of the crisis. When you write your crisis procedures, keep these Be CALM steps in mind as a checklist for what you want to include.

> **M:** Manage the crisis, maintain the responders (food, water, etc.), and modify the plan afterward, based on what you learned.

Recovery guidelines tell us how to support staff, students, and families in the days, weeks, and months following a crisis. Often overlooked after a crisis are two final components of comprehensive crisis plans. *Debriefing and evaluation* procedures remind us to examine the crisis and the crisis responses. During this phase, responders meet to review the team's response and to get help for their personal reactions. Recovery also includes looking at how we responded and making plans to improve our efforts. Crisis plans and policies should be reviewed regularly to confirm their effectiveness (SVRC Fact Sheet, 2004). This ensures that we learn from our experiences, mistakes, and successes.

POLICY AND PROCEDURES: AN ILLUSTRATION

To help you understand how school crisis policies and procedures interrelate, we provide in this section an example for suicide prevention, mitigation, response, and recovery (postvention). Figure 2.1 shows the sample suicide policy and procedures suggested by the Services for Teens at Risk (STAR-Center), a nationally recognized suicide prevention and treatment center. Although some of the specifics of this policy will not fit your situation,

Figure 2.1
Example of Suicide Policy and Procedures.

1. **Purpose**
   The *[Board of the School District]* in recognition of the need to protect the health, safety and welfare of its students, to promote healthy development, to safeguard against the threat or attempt of suicide among school aged youth, and to address barriers to learning, hereby adopts this policy. This policy corresponds with and supports other federal, state, and local efforts to provide youth with prevention education, early identification and intervention, and access to all local resources to promote health and prevent personal harm or injury.

2. **Prevention Education**

Prevention:
Awareness
Assessment
Mitigation/Education

   Students will receive age appropriate lessons in their classrooms through health education on the importance of safe and healthy choices, as well as help seeking strategies for self or others. Students are taught not to make promises of confidence when they are concerned about a peer or significant other. Lessons will contain information on comprehensive health and wellness, including emotional, behavioral, and social skills development. Lessons are taught by [health and physical education teachers, community service providers and Student Services staff]. Students who are in need of intervention will be referred to the Student Assistance Program (SAP) team for screening and recommendations.

3. **Staff Training and Responsibilities**

Preparation:
Planning
Preparation (training)
Crisis communications plan

   All staff are responsible for safeguarding the health and safety of students. All staff are expected to exercise sound professional judgment, err on the side of caution and demonstrate extreme sensitivity throughout any crisis situation. All school personnel should be informed of the signs of youth depression/suicide.

Any staff member who is originally made aware of any threat or witnesses any attempt toward self-harm, that is written, drawn, spoken or threatened, will immediately notify the principal or their designee.

Any threat in any form must be treated as real and dealt with immediately. Suicidal behavior has been shown to have a contagion effect, thereby heightening the risk of suicidal behavior in others. Because of this contagion issue, suicidal behavior differs from other crisis situations.

No student at risk for suicide should be left alone, nor confidences promised. Thus, in cases of life threatening situations a student's confidentiality will be waived. The district's suicide crisis response procedures will be implemented.

4. Suicide Crisis Response Procedures

Response:

Immediate actions to restore
security and safety

Suicide Threat

Definition—A suicide threat is a verbal or non-verbal communication that the individual intends to harm him/herself with the intention to die but has not acted on the behavior.

  a. The staff member who learns of the threat will locate the individual and arrange for or provide constant adult supervision.
  b. The above-mentioned staff member will immediately inform the principal/designee.
  c. The principal/designee will involve staff, school nurse practitioner or in their absence. *[Insert appropriate numbers for school and non-school hours.]*
  d. The appropriate staff or approved agency provider will determine risk and intervention needed by interviewing the student, and gathering appropriate supportive documentation from teachers or others who witnessed the threat. Because of the contagion issue, these witnesses should have some follow-up monitoring as well, especially if they are considered to be at risk themselves.
  e. The principal/designee will:
  • Contact the parent/guardian, apprise them of the situation and make recommendations.
  • Put all recommendations in writing to the parent/guardian.
  • Mail the recommendations through certified mail.
  • Maintain a file copy of the letter in a secure and appropriate location.
  f. If the student is known to be currently in counseling, the principal/designee will attempt to inform their treatment provider of what occurred and the actions taken. [Before contacting the outside treatment provider, the school should be sure that consents are on file and current.]
  g. If the parent refuses to cooperate, and there is any doubt regarding the child's safety, the school employee who directly witnessed the threat may pursue a mental health assessment by calling *[County Emergency Services at xxx-xxx-xxxx]*.

    h. Do not drive the student to a hospital in a personal vehicle. Do not leave the student alone at any time.

    i. Involve the SAP team for follow-up and support.

Note: If a threat is made during an after-school program, and no school or district personnel are available, call [*Insert telephone number for County Crisis Emergency Services or* 1-800-SUICIDE or 1-800-273-TALK] for help. Inform the principal of the incident and actions taken.

Suicidal Act or Attempt on School Grounds or During a School-Sponsored Activity

Definitions[1]

Suicidal act (also referred to as suicide attempt)—a potentially self-injurious behavior for which there is evidence that the person probably intended to kill himself or herself; a suicidal act may result in death, injuries, or no injuries.

The first district employee on the scene must call for help from another staff member, locate the individual and follow district emergency medical procedures, such as calling 911.

    a. A staff member must notify the principal/designee.

    b. Staff members should move all other students out of the immediate area and arrange appropriate supervision. Students should not be allowed to observe the scene.

    c. Principal/designee will involve Student Services personnel to assist as needed.

    d. Principal/designee will contact parent/guardian and ask them to come to the school or hospital.

    e. Principal/designee will inform [*Insert name of central office*] Office, or call for assistance from the District's or County's on-call crisis response team at *[24-hour number].*

    f. Principal/designee will document in writing all actions taken and recommendations.

    g. If the student is known to be currently in counseling, the principal/designee will attempt to inform their treatment provider of what occurred and the actions taken. [Before contacting the outside treatment provider, the school should be sure that consents are on file and current.]

    h. Principal/designee will involve the Student Assistance Program team for follow-up and support.

    i. Principal/designee will request written documentation from any treating facilities prior to a student's return to school.

    j. Student Services staff will promptly follow up with any students or staff who might have witnessed the attempt, and contact their parents/guardians. Student Services staff will provide supportive counseling and document all actions taken. Guidelines are available in the *STAR-Center's Postvention Standard's Manual.*

    k. Media representatives should be referred to the appropriate school spokesperson [e.g., Superintendent, or Communications Coordinator]. School staff should make no statements to the media.

Suicide Act or Attempt Not on School Grounds or During a School-Sponsored Activity but Reported to a School Employee

Follow the procedures outlined under Suicide Threat.

Suicide Completion of a Student or Employee on School Grounds or During a School-Sponsored Activity

Definition

Suspected Suicide (also referred to as suicide completion)—death from injury, poisoning, or suffocation where there is initial indication evidence that a self-inflicted act may have led to the person's death. **Note:** Only the coroner's or medical examiner's office can confirm that the death was a suicide. This information should be considered very carefully in the postvention planning. Mental health specialists should be consulted about how to announce the death. Schools should also consider the wishes of the family in this regard.

When a sudden unexplained death of a student or staff member occurs, the principal/designee will confer with the Office of *[insert appropriate office here]* and promptly implement crisis response procedures as outlined in the District's Safe Schools Plan. These actions may include the following:

a. The first district employee on the scene must call for help from another staff member, locate the individual and follow district emergency medical procedures, such as calling 911.

b. A staff member must notify the principal/designee.

c. Staff members should move all other students out of the immediate area and arrange appropriate supervision. Students should not be allowed to observe the scene. Because of the contagion issue, these witnesses should have some follow-up monitoring as well.

d. Principal/designee will involve Student Services personnel to assist as needed.

e. Principal/designee will contact parent/guardian and ask them to come to the school or hospital.

f. Principal/designee will inform [Insert name of central office] Office, or call for assistance from the District's or County's on-call crisis response team at [24-hour number].

g. Principal/designee will document in writing all actions taken and recommendations.

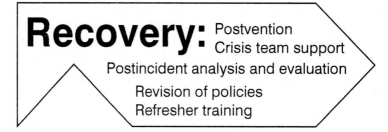

The principal or his/her designee will:

a. Immediately notify, regardless of the day or time, the [*District Office*] at the [*insert 24 hour number*]. They will notify others in central office.

b. Verify and obtain as much factual information as possible via school police, the parent/guardian, or others who may have the facts depending on circumstances.

c. Assemble the response team using school-based and community resources and the school's service providers that are part of the SAP teams; use the procedures outlined in the [*Safe Schools or Crisis*] Plan if in the evening or over the weekend to insure that everyone is informed of what occurred in a timely manner.

d. Do not describe the death as a suicide with the general public, parents, staff or students unless you have written confirmation from the coroner or medical examiner. Decisions about whether to share the coroner's findings should be made in accordance with the guidelines outlined in *STAR-Center's Postvention Standards Manual*.

e. Promptly collect and safeguard the student's belongings from desk or locker, any student work or photo or staff belongings from his/her desk (in the event of a staff death). Consult with family members and determine a mutually agreeable date and time in private, to return these belongings.

f. Inform the faculty that a sudden death has occurred using written communication if school has already begun, followed by a staff meeting at the conclusion of the day. If the death occurred in the evening, convene a staff meeting prior to the start of school the next day. Outline procedures that will be followed per the School Safety Plan.

g. Designate space for all postvention activities.

h. Once obtained, provide funeral arrangements and related details to students, staff via Main Office and parents via written communication.

i. Refer staff to district's EAP (Employee Assistance Program) for additional support.

j. Prepare and send a parent information letter home with students following the district's protocol and guidelines in the *STAR-Center's Postvention Standards Manual*.

k. Prioritize classrooms and students who will need immediate attention and connect them with the response team or other appropriate resources as determined by Student Services staff.

l. Refer media requests to district spokesperson.

m. Do not disclose any information or details to the media.

n. Meet with the response team at the end of the day or days during crisis management activities to insure the exchange of important information, as well as to insure communication and further planning of activities.

o. Check in periodically with the family, staff, and students to insure that everyone is supported as much as feasible with the context of the school setting.

p. Thank those who assisted in the postvention, including the faculty, ancillary staff, crisis team, and any outside agency or community members.

Actions to Avoid

a. Do not announce the death of anyone over the public address system, as this conveys an impersonal tone.

b. Do not hold an assembly program or bring large groups of students together in one place to discuss suicide, because of the suicide contagion risk following a suicide.

c. Avoid canceling school, classes or pre-planned activities unless absolutely necessary; students find comfort in following their normal routine when they are under stress, within reason. Discuss with supervisor prior to proceeding with any cancellations.

Memorials

It is recognized that grieving individuals need a variety of opportunities to personally express their emotions and reactions to this type of death. Nevertheless, suicidal behavior is contagious, and a high-profile memorial can glamorize the suicide act. Because of the contagion issue, any memorial should be the result of careful consideration by a team that includes experts in mental health.

[1]Definitions from *National Strategy for Suicide Prevention: Goals and Objectives for Action*. Rockville, MD: U.S. Department of Health and Human Services, Public Health Service, 2001.

Source: From *Suicide Prevention and Postvention Template*, 2007, Pittsburgh, PA: STAR-Center Outreach. Retrieved October 31, 2007, from www.starcenter.pitt.edu/PDFs/STAR_Template.pdf. Reprinted with permission.

see if you can locate the preparation, prevention/mitigation, response, and recovery elements. Note that suicide prevention and response (including the highly sensitive issue of memorials) are addressed in more detail in Chapter 9 on postvention.

COMMON PROBLEMS IN CRISIS PLANNING

Crisis planning is complex work, with many opportunities for mistakes. Let's review some common errors. First, you may find that your school has *procedures without supporting policy*. When crisis team members take actions, they do so without the support of the school board. This situation may provoke second-guessing by board members, disruptions, or delays in the response while board members debate policy and procedures. In some situations, employees have been prevented from taking any action or seeking outside resources because they lacked the authority imbedded in a district policy. Conversely, you may locate policies without any implementing procedures.

Some districts make the mistake of *focusing all their planning on one phase*. For example, they may assign all their resources to prevention, overlooking how they will respond to an emergency. Still others focus on crisis recovery (the actions we take after a crisis has occurred), but they do not have a prevention strategy to keep crises from happening in the first place. As one principal observed, "We know exactly what to do if someone dies. However, we have no ideas about how to keep them from getting hurt in the first place!" In summary, a good crisis policy and plan includes steps to take before, during, and after a crisis.

Some policies and procedures overlook the *needs for space, directions, and parking in a crisis*. We have found it very helpful to decide in advance how space will be used in crisis response and recovery. For example, after a tragedy, you must provide privacy for individual screenings and small-group discussions. It is helpful to choose rooms that are close to one another and have access to telephones. On the other hand, in an evacuation, you need specific procedures for moving students to a safe shelter. A floor plan for the school and directions to the in-shelter site belong in each school's plan. In congested areas, the plan also should include arrangements for crisis team members to park their cars.

Another mistake districts make is that of overlooking technology (Dorn, 2001), the subject of our final section.

TECHNOLOGY'S ROLE IN CRISIS PLANNING

Technology can facilitate the sharing and safety of information needed in a crisis, saving invaluable time. The National Education Association recommends that schools pay special attention to their computer files and suggests that schools

> have agreed-upon guidelines for saving and naming documents and organize them on a shared network for everyone in the communications office to access. Placing documents on a shared network is vital to sharing information quickly and effectively. Many times communication crisis response team members will be fielding questions and requests for information via phone. Being able to navigate filing systems and having access to important network documents will provide necessary information efficiently, eliminating the need to take messages, search through files, and return calls. In a crisis, the extra seconds, minutes, and hours that this planning will save will make your operation more responsive and proficient. (National Education Association, 2000)

A real-life example that demonstrates the importance of technology in crisis planning comes from the events of September 11, 2001. Crisis responders utilized computer software to inventory much needed supplies, coordinate their activities, and track raging fire hazards (Percy, 2004). The use of these applications helped the crisis responders work more efficiently and swiftly.

You do not want to depend completely on technology because in disasters your technology may not be reliable. However, in most cases, you will be able to use technology to speed your communications and callout procedures and to inform others rapidly about their roles and responsibilities. As you develop your crisis procedures, consider how technology might enhance your efforts. Table 2.2 offers some ideas.

Table 2.2
Watson School District Technology Division Proposal for Crisis Support

Technology	Purpose	Notes
1. Computers	Computers in the schools, including those in classrooms and labs, can be used to retrieve information from the district's crisis response website or for communications.	Computers in each school are set to allow access to any crisis responder from the district. The computers in the classrooms and labs will sound a special signal when an all-school communication is sent out.
2. Website	Crisis policies are posted on the website with their accompanying procedures. Users will find links to essential district and community resources: • Directory of district employees with their contact information. • Directory of on-call crisis team members with emergency numbers, etc. • Links to community agencies that collaborate during crises. • Links to critical district departments such as medical, security, and transportation.	The crisis response page is protected by a firewall and requires authentication for log-on. *Only selected crisis team members (including building administrators) can access this page site.* The files are read-only to prevent unauthorized changes.
3. E-mail	District e-mail includes distribution lists for crisis notifications.	District e-mail requires use of a password as well as other security safeguards. Messages carry a statement at the bottom that the information is confidential.
4. CD-ROMs and memory sticks	Responders can access sample communications and forms such as letters to parents, press releases, guidelines for conducting a grief group, parent consent forms, screening logs announcements.	These forms and communications can be edited by users for the particular situation.
5. Cellular phones	Cell phones are for callout and communications during nonschool hours or offsite.	District crisis responders receive reimbursements for use of their personal cell phones.

(continued)

Table 2.2 *(continued)*

Technology	Purpose	Notes
6. Pagers	Pagers are for callout and communications during nonschool hours, offsite, or when cell phones cannot be used.	District crisis coordinators also carry pagers when oncall. Collaborating agencies have the pager numbers.
7. PDAs	Crisis coordinators and administrators can download information from the website through PDAs and can beam this information to those at the incident site.	
8. Walkie-talkies	Each school is outfitted with walkie-talkies to use within the building and in the event that cell phones are shut down.	
9. Ham radios	These are used to communicate in disasters, when other forms of communication are not working.	Each building has a ham radio set up and at least two trained users.
10. Severe weather alert system	Each school has a severe weather alert system that sends out a signal in bad weather.	At least two staff members in each building are trained to use the system.
11. Security systems	Each building has security systems that allow authorized individuals to secure certain areas, lock certain access doors, and to screen visitors. Buildings also have required smoke, fire, and exit door alarms.	At least two staff members in each building are trained to use the systems.
12. Crisis hotline system	The district has a crisis hotline system that allows anonymous reporting of threats or concerns.	This number is publicized on the district's main Web page. Schools send out refrigerator magnets and helpcards to students and residents each year. The system is supported by an answering service that calls the crisis coordinator or administrator on-call according to the protocol.
13. Electronically stored student records	This information is needed to release students in emergencies, as authorized adults are listed in the student records.	In custody disputes, a court order may be referenced in the student files.

SUMMARY

A comprehensive crisis plan begins with focused goals, supported by policies that authorize a response consistent with the district's position. Procedures flesh out these policies with specific protocols that tell employees and collaborating agencies what to do. Technology can support a crisis response effort.

Let's reflect . . .

As we conclude our opening case study, we find out how Connie (the principal) used technology and the "Be CALM" response steps to pull together a response for an unusual situation. Read over the goals of effective crisis policies and procedures at the beginning of the chapter. Can you identify the goals of her crisis plan? Can you spot the "Be CALM" steps Connie followed? If you were helping Connie's district revise their policy and procedures for bus incidents involving community incidents, what would you suggest?

CASE STUDY CONCLUSION

I took three deep breaths and then remembered our crisis motto: *Be CALM.* I quickly jotted some notes about what I needed to know and do, grabbed the phone, and called the head of transportation.

"Dave, Connie here. I need some facts. Where is the bus now? Give me the exact location. What is the bus number? Do you have a head count of kids on the bus? Am I right that none of the kids are hurt? Is the bus driver okay to drive? How do I reach the police at the scene?"

Once I got the facts, I called for help. I scanned our list of faculty and spotted three who lived near the corner where the bus was stopped. I called the first teacher, filled her in, and directed her to call the other two.

"When you get there, check in with the officer on duty. Her name is Samantha Ryan. I told her to expect you there. She will let you on the bus, but you must have identification. Try songs, hugs, and simple games to distract the kids and calm them down. Don't talk about the incident because we don't really want the kids dwelling on that. After all, most of the kids on that bus are first and second graders. Dave is dispatching another driver to help out, in case the bus driver is too upset. The police will escort the bus along a different route just in case. They will personally walk each kid to his house and reassure the parents. They will not leave any child at home alone. I have your cell phone number, and you have mine, so check in as soon as you get there."

I then checked my e-mail. The transportation office sent me a list of the kids on the route, so I could figure out who remained on the bus. I called our school counselor.

"Fred, this is Connie. We have a crisis and I need your help right away. I'm sending you an e-mail list of kids on a bus that witnessed a shooting. You will know some of the families. Call them and tell them exactly what I write in the e-mail. We want them informed that their kids are safe but they will be delayed. Start calling parents of the kids who will get off the bus last. Their kids will be the most delayed. I will start calls with Jose Llano and his sister and work toward the end of the list. Let me know if you can't reach a home. No, better than that, call Betty on her cell phone if you can't reach someone. She is working late, so she's at school. I reached her on her cell phone. She has the emergency contact numbers. If we are not able to escort a child to his home, we will have to get Betty to check on who else is authorized to receive the child."

I dashed off an e-mail, including a few lines about the incident for Fred to share with parents. Betty called to say she was ready with emergency cards, so I asked her to start calling parents at the end of the list. Then I called the superintendent and began mapping out plans for the next morning.

Let's reflect . . .

As you consider this case, consider what steps supported the students and their families. Were there steps that could have been improved or added? If this event happened in your district, what policy and procedures would you follow?

DISCUSSION AND APPLICATION IDEAS

1. How would your current school policy and procedures address these crises?

    - A member of the high school football team collapses and dies during a practice. The police and reporters arrive immediately. One reporter asks the coach about the protocol for preseason physical exams.
    - A car full of teenagers careens off a highway in a rainstorm, leaving three dead and two in serious condition in the local hospital. The students had left the pep rally and driven themselves to a school football game, where a new administrator noticed they seemed intoxicated. When the administrator went for help, the students fled to avoid disciplinary consequences.

2. Discuss these comments about crisis planning with your colleagues. What problems do they reflect? How might good crisis policies and plans address their concerns?

    - *"Not until after a suicide did we realize that our suicide policy never addressed prevention or mitigation, only postvention and memorials"* (a board member).
    - *"We thought we had a crisis plan, until we had to use it. That's when we realized that all we had was a bunch of guidelines no one had ever used"* (a school social worker).
    - *"You should have seen the look on the face of the telephone company rep when he realized that their telephone tapping procedure didn't work on our school phones. Thank goodness the bomb threat was only a threat. We learned to collaborate on plans after that"* (a superintendent).
    - *"We had lots of plans for what to do if we had an intruder or a weapon in school. But looking back, we realized that we had not ever sat down and discussed prevention or threat assessment. We had a lot of explaining to do with the community"* (a principal).

- *"No one ever taught us in graduate school how to deal with a murder or a suicide. The only training I ever had was in the military"* (a teacher).
- *"I never dreamed it could happen here"* (parent of a kidnapped child).
- *"The procedure may look good but not work after all. We learned the hard way . . . all this time we had the wrong phone number in our procedure for a mental health crisis"* (a principal).

REFERENCES

Canevit, S., Lovell, R., & Pope, C. E. (2005). *Integration of law enforcement into school safety: The Milwaukee initiative.* Milwaukee: University of Wisconsin-Milwaukee.

Dorn, M. (2001). Are you prepared for the next crisis? *School Planning and Management, 40* (4), 35.

Knox, K. S., & Roberts, A. R. (2005). Crisis intervention and crisis team models in schools. *Children & Schools, 27* (2), 93-100.

Lerner, M. D., Lindell, B., & Volpe, J. S. (1999). *A practical guide for crisis responding in our schools* (5th ed.). Commack, NY: American Academy of Experts in Traumatic Stress.

Montana Healthy Schools Network and Office of Public Instruction and Montana Division of Health Enhancement and Safety. (2005). *Bullying, intimidation, and harassment prevention school policy.* Helena, Montana: Author.

National Education Association. (2000). *Crisis communications guide and toolkit.* Washington, DC: National Education Association.

Newgass, S., & Schonfeld, D. (2000). School crisis intervention, crisis prevention, and crisis response. In A. R. Roberts (Ed.), *Crisis intervention handbook: Assessment, treatment, and research* (pp. 209-228). New York: Oxford University Press.

Percy, B. (2004). Technology to the rescue. *T.H.E. Journal, 31* (6), 56.

SVRC Fact Sheet. (2004). School preparation to the terrorist threat. *School Violence Resource Center.* Retrieved September 21, 2007, from http://www.svrc.net/Files/TerroristThreat1.pdf

Trump, K. S. (2002). The impact of terrorism on school safety planning: Whether school violence, terrorism, or a natural disaster, the lesson remains the same: Plan, prepare, and practice. *School Planning & Management, 41* (7), 22-23.

U.S. Department of Education. (2003). *Practical information on crisis planning: A guide for schools and communities.* Retrieved September 21, 2007, from http://www.ed.gov/admins/lead/safety/crisisplanning.html

Vermont School Crisis Planning Team. (2004). *Vermont school crisis guide.* Retrieved June 25, 2006, from http://www.state.vt.us/educ/new/html/resources/model_policies/crisis_guide_04.html

CHAPTER 3

CRISIS TEAM PREPARATION

CASE STUDY

It was a hot August afternoon. As the new director of pupil services for a large district, I was unpacking my new office downtown when the call came.

"GET OUT HERE! A kid has gone down! We have no idea what happened. What do we do? We called 911 but they aren't here yet! You have to get out here!" screamed the panicked principal on the phone.

In the background I could hear the chaotic clamor of adult voices.

"Where is the nurse?"

"Does anyone know CPR?"

"She's not breathing...SOMEONE HELP!"

Before I could go through my mental checklist of Be CALM crisis steps, the principal had hung up. I grabbed my keys and dashed to my car.

I arrived at the school and found my way to the scene; it was chaos. Stunned teenagers huddled next to the lockers. A crowd of adults stood immobilized. Some were whispering prayers. Others were crying. I could barely make my way through them. When I did get through, I spotted an ashen-faced adolescent girl who appeared to be going in and out of consciousness. Leaning over her, a paramedic was asking questions but getting no responses.

"Can you hear me?"

"What is your name?"

"Take a deep breath."

I raised my voice to disperse the crowd of onlookers.

"Teachers! Please return to your classrooms. Let the paramedics do their work! Please get the other students back to their classrooms. We need space here. P-1-e-a-s-e, move back!"

I turned to a nearby teacher by the arm and directed, "Go to the office. Get the emergency card for this student and bring it back to me. HURRY!"

The bewildered young teacher stammered, "I'm a sub. I don't know this student. I'm not even sure where the office is from here. I'm sorry. What do you want me to do?"

In frustration, I shouted to the crowd, "SOMEONE GO TO THE OFFICE AND GET THIS GIRL'S EMERGENCY CARD. NOW!"

Minutes later, a teenage boy clutching the card ran back to me, his hand shaking with fear. A school secretary ran behind him, calling to someone on her walkie-talkie. The deep-voiced custodian began to direct the crowd, pushing them to clear a path for the stretcher.

"Call your crisis team," I shouted to the flustered principal as he returned from calling the victim's parents.

Lowering his voice, he responded, "This school was just reorganized over the summer. I just got here. We don't have a crisis team yet. I'll pull some people together."

Let's reflect . . .

Consider what went wrong in the opening case study. Think about the model for crisis we outlined in Chapter 1. What crisis *preparation* tasks did this school overlook? In terms of crisis *response*, what tasks required an adult's attention right away?

This chapter helps you select, assign, orient, and train a crisis team. We begin with a general discussion of crisis team qualifications and then examine individual roles that might apply across different situations. After addressing the "who" of crisis teams, we focus on the "what": crisis team orientation and training.

CRISIS TEAM MEMBERS

Let's first consider general personal and professional qualifications of effective crisis teams. We mention these requirements first because you may find that some crisis team volunteers are not suitable. Whether they volunteer or are assigned as part of their contractual duties, crisis team members should:

- Have the capacity to accept direction and execute diverse functions under pressure ("multitask").
- Be willing and available to leave their immediate work location to work elsewhere in the school or district. Teachers with responsibility for student supervision, for example, might not be able to serve on a district-wide team.
- Be knowledgeable about the age groups they may serve in a crisis because children and teens respond differently to a crisis or tragedy. For example, those with only elementary school experience might not know how to comfort or support young teens.
- Be committed to continued professional development to improve their competency for crisis responses (Blythe, 2001).
- Communicate clearly and sensitively even under stress. Some members should be bilingual if you have non-English-speaking students, staff, or families.
- Demonstrate that they can complete assigned tasks calmly, without experiencing undue personal stress or creating stress for others.
- Safeguard confidential records and exhibit good judgment about sharing other information.
- Possess skills that are needed in a crisis (although not necessarily formally trained in counseling or crisis responding). For example, your team might include an English teacher who agrees to edit all communications, a paraprofessional who has close ties to the local community, and a disability specialist who can design specialized communications.
- Know the community and school or able to establish rapport quickly and meaningfully (Blythe, 2001; Smith, 1997, cited in NEA, 2005).

Let's reflect . . .

Read over the list of qualifications again. Imagine how an individual lacking some of the qualifications might impede a crisis response or create more stress. Can you identify additional qualifications that your crisis team should possess?

Different age groups need developmentally appropriate responses. In our district we have three teams of counselors—one for each level (elementary, middle, and high schools) who respond to crisis in those specific schools. The team finds this most effective in that most high school counselors don't often understand the unique needs and approaches required for kindergarten through fifth-grade students. The reverse is also true. I have found that most young students process the news of a death for a fairly short time (20 to 30 minutes) before they need a break and then want to move on with their day. They often come back to the death via short conversations, brief questions, or comments, but unless emotionally close to the individual who dies or if they have recently experienced the death of someone else they are close to, the younger students do not spend a great deal of time emoting or intellectually processing the news. High school students, however, can spend an entire day grieving the loss of a friend and tend to go through the initial stages of shock and grief, rather slowly needing support for expressing their feelings in verbal, physical, and artistic ways over a period of time. They also grieve in the context of their peer group, forming internal support groups with one another. This process takes several days to go through and even though routines may return to normal rather quickly, students often take a sustained grieving period into their own hands (impromptu memorials, poetry readings, sing-alongs, making and selling T-shirts and buttons to raise money for the family, etc.). If counselors are not used to the style of grieving that differing age groups may need to experience, they may unintentionally intervene and impede the process. It is very important for teams to have experience with the age group they serve. (Pam Wilson, Principal and former Director of Student Services, Portland Public Schools, Portland, Oregon)

Crisis Leadership Team

Each school should identify members of a crisis leadership team who will take over the coordination and delegation roles in a crisis. This group also meets with others after a critical incident to review the response and revise the plan. We suggest that this team include members such as:

1. Crisis team leader (principal or other administrator).
2. Crisis team leader designee (in the event that the leader is absent or offsite).
3. Offsite manager (a senior staff member without direct student responsibilities who can do the advance work needed to prepare in-shelter facilities in an evacuation).

4. Security coordinator (a school resource officer, security guard, or other staff member who can work with others to secure the school until law enforcement arrives and who can assist law enforcement in moving visitors, media, and parents).
5. Medical responder (in most schools, the school nurse; in schools where no nurse is on duty, someone on the staff trained appropriately, such as a teacher who is also a paramedic or firefighter).
6. Communications coordinator (someone who can manage the communications internally and externally until the district's information officer or designated spokesperson takes over). This individual may need to call language and disability experts for some communications.
7. Mental health specialist (the school counselor, psychologist, or social worker who can focus on psychological first aid).
8. Facilities manager (usually the custodian or building manager who can address utilities needs, direct traffic, and provide floor plans to public safety responders).
9. Other staff members, including teachers, play important roles in a crisis, but they usually cannot lead a crisis response because of their responsibilities for students.

School crisis response and recovery teams cannot operate without help from vital community resources. Next, let's examine the roles of those who respond from the community.

Community Members of the Crisis or Public Safety Team

School crisis response and recovery teams cannot operate without help from vital community resources. Do you recall from Chapter 1 the advice to host an interagency advisory group? That group should represent the other crisis responder agencies that will assist with crisis team formation, training, and maintenance (Kline, Lichtenstein, Schonfeld, & Speese-Lineham, 1995). These community members include: mental health specialists from the local mental health clinic or hospital; law enforcement officials (e.g., local police, transit authority police, sheriffs' department and state polices); fire, health, transportation, emergency management, victim assistance, and child protection officials (Blythe, 2001). In addition, consider your district's need for support services such as interpretation and translation of parent communications, assistance in responding sensitively to members of different ethnic groups, accommodations for students and staff with disabilities, and responders with specialized expertise needed in your area (e.g., weather-related disaster support, snow removal, towing companies to move vehicles blocking the school entrance).

When a school district collaborates with outside crisis responders, written agreements should specify the guidelines under which those responders or counselors work. For example, outside agencies may require parental consent to see students. Agency providers should be familiar with the school system and its regulations regarding confidentiality of student records.

Each school has a slightly different configuration for its crisis team, given its staff, their schedules and qualifications, and its needs. Let's consider some of the essential roles.

School Crisis Team Coordinator

The coordinator may be a superintendent, principal, school psychologist, counselor, social worker, or other support personnel. Whoever coordinates the crisis response efforts must be a calm and quick-thinking leader in crisis, with enough authority to organize and delegate simultaneous efforts to meet the needs of diverse populations. In the event of a crisis, the coordinator is responsible for carrying out or delegating the following tasks. We use the Be CALM checklist introduced in Chapter 2 to help you remember these functions (see bracketed hints).

> **Be:** Before you act, be sure you get the facts.

- **[Before you act, be sure you have the facts.]** Receive the first call and gather facts about the incident; get the exact location of the incident, identify those affected by the incident and their whereabouts and conditions, identify the assistance needed.

> **C:** Call for help, communicate the instructions, and collaborate with other responder agencies.

- **[Be sure you call for help.]** Call for additional help from the district's crisis response team, including community members and the communications coordinator.
- **[Coordinate, collaborate, contact, and communicate.]** Coordinate responders, each of whom should have a predesignated assignment, based on the crisis response plan. Collaborate with other agencies on the scene and those you will need. Contact other schools where the incident may have an impact. Communicate through walkie-talkies, telephones, faculty meetings, crisis team briefings, letters and e-mail updates to parents.

> **A:** Anticipate what could happen next and adjust the plan accordingly.

- **[Anticipate, avoid, adjust, and activate.]** Anticipate what will happen for the next 24, 48, and 72 hours. Avoid getting stuck on the present situation; ask the "what-if" questions. Adjust the crisis plan as the situation demands. Activate the crisis recovery plan (supports for the aftermath of the crisis). As you move from crisis response to recovery, look for signs of things getting worse or better, of new crises, or of the restoration of routines.

> **L:** Listen to your audiences and learn what they need.

- **[Look and listen.]** Listen to the stakeholder "audiences."

> **M:** Manage the crisis, maintain the responders (food, water, etc.), and modify the plan afterward, based on what you learned.

- **[Manage, maintain, and modify.]** Manage and maintain the crisis team, ensuring they have the information, supplies, nutrition, and equipment they need. Make sure they have psychological supports following the crisis and an opportunity to meet for the purpose of modifying the plan.

Mental Health Specialist

Many crises require special mental health expertise because those affected need psychological first aid. Your school psychologist, counselor, and social worker most likely have specialized training for this role. Moreover, they are familiar with your school and community, which is another advantage, as traumatized individuals should not have to relate the story of their experiences to many strangers. However, it is unrealistic to envision that these few individuals will be able to manage a crisis response and also meet the psychological first aid needs of a large number of students during a widespread crisis or disaster (Allen, Ashbaker, & Stott, 2003). In such situations, your internal mental health specialists may call in trusted community or national specialists. Here are some additional Be CALM functions undertaken by the mental health specialist:

- Coordinate the screening and referral process for students experiencing acute stress reactions. Co-lead support/education groups for students (either students who self-identify or those who are referred by school personnel). Collaborate with mental health agencies to secure support for affected students and staff. Communicate with the hospitals, if students and/or staff are hospitalized because of an incident. Coordinate with mental health staff in other districts that may be affected by the tragedy.
- Anticipate the psychological needs of staff, students, and parents as the school prepares homeroom announcements of a death or tragedy, communicates with the family of the injured or deceased, composes letters home, plans the agenda for a community meeting, and considers memorials. Anticipate the information needs of the media while balancing those needs with the needs of those affected. Anticipate needs and arrange support services or referrals for the family members of the victim.
- Listen to the voices of those involved in the crisis and interpret their psychological needs. Line up new community resources for future situations.

- Maintain and manage the psychological first aid needs of district employees by sharing information about employee assistance programs (EAPs), by helping them with post-incident analysis, by calling in outside resources to relieve them, and by touching base with them as they work. Familiarize staff with the developmental tasks associated with recovery from loss and the dynamic nature of trauma and loss (immediate reactions as well as reactions over the weeks and months to follow). Make suggestions for improving the postvention policy and procedures.

Other School Employees

Although administrators and pupil services staff may lead the crisis team, it is important to train and involve *all* adults, including general and special education teachers and paraprofessionals, in crisis response drills (Brock, Sandoval, & Lewis, 2001). The exact duties assigned to other school staff will depend on the crisis. However, these roles should be spelled out clearly and listed in the crisis plan. Table 3.1 shows an example for outlining the roles for staff in general. If you look ahead at Table 5.4 from the *Vermont School Crisis Guide*, you will notice that the guide outlines roles in a similar format for each potential crisis. The advantage of having such a visually uncluttered format is that anyone can quickly scan the page and see what to do. (Recall that the opening case study involved a substitute teacher with no preparation. If this plan had been available, even a temporary employee could follow it.)

As you review this crisis plan, notice that the high-priority tasks appear first. Also, notice that the plan makes no assumptions about who might be first on the scene but rather tells everyone what to do should they arrive first.

Let's take a look at a few roles that easily are overlooked in the *recovery phase* of a crisis, *after* the initial response. Brock et al. (2001) recommended that one team member should serve as an evaluator whose job consists of collecting data on crisis team performance, conducting structured interviews, and administering questionnaires about the effectiveness of the response.

After some events, students may need to move throughout the building for individual screenings in an organized and expedient manner. An office "escort or coordinator," usually a school secretary, paraprofessional, security aide, or crisis team member, can keep a confidential list of students, looking up schedules, and calling students to the office. Coordinating the movement of students minimizes disruptions, deters students from congregating in large groups, and saves valuable time for the counselors and students. Although the role of the escort/coordinator is largely managerial, it is best to designate someone who is sensitive to the students and faculty. This individual will need to be aware of his or her role *before* a crisis occurs. Clerical staff who will be answering phones, receiving visitors, or escorting students should participate in crisis response training.

Building security staff can help prevent problems. Security staff might also do the following:

- Make arrangements to safeguard the victim's belongings.
- Be sensitive to the timing but move the mementoes left at the locker of the deceased after a process has been announced to students. (These items would be given to the family.)
- Escort distressed students to the guidance office for proper support.

Table 3.1
Vermont School Crisis Guide Excerpt on School Crisis Team

School Crisis Team	Team Member Name	Phone # or Extension
Principal (Team Leader) Responsible for all planning meetings. Coordinates the broad and specific functions of the team during a crisis. (Principal passes team leader role to fire chief during a fire/hazardous material incident and law enforcement commander following criminal act.)		Phone: _____ Email:
Designee (Backup Team Leader) Will assist or substitute for the Principal. Oversees reporting of any missing students or staff to the Principal during a drill or crisis.		Phone: _____ Email:
Communication Coordinator The sole contact person for all media and staff to communicate the nature of the crisis and keep the community informed about the school's response. The Superintendent may assume this role, but if not, the communication coordinator shall discuss the message to be conveyed with key school administrators in advance. Always coordinate message with law enforcement or fire commander prior to release of public information.		Phone: _____ Email:
Custodian/Maintenance Staff Head custodian or maintenance director works with the school crisis team using blueprints and an advance video tape/DVD of the school to identify specific sections of the building. Custodian/Maintenance staff members, wearing fluorescent vests, work with law enforcement to keep incoming and outgoing travel lanes clear for emergency vehicles and to prevent unauthorized people from entering school.		Phone: _____ Email:
Information Site Manager Provides information to parents when they call pre-designated cell/land line phone number(s). Works directly with the Communications Coordinator, or in a small school, roles may be combined.		Phone: _____ Email:
Relocation Site Manager Coordinates logistics at relocation site(s) and works directly with the Information Site Manager.		Phone: _____ Email:

(continued)

Table 3.1 *(continued)*

School Crisis Team	Team Member Name	Phone # or Extension
School Counselor Coordinates the scheduling of support meetings and counseling sessions, and organizes other grief management resources.		Phone: _____ Email:
School Nurse Coordinates advance procedures with EMS, doctors and hospital emergency room staff. Prepares inventory of students and staff who have CPR and other emergency medical training. Remains the medical point person during a crisis.		Phone: _____ Email:
Staff Notification Coordinator Responsible for activating the telephone call tree to notify school crisis team members and other school staff about the crisis. Becomes the staff communication liaison during a crisis. Works with the Principal or designee and office secretary in advance to establish an internal classroom telephone/intercom communications procedure for use during crisis.		Phone: _____ Email:
Teachers and Staff Provide supervision of students and assist other staff as needed. Manage student communication via cell phones per local school board policy. Report any missing/injured students to the Backup Team Leader/Nurse.		Phone: _____ Email:

Note: These materials will help to make schools safer. However, in no way can a school district guarantee the safety of all students, all the time, using the *VT School Crisis Guide*.

Contributors include: Vermont State Police, Essex Police Department, Vermont Department of Education, Vermont School Boards Association, Montpelier Police Department, and Vermont Emergency Management.

Source: From *Vermont School Crisis Guide* (pp. 55–56), by Vermont School Crisis Planning Team, 2004. Reprinted with permission.

- Monitor students congregating in large groups during regularly scheduled activities. For example, after a tragedy, security staff can empathize with students but set limits on their spontaneous gathering. If the group is a natural occurring group, security can arrange for them to meet with a counselor. If the group has already met, security can monitor them and direct them to a member of the team if they become disruptive or very distressed.
- Approach representatives from the media and refer them to the school's media representative, and, if necessary, escort them to an appropriate waiting area off the school campus.

- Prevent media representatives from interviewing students or teachers on the school grounds, unless a special arrangement has been authorized.

In the absence of security, teachers or other adults in the building may monitor hallways, stairwells, bathrooms, locker rooms, entrances/exits, and other areas where students may congregate or attempt to leave.

Let's reflect . . .

Read over the opening case study and the crisis team functions again. Would your school be staffed for a student who became suddenly ill? Would you be prepared for *dozens* of students who became suddenly ill from food poisoning or an environmental hazard? How would you staff and organize the release of an entire student body in a crisis?

INITIAL CRISIS TEAM TRAINING

Training is crucial to the success of any crisis response team. This section helps you understand the preparation a crisis team should undertake before responding to its first crisis. A lack of preparation within a crisis team can cause response delays when responding to a real-life crisis (Knox & Roberts, 2005).

Orientation and Introductions

Because crisis team members must communicate and interact under highly stressful circumstances, training should begin with an orientation to the challenges ahead and introductions of the individuals who make up the team. Introduction activities should extend beyond mere names and titles because crisis team members who may be strangers must be ready to face significant stresses together. The more they can learn about one another's strengths, vulnerabilities, and stress reactions, the more effectively they can support one another. Such introductions also allow the coordinator to spot potential problems, as evidenced and illustrated in this anecdote:

> As I moved around the room listening to introductions that first day, I noticed that all the members of Team One introduced themselves as people whose typical response to stress was to take charge, make decisions, and become more controlling. In contrast, members of Team Two described themselves as laid-back in a crisis and eager to let others give the orders. At least they were honest, I thought. Yet, I could just imagine what conflicts might arise during the heat of a crisis! One group might fight for control, while the other group might never arrive! The best revelation came from the third group. Every one of them admitted that they grew faint at the sight of blood. They'd have been a big help at a playground or bus accident! Needless to say, we reorganized the teams.

Initial Training

Prior to conducting crisis team training, those in district and building leadership positions (including the mental health specialists in the district) should review the contents of this book to develop an in-depth understanding of their responsibilities. For example, the district spokesperson should be very familiar with the material discussed in Chapter 4 (on crisis communications) and principals should learn about crisis prevention and response in the specialized chapters on illness, injury, violence, and disasters. Mental health specialists may want to review the information on postvention after a death and on psychological supports. Together, these leaders can plan the training agenda for both crisis teams and building staffs. Table 3.2 illustrates a training agenda for a new district team.

Let's examine this agenda. Notice that all members first receive authority for their work through the superintendent's message, copies of the school board policy, and pertinent regulations. Next they get acquainted with their internal crisis team organization and their external crisis responders. Understanding stress reactions can help them support one another and safeguard against risk factors for secondary stress reactions seen in responders (see Chapter 10).

The Be CALM steps introduce a mnemonic device to help teams respond when there are no specific protocols, when they "freeze" and do not have their procedures in front of them, or as a mental checklist in unfamiliar situations. Vignettes with unusual crises form the basis for tabletop exercises where team members must respond in the absence of a specific written protocol. Mastering these simulations gives team members a conceptual framework and confidence in their abilities to respond even when they do not have a protocol with step-by-step directions before them. Although unusual, such situations can happen. We have also seen members become so anxious when they receive a phone call that they cannot recall where their crisis plan is or how to get started. Be CALM can focus an anxious individual and move them along a bit until they regain their composure, just as the ABC device reminds us how to give first aid to someone who has stopped breathing.

Specific protocols are the focus of the next day's agenda when members study their roles and discuss how these protocols will unfold in their schools or offices. Notice that we add complications to these simulations after participants have role-played several times. These complications provide a deeper understanding and opportunities for members to simulate what they will do under unpredictable circumstances such as the absence of a principal or mental health specialist. We added these special scenarios after watching some teams struggle in situations where leadership was not available immediately or things didn't go as planned. Every crisis is unique, so team members must be able to problem-solve rapidly.

The EAP is included here to remind us to take care of our crisis team members. If your district does not have an EAP, you will want to plan a session based on the information in Chapter 10. From the onset, crisis team members must not only understand the psychological and physical stresses of their work but be able to identify self-care strategies.

Identification in a crisis is critical, so take some time during training to photograph members and prepare their crisis responder identification badges. In a large-scale crisis, ordinary school employee IDs will be insufficient to cross into certain areas, in our experience. Identification, self-care aids, crisis protocols, and contact sheets comprise a crisis team kit, as described in our next section.

Table 3.2
Agenda for Initial Crisis Team Training

Activity	Rationale	Handout or Training Activity	Notes
Welcome and distribution of training and crisis response materials		Distribute Crisis Kits (including policies and crisis procedures, contact lists, maps, floor plans, and CD-ROMS with this information).	
Superintendent explains the role of the crisis teams and reviews policies and relevant regulations.	Team members need to understand the authority for their work; any legal or insurance issues need to be addressed.	Distribute and review board policy approving the crisis teams.	Review the state regulations that provide protection from lawsuits in case anyone asks. Review other regulations as they are referenced in the policies.
Other agencies introduce themselves and explain their roles.	Team members need to understand the interagency nature of a crisis response.	Share contact information and overview of each participating agency.	Invite police, fire, and emergency response team members from each municipality; county emergency response and health officials.
Leader explains how the team is organized: • Organizational chart • Lines of authority and decision making • Where each member works • Role descriptions (e.g., office support; nurse; custodian; security; counselor; communications)	Crisis team members need this information to situate themselves within the larger team and to understand their particular duties.	Share contact information (as determined appropriate for each team member). School leaders receive information for each member, including cell, home, and work phones, e-mail and regular addresses.	Mark this handout confidential and remind everyone to keep this information in a secure place.
Team member introductions	Team members need to have a level of trust and familiarity with one another.	Each member of the team answers these questions by way of introducing themselves to the others. Members take turns going around the group. Everyone answers the first question; then they move to the second, etc.	Observers or trainers should observe for potential problems. For example, a group with many members who admit that they faint or gag at the sight of blood or vomit will not function well at a crash site.

(continued)

Table 3.2 *(continued)*

Activity	Rationale	Handout or Training Activity	Notes
		1. "The assets I bring to a crisis are . . ." 2. "The weaknesses I bring to a crisis are . . ." 3. "You will know I am feeling stressed if you observe . . ." 4. "What helps me to remain calm is . . ."	A group with too many members who see themselves as followers will not be able to mobilize.
Be CALM: Essential steps in crisis responding	This is a conceptual approach that supports the step-by-step crisis procedures in the plans that will form the basis for drills.	Using a worksheet that reviews the Be CALM steps, participate in a tabletop simulation exercise that allows members to plan a response to hypothetical scenarios.	
Review of the day Preview of day 2 Homework assignments		At home, team members should become familiar with their crisis response kits and begin adding their personal items.	Crisis team training can be emotionally draining, so teams should not work longer than their normal work schedule.
Review of team assignments	Members review their specific responsibilities in common crises.	List of crisis team roles and responsibilities	Be sure that each team has the skills it will need to respond to crises.
Review of crisis protocols	Members must become familiar with the specific protocols to use. This also provides opportunities to clarify or review information.	Crisis plans, including the step-by-step protocols.	Remind members not to share their plans outside of the school. Some of the information (e.g., codes for hostage situation) is confidential. Disclosure could compromise safety.
Break [Teams practice group decision making by determining when they will take a break.]			
Employee Assistance Program speaker on stress management for crisis team members.	Involving the EAP normalizes help-seeking behavior by crisis responders.	EAP tips on taking care of yourself.	

Table 3.2 *(continued)*

Activity	Rationale	Handout or Training Activity	Notes
Review of the day Preview of day 3 Homework assignments		At home, team members should become familiar with their crisis plans and begin adding their personal notes.	
Continuation of the simulated exercises, with guidance from the facilitator, who debriefs each situation.			
Break			
Continuation of the simulated exercises, with unannounced complications choreographed by the facilitator during the exercises: 1. Remove principal from a school-based team to see how well they can respond without their leader. 2. Shorten the time allowed, to give teams a more realistic crisis experience. 3. Put panel up front for questions from "reporters" (other teams pose these questions). 4. Announce that half of the team is away at a conference, to see how teams call out others to help.	Responders must be ready to act when critical members are absent, when a second crisis arises, and when the situation becomes complicated. Shortening the time allows responders to practice rapid decision making under stress.		
Continuation of the simulated exercises, with unannounced complications choreographed by the facilitator during the exercises: 5. Change the time of day in a scenario to a week			

(continued)

Table 3.2 *(continued)*

Activity	Rationale	Handout or Training Activity	Notes
end or very early morning, as a test of team's ability to call out members. 6. Give teams a "second crisis," to see how well they can redeploy members or get additional help. 7. Add a scenario requiring travel (e.g., chaperone in London becomes gravely ill during a school trip), to test team's ability to mobilize offsite. 8. Require written communication (announcement, script, letter home, press release) to test writing skills.			
Lunch followed by recognition of crisis team members and individual and group photos.	Team members need recognition and encouragement.	Certificates ID badges Armbands or other identifying clothing	
Closing Reminder of refresher dates in schools and next district-wide training. Review of deadlines for turning in crisis team contact information.	Members must understand that their obligation does not end with this training.		

CONTENTS OF A CRISIS RESPONSE "GO-KIT"

Consider for a moment how emergency responders equip themselves. Fire companies conduct regular checks of their personal equipment and their vehicles. Ambulance services restock their inventory after each run. In short, they are prepared for the next crisis.

School crisis response teams share this obligation to be prepared always. After all, if a team must scramble to search for contact numbers, driving directions, or protocols, that team will delay its work. Recognizing the importance of preparation, the U.S. Department of Education has developed guidelines for school-level and classroom-level "go-kits." A brochure describing these kits is available on the U.S. Department of Education Emergency Response and Crisis Management Technical Assistance Center website and on our website. For example, the administrator's "go-kit" would include:

1. Clipboard with lists of:
   a. All students
   b. Students with special needs and description of needs (e.g., medical issues, prescription medicines, dietary needs), marked confidential
   c. School personnel
2. School emergency procedures
3. Key contact information for the district crisis team
4. Parent-student reunification plan
5. Whistle
6. Hat or brightly colored vest for visibility and leadership identification
7. Battery-operated flashlight and batteries
8. Utility turnoff procedures
9. Emergency communication device
10. First aid kit with instructions (U.S. Department of Education Emergency Response and Crisis Management Technical Assistance Center, n.d.)

"Go-kits" should be designed and stocked according to the roles of those who carry them. For example, one school outfitted its teachers with neon-colored backpacks as their go-kits, a practical decision that freed teachers' hands for making notes and made it easy for teachers to move about. To illustrate a different kind of preparedness, Figure 3.1 provides an inventory of a crisis kit used by one regional crisis response team. This kit is designed to help those who come in *after* the immediate crisis to provide ongoing recovery support such as counseling and communications.

Let's explain some of the recommendations for the crisis team kit. For example, you'll notice personal items such as food, clean socks, and contact lens solution. A school crisis may occupy team members for many hours, making "creature comforts" important for sustaining one's physical and psychological stamina. That's why you'll also see personal photographs and reading material. These can help a team member through a tough time. Being efficient depends on having one's tools. That's why you see copies of protocols, sample letters, directions, and announcements on a CD-ROM or memory stick (in both PC and Mac formats because you don't know what type of computers the school uses).

You may want to create a "virtual crisis kit" for the documents you need. This computer-based crisis file could be placed on computer desktops, to enable staff to access the documents, list, and forms they need.

In addition to personal crisis responder kits, schools and offices should also have emergency supplies on hand, such as water, blankets, flashlights, and other gear. These supplies should be on hand in buildings, in accordance with a district's emergency preparedness plan. Moreover, new and substitute staff should receive general instructions each year about what to take with them in case of an evacuation. As one veteran teacher explained,

Figure 3.1
Sample Inventory for Crisis Responder "Go-Kits."

Phone Lists including:

    Phone chain for the crisis team and faculty

    Student emergency numbers to reach parents (and out-of-town emergency contact numbers for students, as recommended by FEMA and the Red Cross)

    Agency, emergency, and community response numbers

    Personal numbers (i.e., team member's child-care center, next-door neighbor)

Floor plans for schools, if you will have to orient emergency workers to your building

First-aid kit, rubber gloves, mask

Backup batteries for pagers

Walkie-talkie or other emergency communication device; charger

Battery-operated radio

Personal hygiene products (feminine products, toothbrushes and toothpaste, deodorant, liquid soap)

Contact lens case/solution

Eyeglasses

Sunscreen (in the event of an outside assignment)

Hearing aid batteries

Warm clothes, in the event you lose heat or have to walk a distance

Quarters for pay phones

Directions for using collect call service

Prepaid phone card

Pens/pencils/erasers

Paper, self-stick removable notes

Facial tissues

Peanut butter or cheese crackers, energy bars, Ensure or other nonperishable nourishment

Bottled water

Preferred over-the-counter medication

Prescribed medications

Clean socks and underwear

Spiritual or religious materials

Playing cards

Cash

Searchlight (can illuminate a room if the power goes off)

Boots or warm shoes

Photographs of family and friends

Reading materials

Matches

In addition to these individual crisis team boxes, check our website for lists of items that each building should have on hand and available to the crisis team.

Last year, we had to evacuate our school after a bomb threat. After two hours of sitting on the stadium bleachers in the hot sun, we were released. However, the police determined that no one should reenter the building. I felt so bad for the new teachers who had forgotten to take their car keys with them. Stranded, they had to get rides home. To make matters worse, students and staff returned the next day with sunburns. Now we tell everyone to pack sunscreen and grab car keys!

DRILLS

Training for crisis teams and school staffs must continue with drills. Conducting dry runs is essential but complicated. On the one hand, if a crisis team is to discover weak aspects of its response, it must undergo a realistic and rigorous examination. After all, "reactions of individuals to a crisis event are one of the valuable assets of a simulation—especially if the crisis is life-threatening" (Degnan & Boseman, 2001, p. 300). Studies conducted by the Department of Defense showed that over 50% of those who did not prepare through simulations failed to accomplish their missions (McArthur, 1989). On the other hand, we do not want to disrupt schools unnecessarily or cause alarm in the community. This section offers guidelines for holding reasonable simulations without creating an internal or external public relations nightmare. One approach is to use pencil-and-paper or computer-based simulations (see Degnan & Boseman, 2001, for a detailed account of computer-based simulations for school crisis teams and the costs incurred).

Regardless of the format you choose, base the rehearsal on threats the district is likely to face (Blythe, 2001). Some teams expend great energy on highly unusual events while overlooking those most likely to take place. Do some research by contacting your local law enforcement and emergency response agencies. Ask officials what scenarios are likely to challenge the skills and knowledge of your team. Examine the past five years of records in the school or district. Don't forget about community-based crises that in turn would create a critical school event. For example, if a district is located in a low-lying area, flooding might create a crisis. A district experiencing severe winters could expect that students might have to stay at the school overnight. Any district can expect vehicular accidents involving students, their parents, or employees.

Conducting a dry run is more sensitive than a paper-and-pencil or computer-based drill as it happens in the field. If you decide to conduct drills involving your entire staff, involve your local emergency management agency and public safety officials. They are expert in these drills and have the resources to make them manageable. Such drills would be announced in most cases so the community is likely to be aware of them.

Here are some guidelines for in vivo drills. These focus on crisis team participation without direct involvement of the school staff or community.

Do not announce all drills in advance. Prepare your team to expect drills, but do not always inform them of the date and time. After all, you want to gauge their response to an unexpected event. Remember, these drills do not involve students.

Limit the number of personnel who know about the drill. Without disrupting school, you can test the response time of your team when you call out the team, mobilize them to meet for a briefing, assign duties, and review the responses. Figure 3.2 shows the journal entry of a crisis team leader following a dry run.

Figure 3.2
Journal Entry.

> **Notes on October 12th drill for southwest crisis team.**
> The district crisis coordinators decided to conduct a drill for the southwest team, because that team has several new members this school year. In addition, several of the principals in that area are new to their schools.
>
> On October 12, around 6 A.M., I arrived at Tryon Middle School where I called the principal at her home. I alerted her that we in Central Office had received a call that a custodian had found a threatening message on a rest-room mirror. I explained that the police had been called, had photographed the mirror, and had removed the writing. I asked her to alert her in-school team to meet in the designating briefing area (the conference room adjacent to the school library) and not to discuss the situation with anyone but her crisis team members. I noted the time when I hung up [6:08 A.M.]. As each team member and the principal arrived, I noted their arrival time, whether they had their crisis response kits (two forgot theirs), and whether they went directly to the briefing room as directed (one had to ask me where we were meeting).
>
> Once assembled, I described the situation and passed around photos of the mirror. (The night before, I had written on the mirror, then immediately photographed it and removed the writing, without telling anyone except the superintendent.)
>
> The principal and I assigned duties to the crisis team members: preparing a letter for parents, drafting an announcement for students about the incident and where they could get support or talk with an adult, meeting with the detective assigned to the case, preparing an agenda for a faculty meeting, reminding staff how to be on the alert for unusual behaviors, and alerting office staff how to answer the phone.
>
> To extend the drill, I had arranged for the principal to receive a call from "a local reporter doing a story on school acts of terrorism." (The superintendent had recruited a friend who works as a freelance writer to play the role of reporter.) The writer had prepared some questions that she posed. Then she took notes on the principal's responses, before explaining her actual role in the drill.
>
> Minutes before the first teachers arrived, I called off the drill by reconvening the team and explaining that this had been a drill. (By then my adrenaline was really rushing, and I was feeling a little bad about the necessity to keep the drill a secret!) Then I broke out the coffee and bagels and scheduled a time for an evaluation of their response. In all, they did well. We had a rapid response time and only a couple of team members forgot their kits.

INITIAL CALLS AND BRIEFINGS

This section addresses the onsite communications and briefings that a team issues and receives during a crisis. In any school crisis situation, someone must take change immediately. Typically this is the building administrator, who may call 911 with the specific location of the problem (e.g., fire or chemical spill) and the status and specific location of anyone injured or involved.

Providing essential information calmly and clearly in a highly stressful situation is difficult and requires practice. Invite the local 911 dispatcher to a team meeting to explain how best to convey information over the telephone in a crisis. Then arrange role plays for the crisis team members, who take turns asking and providing information about scenarios. After all, in a crisis any team member may be the one who must summon emergency aid.

If called in to a critical incident, the emergency responders take over the initial response. As they shift the onsite responsibilities to the school team, the police, fire, or emergency medical responders should share essential information with, or brief, whoever is in charge at the school or incident site. (In a large-scale crisis or disaster, this ongoing process of sharing information and coordinating responsibilities takes place in a special command center set up for that purpose.) The team leader should be prepared to receive this critical information, which would include status of those involved, next steps, contact persons, their titles, badge numbers, telephone numbers, and who to contact after those responders go off duty.

The team leader must gather essential information to share, in turn, with the team members, in a formal **briefing** (a meeting to inform the crisis team about the incident and to give them their instructions). The briefing allows the team director to share with the team specific details about the critical incident. We suggest that the briefing follow a standard format, or **protocol**. A protocol ensures that information is not overlooked and helps each member of the team to comprehend the information, take notes, and go into action most efficiently. Blank briefing protocol sheets for taking notes should be in the crisis response kits. The briefing protocol should include a description of the event, the status of those involved, what the team can expect within the next few hours, immediate assignments for crisis team members, and a time and location for the next briefing. At the conclusion of the briefing, the leader should answer any team questions. Never conduct briefings in public areas, as the information is highly sensitive and often confidential. Depending on the severity of the crisis, additional briefings should be held each hour or at designated periods (e.g., at the end of the day). The team leader should also brief those in supervisory positions (e.g., the superintendent or principals in other buildings) so that they can handle questions from the community and the media. On our Companion Website, you'll find a protocol for briefing a crisis team.

REFRESHER TRAINING

Teams often begin their work with a burst of enthusiasm only to find that they quickly lose their energy as the crises demand more and more of them. Effective school crisis responders, like emergency responders, need to meet regularly to maintain their focus and commitment. Yet time is difficult to schedule during the school year. If schools find that they do not have the time for extensive drills, they should then conduct shorter tabletop exercises of school crisis guidelines (Trump, 2002). Table 3.3 lists refresher activities that can fit into a 30- to 45-minute period before or after school.

COMMON PROBLEMS IN CRISIS TEAM PREPARATION

This section will help you understand and avoid typical problems in crisis team preparation. For each problem, we will share an illustration.

Table 3.3
Sample Refresher Activities

Activity	Goal	Rationale
1. The school office manager conducts a "guided tour" of the office, explaining how to operate the copier, fax machine, phone, and public address system.	Team members learn how to make copies, transfer phone calls, and use the public address system.	School employees can become overly dependent on the office staff during a crisis. This can be a real problem when the phones are ringing off the hook, the office staff is absent or busy, or multiple tasks require additional help.
2. The custodian leads the team on a tour of the building and grounds.	Team members learn how to shut off utilities, to operate an emergency generator, to locate the hazardous chemical fact sheets, to remove graffiti, and to find their way around the building.	School employees can become overly dependent on the custodian, who may be absent during a crisis.
3. The team leader facilitates a discussion of scenarios taken from the news or from the Companion Website.	Team members go through simulations, assuming the roles they'd take if the scenario happened.	Team members can forget their responsibilities if they do not practice regularly.
4. Team members draft sample letters to parents and announcements. English teachers (and others familiar with foreign languages) aid in revisions and translations.	The team is prepared for the communications demands of a crisis.	Many people do not write well or easily, especially during a crisis.
5. The team reviews its crisis handbook to see if everything is up to date.	The contact numbers and protocols are correct.	Contact information changes over the period of a school year. Incorrect information can delay a response.
	Members receive new copies of missing pages.	Protocols are revised in response to evaluations after crises.
		Pages may get lost during a crisis.
6. Crisis team members check the contents of their crisis kits.	Everyone has what he or she needs.	Items used during a response must be replaced. Batteries, cameras, personal medications, and nourishment may expire.
		New items may be identified.

First, some teams based their responses on unfounded assumptions about how other agencies will respond. Here is an example:

Imagine our frustration when we tried to get help for a student with serious mental health issues. Little did we know that the mental health regulations had changed. The student was old enough to refuse a psychiatric assessment. When we telephoned the local clinic, they seemed almost annoyed. We had to go back to the drawing board with the mental health agency to plan a different response in the future.

Reliance on one essential person is another common problem, as illustrated in this anecdote:

There we were in the middle of a snowstorm. Our small elementary school had only one administrator, and she was stuck across town. We had never planned how to respond if she wasn't at the school. To make matters worse, the custodian was out with the flu. We had no keys and no idea how to operate the emergency generator. The police got through, but they had none of the information or keys either. After that night, we got busy writing Plans B, C, *and* D!

Some team leaders make benevolent assumptions about others' behavior, not recognizing that team members reacting to stress may abandon their duties. Consider this example:

We were called to a school that had received recurring bomb threats for months. As the team leader, I headed into the building, calling out directions to my team members. Each of us was assigned an area of the school to search. Imagine my surprise when I reached the top of the stairs and realized I was alone! That's when I learned that people will react to fear, and you cannot always count on their help.

Finally, teams have a tendency to overgeneralize from one incident to others. This means that they count on a crisis response to follow the pattern of similar episodes, failing to realize that each crisis is in some ways unique.

We are in a large urban district, so we'd had experiences with students threatening others in the building. We felt prepared when a school called to report that a terroristic threat had been scrawled across a rest-room mirror in one of the high schools. The police got involved, and we tried to reassure the staff and kids. A couple of dozen students were interviewed about what they'd seen and heard. Imagine our shock when the police discovered that the threats came from a disgruntled member of the staff. That possibility had never crossed our minds.

EVALUATING THE RESPONSE AND IMPROVING THE PLAN

Fortunately, most schools experience few serious crises because schools in the United States are generally safe. Therefore, unless you are a full-time crisis response specialist, you will not have the opportunity to build firsthand knowledge every day or even every week. To counteract this lack of experience, it's important to learn as much as you can from each crisis response. *In many ways response evaluation is a form of continued professional development for crisis team members.* As soon as is practical, the team leader should reconvene the team to review the response. In a very busy district where teams have little time, this review might take place by telephone conference call. What's important is that each member of the team has an opportunity to share their views on what worked, what didn't, and what should be modified in future responses. If other agencies joined the response, you may want to include them in the review. If there were problems in the interagency coordination, the other agency should join an all-team review or meet with the team leader. Someone in the review meetings should take notes and make any agreed on changes in the crisis response plans.

SUPPORTING A CRISIS TEAM

> All the parents watching the practice were hysterical and running onto the field. At first, I couldn't think. Everything was a blur. I couldn't even remember where I kept the emergency cards. Then it was like I just went on autopilot, doing what we had rehearsed. It had all happened so fast. The kid just collapsed on the field. That was a lot of years ago, but it still feels like yesterday.

As this narrative reminds us, crisis team members experience powerful emotions during and after a critical incident. They require ongoing support to do their work effectively. This section offers guidelines for *basic sustenance* of a crisis team, while Chapter 10 explores psychological reactions and supports.

Basic Supports

In addition to the items in their crisis response kits, team members should have access to healthy nutrition and water whenever possible. Discourage responders from drinking too much caffeine because it can contribute to dehydration and make some people jittery.

In addition to nourishment, try to schedule breaks for crisis team members, during which they can telephone home or merely relax. Protect team members from having to answer questions from the press. For example, if team members take a walk outside the school, they may want to remove their identification so that reporters do not assail them with questions.

Rotations

Although not always possible or necessary, rotating a crisis team member off for a year or six months can help sustain a team. Whether to use such a strategy depends in part on the number of crises a team has managed, the size and experience of the team, and the supports available to the team between and during incidents. Such rotations are essential when a crisis team member experiences a crisis in his or her personal life: Death, divorce, serious illness, or other hardship can interfere with an individual's ability to respond effectively or make good judgments during a critical incident. Similarly, if the incident involves the team member, a loved one, or close colleague, the team member should be relieved of duties. This leave of absence may be for hours, days, or months. Sometimes, a crisis team member experiences a brief stress that requires reassignment. Consider this vignette:

> Cheryl was one of our best crisis responders. Always calm, she was willing and capable of any role I assigned. Therefore, I was surprised when she left the room before interviewing a sobbing teenager.
>
> "You'll have to take over," she told me.

"Why? What's wrong?"

"That ninth-grader . . . she looks just like my daughter. They're the same age. All of sudden, I realized that she could have been in that car. It just got to me."

I went to reassure the student and returned twenty minutes later to find Cheryl editing the parent letter.

Months later, I responded to a kindergarten fatality. Cheryl, recalling that my son had just begun kindergarten, rescued me from that assignment.

"Hey, it's my turn. Go call Rob and see how he liked his little Pumpkin Patch field trip."

Employee Assistance Services

In addition to the informal supports that crisis team members extend to one another, many can benefit from formal support or professional counseling. One veteran crisis responder puts it this way: "I keep a good therapist on call, just in case. There is no way I am going home and reliving these scenes with my husband and kids. This work requires a professional listener!"

Districts with EAPs can involve those providers in regular meetings with the teams. A well-qualified employee assistance provider can review the signs of psychological distress and offer coping strategies. Those providers should have some crisis response experience so they can understand the perspectives of team members. Chapter 10 describes in more detail the personal stresses associated with crisis responding.

SUMMARY

This chapter outlined steps in selecting and preparing crisis responders to be effective and efficient under highly stressful conditions. A well-planned initial training includes orientation to the crisis model and to the policies and procedures of the district. New responders need time to familiarize themselves with one another and with their specific duties in a crisis. Joint training with responder agencies, tabletop simulations, drills, and postincident reviews can upgrade a team's competencies. Tools such as crisis kits and computer-based documents can give responders ready access to information and basic sustenance while instilling confidence.

CASE STUDY CONCLUSION

Let's return to the case study that opened this chapter. As you recall, a high school student collapsed during one of the first days of school. Chaos broke out, making the emergency response more difficult. The principal had no crisis team in place.

As a new director of pupil services, one of my first assignments was to design a crisis response plan for the district's nearly 60 schools. I was still unpacking that day when the student collapsed. Suffering from dehydration, she had fallen and hit her head on a hardwood floor. One chaotic scene led to the next. Word got out that she had been shot. Parents began calling the school and showing up. The reporters and camera operators quickly followed, stopping kids on the way to their buses to get interviews. It was bedlam. I went home that night determined to have crisis teams in place by the end of the week. No way was I going through an ordeal like that again!

The next day, I sent out a memo, asking nonclassroom staff to volunteer to serve on district-wide crisis teams. (I figured that teachers would not be able to leave their classrooms and students to respond to crises, so their role would have to be different from the team members.) I prayed that staff would respond. The first calls came from the school with the recent incident, showing I was not the only one unwilling to repeat that episode! By week's end, 30 people had volunteered. We had our first crisis team.

Next, I had to convince principals to release their volunteers to respond to crises in other buildings. However, why should they? Our schools were short staffed, and many served children with many needs. How could I persuade a principal to relinquish a counselor or social worker for a crisis that might require days to resolve? I could imagine the response: "What's in it for me?"

The answer came in a telephone conversation with the still-shaken high school principal.

"I only hope that none of my colleagues ever have to live through a nightmare like that. We still have press calling to ask about a gun that never even existed! You cannot believe how much time this has taken from everything else I have to do. I was up until two in the morning doing paperwork."

Let him tell his story. He will convince them. A crisis like that could happen in their school. Then what would they do?

The principal agreed. At the next administrators' meeting, we shared his story. All but three principals signed on to share their building's crisis team volunteers.

By the end of the first year—a year in which a plane crashed near a middle school and a preschooler came down with meningitis—those holdouts joined their colleagues. By then we had formed a regional crisis team comprised of volunteers who could work for a brief period in another building.

A central office employee joined each regional team to help with communications. They sat by the phone, ready to relay messages to the superintendent or district PR person. Sometimes they gave driving directions or called the bus garage for a list of students on a particular route.

The teams trained together initially for two days, then met for refresher sessions every other month. We had planned a number of dry runs, but reality beat us to them: By the end of the first semester, we had responded to 13 emergencies.

DISCUSSION AND APPLICATION IDEAS

1. Why is it important for crisis team members to have standard inventory kits? What *personal* items would you include in yours?
2. Write the script for dry runs involving (a) an elementary school, (b) a vocational-technical school, and (c) a middle school.
3. Check our Companion Website, the Internet, or newspapers for stories about school crises. Can you identify the district and community team members you would need for each situation?
4. Using the stories you located in the preceding activity, role-play a briefing for the crisis team involved in the response.
5. Interview an emergency responder from your local law enforcement agency, fire department, emergency response agency, victim assistance program, or emergency rescue team. Invite the professionals to share how they were trained to respond to emergencies. For example, ask about their inventory of supplies and equipment, their briefings, their response protocols, and their evaluations of responses.
6. Can you design a 40-minute refresher activity for a school-based crisis team?

REFERENCES

Allen, M., Ashbaker, B. Y., & Stott, K. A. (2003). Strengthening rural schools: Training paraprofessionals in crisis prevention and intervention. In *Rural survival*, Proceedings of the Annual Conference of the American Council on Rural Special Education (ACRES), Salt Lake City, UT, 258–263. (ERIC Document Reproduction Service No. ED 476220)

Blythe, B. (2001). Creating your school's crisis management team. *School Business Affairs, 67* (7), 16–18.

Brock, S. E., Sandoval, J., & Lewis, S. (2001). *Preparing for crises in the schools: A manual for building school crisis response teams*. New York: Wiley.

Degnan, E., & Bozeman, W. (2001). An investigation of computer-based simulations for school crisis management. *Journal of School Leadership, 11*, 296–312.

Kline, M., Lichtenstein, R., Schonfeld, D. J., & Speese-Lineham, D. (1995). *How to prepare for and respond to a crisis*. Alexandria: Association for Supervision and Curriculum Development.

Knox, K. S., & Roberts, A. R. (2005). Crisis intervention and crisis team models in schools. *Children & Schools, 27* (2), 93–100.

McArthur, D. (1989). *Developing computer tools to support performing and learning complex cognitive skills*. Santa Monica, CA: RAND Human Resource Management Center. (RAND Document No. 2675-FMP)

Smith, J. (1997). *School crisis management manual: Guidelines for administrators*. Holmes Beach, FL: Learning Publications.

Trump, K. S. (2002). The impact of terrorism on school safety planning: Whether school violence, terrorism, or a natural disaster, the lesson remains the same: Plan, prepare, and practice. *School Planning & Management, 41* (7), 22–23.

U.S. Department of Education Emergency Response and Crisis Management Technical Assistance Center. (n.d.). *Helpful hints for school emergency management: Emergency "go-kits."* Retrieved July 7, 2007, from http://www.ercm.org/views/documents/HH_GoKits.pdf

CHAPTER 4

CRISIS COMMUNICATIONS

CASE STUDY

I started my first year of teaching at the age of 22, my school located about 15 miles south of Washington D.C. The first week was fantastic. I had introduced myself to the staff, made a good impression on my principal, and set the stage for a wonderful year of learning and growth for my students and me. I was feeling good about myself and what I had accomplished in the first week of my career.

On Tuesday of my second week of school, my students and I were discussing the place value of decimals and there was an unexpected visitor. The principal, Mrs. Pinckney, dropped by my room and said, "Good morning, boys and girls."

My students responded in unison, "Good morning, Mrs. Pinckney." Mrs. Pinckney motioned to me and asked, "May I speak with you for a moment, Mr. Fitch?"

We stepped into the hallway, my principal took three steps away from my door, I heard my door click shut, and we stood in the hallway. I was standing in front of my door so I could still see my class until Mrs. Pinckney signaled me to step forward away from my window. She then asked me, "Do you have any friends and family that work downtown or in New York City?" I thought it was a strange reason to pull me out of class, but I thought about it for a moment. My friends and I had scattered throughout the United States and Europe after graduation, and it was hard to keep up with where everyone was headed, so I decided to focus on family.

"Yes," I said, and I saw my principal's face abruptly change to a look of concern. "My aunt works in a federal building in Rosslyn," I continued.

She took a deep breath, almost a sigh and said, "I don't know how else to say this, so I'll just say it. About an hour ago, two planes crashed into both towers of the World Trade Centers in New York. Just a few minutes ago, a plane crashed into the Pentagon. I have no information other than that. Now what you need to understand is that . . . "

I interrupted her, "How close is Rosslyn to the Pentagon?"

She said, "Less than 5 miles, now I need you to understand something, Alex. I have people that I am worried about as well. But a third of our school's population is from naval housing, and the parents of most of the other two thirds are contractors or work for the federal government in some capacity. Under no circumstances should you turn on the television, radio, or any other form of media. I need you to go back into your classroom and teach throughout the day as though nothing has happened. If there is any other important information available, I will have someone bring it to you or send it via e-mail. Can I count on you?"

With a million images going through my mind, most immediately, what impact these tragedies might have on me or my loved ones, the reality hit me. One of my students might have suffered a loss more horrible than I could possibly imagine and not even know it. I managed to nod and respond, "Yes."

As my principal turned and entered the next classroom, I attempted to regain my composure and walked back into my class. I opened the door and faced the innocence of 26 ten-year-old faces. I was running "what ifs" in my mind. What if the students found out something big had happened? How would I answer their questions? When I got to my desk, I pulled out the district crisis plan and skimmed the crisis communications codes, just in case I would need to follow them later.

Let's reflect . . .

Talk with friends about their workplace or school experiences on September 11, 2001. What kinds of reactions did they experience and address? How did their employers communicate with them? As you talk with parents who had children in schools that day, consider their reactions and needs for information. What did they want to know?

THE GOALS OF CRISIS COMMUNICATIONS

Effective crisis communications can foster trust and credibility among school and community members (Covello, Peters, Wojtecki, & Hyde, 2001; Maxwell, 1999, O'Toole, 2001). A crisis communications plan (CCP) outlines how the district will convey information to and receive information from its employees, students, families, and the general public. An exemplary CCP can:

1. Prevent critical incidents by fostering two-way communications with stakeholders to share information on potential risks.
2. Aid in early detection of an impending incident.
3. Mobilize and facilitate the response to a critical incident.
4. Contain the crisis and prevent "spinoff" crises by maintaining responsible communications with stakeholders.
5. Maintain or restore the public's confidence in the school.
6. Support the victims of a tragic incident through sensitive outreach and information.
7. Illuminate and communicate flaws in crisis prevention and intervention, thereby averting future crises.

As one expert observed, "The CCP provides a functioning collective brain for all persons involved in a crisis, persons who may not operate at normal capacity due to the shock or emotions of the crisis event" (Fearn-Banks, 2002, p. 11).

The "crisis continuum" illustrated in Figure 4.1 can help you visualize the goals of a communications plan. At one end, we see human reactions that can exacerbate or extend the crisis; at the other end, we recognize preferred responses, those that can limit the extent of a crisis and reduce risk.

Imagine the written and spoken communications you might have in a crisis. Consider the content, timing, and tone of each one. Ask yourself two questions:

1. "Would this communication move people toward confusion and hysterical reactions or toward calm, rational thoughts and actions?"
2. "Would this communication increase trust and credibility or diminish our reputation?"

Here are three examples to prompt your thinking:

1. [Principal's e-mail to a parent] "We are not sure what kind of hazardous material was released during the construction project, but we are working on finding

Figure 4.1

Crisis Continuum.

Imagine that this is a continuum of human behavior and emotions:

Now imagine the following phrases or words on the continuum, where you think they belong:

Complain	Express Concern	Scream	Speculate	Swear	Rage
Fear	Helpful	Panic	Anxiety	Question	
Informed	Uninformed	Rational	Irrational	Disoriented	

someone who can analyze it for us. If you know anyone who is an expert in assessing hazardous materials, please let us know."

2. [Press release] "The district has followed its usual policy and procedures in addressing this bomb threat. As you know, our staff and students practice evacuations regularly, and these drills are evaluated by our local police and fire departments. All school students and personnel were present and accounted for at a safe relocation site within 10 minutes of the telephoned threat. The state police arrived within minutes of our initial call and have completed a thorough search of the inside and outside of the school, including all cars on the parking lot. We have their complete assurance that the building and school campus are safe for our return. As your superintendent, I want you to know that the safety of your children and of our employees is my primary concern."

3. [Newspaper interview after fight involving 10 students] "We are not really sure what happened at the football game, but we are looking into it. We heard from some of our students that it might have been a gang-related incident. I don't have to tell you that gangs are on the rise in our community. As I said to my fellow board members the other night, a school can only do so much."

Example 3 is likely to raise anxiety, as is example 1. In contrast, example 2 conveys a sense of control and competence.

As one superintendent observed, "No written plan can ever ensure that people will rise to the occasion in a crisis" (Hewitt, 2004, p. 44). However, a solid CCP accompanied by professional development and practice sessions can prevent crises, safeguard individuals, mitigate and contain the crisis, and reduce the inevitable risk of negative public relations. We move now to an examination of the planning process.

PREPARING FOR CRISIS COMMUNICATIONS

This section of the chapter guides you through an examination of seven questions, whose responses will form your CCP.

Let's begin with, *"What are the crises we might avoid if we exchange information with parents, students, employees, and other agencies?"* These so-called risk communications not only reveal information and opinions, but strengthen the relationships between the school and its publics (Fearn-Banks, 2002; U.S. Department of Health and Human Services Substance Abuse and Mental Health Services Administration, 2002). In this phase of planning, schools communicate with law enforcement, health, insurance, community, and emergency response agencies as well as individuals, with a shared goal of identifying risks and prevention strategies. For example, many schools organize alcohol awareness campaigns timed to coincide with their senior proms. Your local health department may provide posters for locker rooms to warn athletes that meningitis and other infectious diseases can be transmitted through shared water bottles. "Stranger danger" and fingerprinting programs guard against child abduction; date rape presentations can protect teens from sexual assaults.

For middle and high school students, we suggest that schools collaborate with local print shops to design and print wallet-sized help cards in advance. The card can include local crisis resources, provide instructions on how to place a pay phone call in an emergency, and provide lines where students write in the contact information for trusted adults. Be sure to verify the phone numbers of resource agencies before printing the cards. Reconfirm the telephone numbers annually (Kerr, Brent, McKain, & McCommons, 2006).

The second step in crisis communications planning is to ask, *"Who are our target internal and external audiences?"* Internal audiences include staff, students, and parents. External audiences are those in the community and those who may read, hear, or see media reports.

Table 4.1 is a worksheet to identify a school's key publics (or stakeholders), what information they need, and when they need it. "Gain a sense of the public's general attitude toward the situation and tailor your presentation accordingly. Are they worried and in need of reassurance? Are they sanguine and in need of a warning? Are they angry and in need of calming?" (U.S. Department of Health and Human Services Substance Abuse and Mental Health Services Administration, 2002, p. 5).

Always keep in mind the goal: moving people toward calm and rational thoughts and actions. The U.S. Department of Health and Human Services Substance Abuse and Mental Health Services Administration (2002) counsels,

> Crisis + heightened public emotions + limited access to facts + rumor, gossip, speculation, assumption, and inference = an unstable information environment. (p. 5)

> Review your remarks to gauge the probable impact . . . and adjust them as necessary; e.g., are you using words, like "crisis," "life-threatening," or "extremely" and can other, less dramatic words be substituted? (p. 5)

The third step is captured in two questions, *"What information will we need to prepare messages and how do we access that information during an emergency?"* and *"How can we safeguard our vital records in the case of a disaster?"* As one security and loss prevention adviser cautioned, "If a vital record is lost, damaged, destroyed, or otherwise rendered unavailable, that loss becomes a disaster within a disaster, affecting critical operations needed to recover from the initial disaster" (Carlisle, 2005, p. 47). The CCP should include the identification, protection, and emergency retrieval of essential records. Carlisle counsels school administrators to ask themselves, "If you had a disaster and you had to reopen the next day, what records would you target?" (p. 47). Some data and crisis documents may be kept on personal digital assistants (PDAs) or laptops.

Table 4.1

Worksheet for Identifying Stakeholders and Their Information Needs

Group	Initial Focus	Priority	What They Need	Your Task
Parents	Narrow	"My children"	• To be with their children • Reassurance that their children are safe • Information about safeguarding their children • Control	• Accurate information • Safe and orderly dismissal
Students	Narrow	Themselves	• Clear directions to ensure safety • Familiar adult present	
Staff	Narrow	Themselves and their students	• Clear directions to ensure safety; control • Frequent updates • Contact with own family especially if they are at risk	
Public	Narrow	Relatives, own safety	• Frequent updates	
Agencies	Depends on role			
Media	Broad			
Board Members	Broad			

The fourth step in drafting a communications plan is to develop templates for your key messages. Be sure your statements are at an appropriate literacy level and in the necessary languages for your audiences to comprehend. Word processing software usually allows you to assess basic readability statistics for documents, while technical information will require more of your attention (see the U.S. Department of Health and Human Services [2003] handbook chapter on communicating complex, scientific, and technical information). Do not overlook the needs of viewers, readers, and listeners with disabilities that might impede their understanding. Project Reassure, founded in the wake of Hurricane Katrina, offers easy-to-read handouts for those comforting children and teens with special needs (www.projectreassure.org).

In crafting your communications, keep in mind the *key messages* you want your audiences to hear. "Under the stress of a crisis it is easy to forget, or at least fail to state properly, the main points you want to convey to publics or to a specific public. Each message must be accurate, brief, easy to use in a quote, and memorable" (Fearn-Banks, 2002, p. 37). You can find excellent examples of templates and accompanying tips in the *NEA Crisis Communications Guide and Toolkit* (National Education Association, 2002). Plan to have sample press releases, announcements, fact sheets, handouts, and letters stored in multiple languages on CD-ROMs for use in a crisis. The National Association of School Psychologists (NASP) website has some handouts in different languages.

Next, discuss among your team the question, *"What is the best timing for this key message?"* For example, parents will get their news from radio broadcasts, the Internet, or local newscasts. If parents have not yet received information from the school and have no way to contact the school (especially after hours), their only information will come from the media, their friends, and their family. But if they know that the district always updates its parent hotline and website at 7 A.M., noon, and 4 P.M. after a critical incident, they will rely on these bulletins.

Next, answer the question, *"Who should be the spokesperson for a particular message?"* Although most districts will assign one person to be the spokesperson, you will encounter circumstances that call for outside specialists. For example, if an incident involves a public heath risk, you should contact the health department to deliver the facts. The general public wants to hear medical information from an expert, not from someone with an education degree!

USING TECHNOLOGY TO FACILITATE INITIAL CRISIS COMMUNICATIONS

What is the use of a crisis plan if staff members cannot easily share information? Undeniably, the effectiveness of crisis plans relies on the ability of staff members to communicate quickly and efficiently (Myers, 2001).

Michael Dorn (2001) offers one of many possible situations that can increase the severity of a crisis resulting from a lack of effective communications:

> In a suburban school, an elderly woman pulls a large revolver out of her purse and holds the main office hostage. Unfortunately, the office staff has no way of contacting staff members outside of the office. To make matters worse, the only crisis kit is in the main office itself. The school had recently spent $100,000 on a brand-new camera system, but the videotapes were not accessible outside of the school.

In Dorn's example, we see how the lack of communication among staff members and the absence of communication with the local police aggravated an already tense situation. If the school were able to initiate contact with classroom staff, for example, the circumstances of the crisis may not have been so alarming.

Two-way radios are cost-effective tools that can help facilitate communications between administration and staff during the initial stages of a crisis. Myers (2001) notes that two-way radios allow security patrols to share information easily with school officials and staff, in addition to allowing the main office to keep in constant contact with teachers. Teachers who take their students outdoors for physical education or other activities should always carry two-way radios so they do not miss crisis communications such as lockdowns or evacuation orders.

In Dorn's example of an intruder with a handgun, the principal could have used a two-way radio to initiate a schoolwide evacuation that would have removed the students out of harm's way. In another example, a staff member patrolling the school parking lot may radio other staff to assist her quickly in controlling a violent fistfight that has broken out among three students.

Setting Up a Crisis Hotline

A school crisis hotline is another tool that can be used to prevent crises. A hotline gives students a safe, confidential outlet where they can express their feelings or concerns about happenings within the school. A successful crisis hotline supplies information about possible upcoming situations and may serve as a barometer of student feelings.

When creating a crisis hotline, schools should invite students and parents to be on the planning team. Involving students is important because they can be very helpful in marketing the hotline to the student body to facilitate its use (McDaniel, n.d.). Another way to market the hotline is to hold a press conference announcing the hotline and its uses. Again, involving the students in the announcement can help get other students' attention. Finally, give the students' wallet cards with the hotline number on one side and safety tips on the other (McDaniel, n.d.).

A crisis hotline should be monitored 24 hours a day, 7 days a week. If your school does not have personnel on call at all times, try rotating hotline duty among staff and community volunteers (McDaniel, n.d.). Supervisors should outline a clear protocol for those monitoring the hotline, so if word of a potential crisis arises, the proper preventative measures are taken into action.

COMMUNICATIONS DURING A CRISIS

This section illustrates how communications during a crisis can mobilize and facilitate the response to a critical incident, contain the crisis and prevent spinoff crises, and maintain or restore the public's confidence in the school.

Naturally, one of the first calls an administrator should make is to any families of those injured or deceased. These may be the most difficult calls of one's career, so we advise that you have a colleague nearby while making them. Be sure this challenging task is listed in your communications checklist because overlooking it can be hurtful for a family. Consider this story:

> A young child was killed in a handgun accident at home. I was called to the school as an outside mental health specialist and got there rapidly. We worked throughout the day to inform staff and children as sensitively as we could. At the end of the day, I sat down with the principal and asked about her conversation with the parents. Imagine how I felt when she responded, "I thought *you* placed that call."

Our chapter on postvention includes guidelines for communicating with families after a death.

Callout Procedures for the Crisis Team and Agency Personnel

To mobilize a crisis team, the coordinator must receive information about a critical event in a timely manner. During school hours, a two-way radio is an economical and convenient communications device. "Unlike . . . pagers and cellular phones, two-way radios have a one-time cost and do not incur monthly charges or service fees. In addition . . . extensive and costly training is not needed" (Myers, 2001, p. 35). During nights, weekends, and school breaks, be sure at least one crisis team member is available for calls from employees and community agencies (i.e., law enforcement, emergency responders, mental health agencies, and the health department). Some districts rotate this duty among several administrators, who share a district cell phone or pager.

Outlining a telephone tree in advance and "sticking to a script" speeds the mobilization of crisis responders. Consistency of the message is of utmost importance during a crisis (Polansky & Montague, 2001). Provide each team member with the same information, ask members to bring their crisis kits, and relay the location and time for the team's first briefing. (For a telephone tree template, see the NEA handbook [National Education Association, 2002].) E-mails can communicate follow-up information, but only if confidentiality safeguards are in place and team members agree to check their e-mails on an agreed on and frequent schedule.

If you believe a critical incident will affect a team member or other staff personally because of a relationship with those at risk or injured, consider having a close colleague break the news in person and relieve the employee from crisis duty. Death or serious injury of a colleague or student can be traumatic, as one superintendent explains: "People become teachers because they deeply care about children, and it is this depth of emotion that makes them so good at what they do" (Hewitt, 2004, p. 44).

Next we turn to initial communications for the internal audiences of a school: its employees, parents, and students.

INFORMING SCHOOL PERSONNEL

Once the crisis team and emergency response personnel receive notice and confirm with the family or law enforcement (if a death or injury occurred offsite), quickly inform school employees. An extended telephone tree managed by a few members of the crisis team may be the best option during nonschool hours. An audible alert or public announcement of a crisis code followed by an e-mail on classroom computers or a personally delivered briefing may be your choice during the school day. As the following vignette from a veteran crisis responder illustrates, you can never assume that staff already know about an incident.

> I arrived at the elementary school minutes after the principal paged me at 2:30 P.M. with the information that a horse-playing student had fallen over a third-floor banister. The paramedics already had taken the student to the hospital, and the school nurse had ensured that the area was secured and cleaned. Parents in the neighborhood who heard the sirens beat me to the scene, followed by local reporters, who heard the 911 call.
>
> Given all that activity, you can imagine my surprise when I realized that many classroom teachers had no knowledge of the accident! I scrambled to put together a short explanation and advisory that teachers should hold students in their classrooms. This was long before e-mail, so we walked these notices around to each teacher. After all these years, I still do not understand how that incident escaped the notice of so many teachers and students.

An emergency meeting of all school faculty and staff should take place as soon as practicable. At a meeting following a death, for example, you would first give the name and grade (or staff assignment) of the victim(s). Whether to describe the cause of death is a decision based on a number of factors. These factors include (1) the wishes of the victim's immediate family, (2) the advice of mental health and public health professionals regarding the risk of contagion, (3) whether the cause of death is already well known in the community, and (4) a clinical judgment as to whether those at risk for contagion will be better protected and served if they are made aware of the incident and its accompanying risks. One should never refer to a cause of death as suicide that the coroner or medical examiner has not confirmed.

Next, express condolences to the staff and recognize their feelings. A teacher might be a close colleague or relative of the victim, a friend of the victim's family, or be involved with the victim through school or community activities. The tragedy may revive memories of a past loss. Inform staff about signs of stress and how they might manage the difficult days ahead. The crisis team may also anticipate which faculty members and staff may need assistance due to unrelated losses or hardships and offer individual support. Some districts provide EAP services for staff and faculty.

Be sure to introduce anyone from outside of the school who is assisting in the crisis response, and share plans for external audiences such as feeder schools and adjacent school districts.

If time allows, give an overview of the crisis response, including plans for contacting the victim's family and funeral arrangements; how the school will inform and assist other students; the availability of counselors to talk with students individually and in groups; signs to look for in students who may need to be seen/referred; and procedures for referring students for individual screening and assistance.

If prepared, share the letter that will be sent to parents of the student body (see Figure 4.3 and our website for sample letters). This letter might form the basis for faculty announcements to students.

Emphasize confidentiality. Remind school staff that much of the information shared during a postvention is confidential. Alert staff that community members will undoubtedly question them for details of the tragedy, and review school district guidelines about sharing of confidential student (or faculty) information.

Finally, announce follow-up briefings or meetings. A follow-up staff meeting should be planned at the end of the day. Intermittent staff meetings may occur depending on the need to share new information or get advice from the faculty (Kerr et al., 2006). In a crisis situation extending across days, you will schedule regular meetings or briefings so employees and responders have all the information they need. "Develop daily checklists and create contact sheets so that no one is left out of the loop . . . One person left out of the loop can create a domino effect of bad publicity and bad information" (Polansky & Montague, 2001, p. 15).

Throughout your communications with staff, don't ignore questions because they seem unimportant to you. People react to crises individually, and their concerns are valid to them (Polansky & Montague, 2001). Acknowledge the difficult task the staff members are facing, affirm their efforts, and thank them for their cooperation.

INFORMING STUDENTS

If a tragedy occurs during the school day, the school may choose to have students return to a special homeroom session for this announcement or make other arrangements to reach faculty and have them announce the event to students. If any faculty member does not feel comfortable announcing the death in the classroom or answering students' questions, have that person inform the principal. Postvention team members then can step in to make the announcement or otherwise support the faculty member.

Of course, in the midst of an ongoing threat, students require step-by-step instructions to remain safe. Optimally, students will have practiced these steps in drills. After the

Figure 4.2
Sample Announcement.

Announcement of Death

On (*date*), a student (*staff member*) from our school, (*name the deceased*), died tragically. (*You may choose to provide facts about the incident, depending on the situation.*) We are all saddened by this loss. A sudden loss like this can cause many strong feelings. It is good to talk to someone about these feelings. We recommend that you speak to your parents about this and share your reactions. It is important to let your parents know how you feel.

In other schools where this has happened, students have also found it helpful to speak to a counselor. The school is sensitive to this need and has arranged to have counselors from (*name of agency*) available to talk with you (*time and place*). Arrangements to see a counselor can be made at the (*guidance office or other location*).

Source: From *Postvention Standards Manual: A Guide for a School's Response in the Aftermath of a Sudden Death* (5th ed., pp. 80–84), by M. M. Kerr, D. A. Brent, B. McKain, and P. S. McCommons, 2006, Pittsburgh, PA: STAR-Center Outreach. Reprinted with permission.

emergency phase has passed, however, students need accurate information about the incident or tragedy and about services the school will provide. Because each student should hear the same information, teachers should rely on a prepared announcement to read to students (see Figure 4.2 for a sample announcement). To the extent possible, while safeguarding confidentiality and keeping the situation calm and orderly, tell students as much factual information as they can handle. Naturally, an advisory would be worded and handled differently for very young children or those with severe cognitive disabilities.

The announcement of a death should never be broadcast over an in-school announcement system or solely in a school bulletin (unless the death or incident involved someone long absent from the school). These approaches convey an impersonal tone that those close to the deceased will resent. Also, avoid announcements in a large-group assembly. Large groups do not allow the school faculty to assess the reactions of students and follow up with personal support. Chapter 9 on postvention provides you with help on informing students about a death.

INFORMING PARENTS

Nearly all parents are single-minded in a school-related crisis; they want their child safely returned to their custody. Many schools learned this lesson on September 11, 2001, when parents stormed schools across the United States, seeking safe reunification with their loved ones.

A letter home to parents not only informs them of the death or critical incident but can serve to educate parents about acute stress reactions as well (see Figure 4.3).

Holding a Parent Meeting

In some situations, a parent meeting may be scheduled. This meeting, conducted by the school, may include presentations by law enforcement, mental health, and/or health professionals. The goal of the meeting is to alleviate community concerns, share facts, and enlist parental support. The meeting may or may not include students.

Figure 4.3
Sample Letter.

Sample Letter for Parents of Elementary-Age Children

(Note: Be sensitive to previous letters that were sent. You want to avoid having your letter look like a carbon copy with only a name change. Send this letter if you are writing to the parents of students in elementary school. Otherwise, revise this letter, and address it to "Dear Student and Family.")

Dear Parents and Guardians,

It is with great sadness that we inform you of the death of a member of our school community, *(Add the name of the student or staff person, if you choose.)* who died on *(Add the date)*.

A sudden loss like this can have an effect on students. For that reason, we hope that you will listen to your child as well as discuss with them their feelings and reactions to this tragedy. Sudden death is always painful to understand, and your child may experience signs of stress. These include:

- Sleep difficulties (i.e., nightmares, trouble falling asleep, and sleeping too much)
- Changes in appetite
- Inability to concentrate
- Absentmindedness
- Irritability
- Thoughts about death or dying
- Isolation
- Withdrawing from normal activities and friends
- Increased aggression or acting out
- Regressive behavior (e.g., thumb-sucking)
- Guilt
- Separation anxiety
- Fearfulness and worries
- Sensitivity to change in routine
- Use of alcohol or other drugs
- Risk-taking behaviors (e.g., riding a bike carelessly; use of firearms, and "dares" to participate in dangerous behaviors)

(Use this paragraph if you suspect that students are at risk for suicide.) We are especially concerned about risk-taking behaviors and strongly recommend that you remove any guns from homes where there are young people experiencing grief and related stress. Similarly, remove from your child's access any medications, drugs, or alcohol. Young people may be overwhelmed by their feelings and not use good judgment, especially if they are under the influence of drugs or alcohol. Your child may resist these restrictions, but safety is our first concern.

Counselors from *(Add the name of the agency here.)* will be available at the school for several days to talk with students who are experiencing stress. If you have concerns about your child, please call. *(Add the name, title, and telephone number of the school contact for parents to call. Add any additional information regarding parents' consent for their child to be seen by agency personnel, according to your school district's policy.)*

If your child was *(a friend of the youth who has died) (close to the staff member who died)*, we urge you to call us for additional suggestions. After school hours, you may call. *(Add the name, title, and telephone number of the after-hours school contact for parents who cannot call during regular school hours.)* If you want your child to be excused for the funeral, we request that you send us a written excuse. Students should not return to school after the funeral service. We encourage you to accompany your child to the funeral home and services.

On behalf of *(name the school)*, I have extended our sincere condolences to the family of *(name the student or staff person, or refer to them as "the student" or "the staff member")* on this sad occasion. We will continue to inform you of the school's steps in supporting students and their families. Please do not hesitate to call us if you have any questions or information that you would like to share.

Sincerely,

(Principal of the school or other school official)

Source: From *Postvention Standards Manual: A Guide for a School's Response in the Aftermath of a Sudden Death* (5th ed., pp. 80–84), by M. M. Kerr, D.A. Brent, B. McKain, and P. S. McCommons, 2006, Pittsburgh, PA: STAR-Center Outreach. Reprinted with permission.

Before the meeting begins, school personnel should ascertain whether there are any representatives in the audience and determine whether they are to remain for any or all of the meeting. Media representatives should not be present if personal information is shared by parents or if the district views media coverage as a barrier to the crisis response. Instead, offer interviews individually to reporters beforehand or afterward when no parents or students are present.

The following agenda items could be included in the parent meeting:

- An update on the critical incident or threat
- The school's crisis response activities to date
- Typical child and adolescent responses to a stressful situation (see Chapter 5)
- How and when parents might identify children who require additional support (e.g., those exhibiting acute stress disorder, anxiety, depression, and suicidal behavior)
- Resources available in the community (e.g., student help cards, school safety hotline number, public health agency contact information)
- How to reach school personnel after hours to share crucial information or get help for a child
- How to handle requests from reporters
- Any prevention or response efforts the district anticipates where parental input is encouraged

Students and parents should understand that their statements to the media might have a negative impact on others and on the family of the deceased. Schools cannot prevent students and parents from talking to representatives of the media, but they can encourage students and parents to refer media inquiries to the designated spokesperson. Media representative should not enter the school grounds to film or interview staff, parents, or students who are coping with a critical incident or tragedy. Excellent handouts for parents and students regarding interactions with reporters appear in the *NEA Crisis Communications Guide and Toolkit* (National Education Association, 2002).

RUMOR CONTROL

Rumors often arise as individuals try to discern the ongoing threats during a critical incident or attempt to figure out the causes following a tragedy. This speculation can exacerbate a crisis by spreading rumors. Reliable information that is easily accessed is our best defense against rumors.

When a new rumor arises, tell the students or staff what you know to be true. If adults cannot immediately refute the rumor, find an appropriate source to address the rumor as honestly and accurately as possible. Sometimes the only answer is "To the best of my knowledge, that is not true," or "If I find out anything about that (rumor) being true, I will let you know. At this time I don't believe that information is accurate." In a widespread disaster or especially threatening situation, you may consider setting up a rumor control hotline or briefings based on frequently asked questions (see National Education Association, 2002). As long as confidentiality and security concerns are addressed, a district may also use its website to post updates about an ongoing situation.

Confidentiality Concerns

Federal laws prohibit the release of personal student and employee information, including discipline, health, and academic records. The Family Educational Rights and Privacy Act (FERPA) states that schools may disclose, without consent, only "directory" information such as a student's name, address, telephone number, date and place of birth, honors and awards, and dates of attendance (U.S. Department of Education, n.d.). However, schools must tell parents and eligible students about directory information and allow parents and eligible students a reasonable amount of time to request that the school not disclose directory information about them. Certain situations such as the enforcement of a subpoena and safety emergencies do allow schools to release other educational information to various parties.

FERPA covers the disclosure of educational records, and the Health Insurance Portability and Accountability Act (HIPAA) provides confidentiality when dealing with medical and health records. HIPAA's privacy rule establishes regulations for the use and disclosure of information about health status and stipulation of health care. This includes information such as axis diagnoses, treatments, and medical conditions (U.S. Department of Health and Human Services, 2003). Administration should never release protected information to the public. *HIPAA Privacy Rule: Disclosures for Emergency Preparedness—A Decision Tool*, a guide for complying with HIPAA during a school crisis, has been posted on the U.S. Department of Education's Emergency Response and Crisis Management Technical Assistance website.

WORKING WITH MEDIA REPRESENTATIVES

Working with representatives of print and electronic media is crucial in a crisis. As one expert pessimistically observed,

> The media to which you have tried to pitch ideas for news stories, the media that toss "perfect" news releases to the trash, the media that never return phone calls—*that media* will

call you in a crisis. They will probably not telephone in advance. They will show up on your premises—"in your face." The media, seeing themselves as advocates for the people, can be the principal adversaries in a crisis. (Fearn-Banks, 2002, p. 3)

But a mutually respectful relationship between the school and the media can improve your crisis response measurably: "Make the press your ally. Use the press to your advantage to disseminate information and curtail panic. One-on-one interviews and other channels of communication are vital during the first few days" (Polansky & Montague, 2001, p. 15).

Understanding the media's role and responsibilities can help you avoid the power struggle that often characterizes unsuccessful relations between school and the press. In this section, we offer advice for making your relationships with the media mutually successful. Understanding media goals, deadlines, and limitations is the first step.

Understanding Media Goals, Limitations, and Deadlines

Conflicts often arise between school personnel and media representatives (U.S. Department of Health and Human Services Substance Abuse and Mental Health Services Administration, 2002). Often these differences are merely the result of different goals. For example, the journalist's job in covering a school accident is to gain and publish information; your goal, however, is to protect the privacy and safety of your students. Therefore, you will need to explain to the media that they are not allowed on school grounds but at the same time try to arrange interviews with your spokesperson off the campus. A good working relationship with the press can help you through these conflicts. First, you need to understand the working conditions of the press.

Reporters cannot allow you or anyone else to define the news for them, as an ethical matter (U.S. Department of Health and Human Services Substance Abuse and Mental Health Services Administration, 2002). Therefore, what you say may not be aired or written. Space and time limitations play a factor in the outcome of a story. On a slow news night, your story may get more attention than you think is warranted, or you may find your interview reduced to mere "sound bites" if yours is competing for airtime on a busier evening.

Be respectful of the deadlines under which journalists are working to cover your story. Ask them when they need an interview and try to accommodate them. If you cannot meet a deadline, offer someone else who is prepared for the interview or suggest a trusted expert who will comment. Using an outside expert can deflect attention away from the immediate crisis and prevent hastily prepared remarks from those on the scene. Hospitals and universities often employ experts with whom you can develop such relationships. Suggest to staff that if approached by the media, they be polite but firm, saying something like, "My first priority is my students right now. I'll let my principal know that you want a statement."

Creating and Maintaining the Message

As we indicated earlier, it's best to plan press releases, press conferences, and other briefings in a general way before a crisis. You can control your key messages even if you cannot predict all of a reporter's "trick questions." Remember: an interview is *not* a conversation. Table 4.2 describes some inquiries for which you can prepare.

Table 4.2
Types of Media Questions for Which You Can Prepare

Type of Questions	Description	Sample
Speculative	Often begin with "if" and will prompt you to consider hypotheticals.	"If the seniors were not out on a field trip, how long would it have taken to evacuate the school?"
Leading	Imply there is already an answer to the question.	"The district will change their protocol after this incident, right?"
Loaded	Designed to bring up strong emotions and feelings.	"If you knew there was a tornado warning in effect, why didn't you move the students to the shelter?"
Naive	Imply that the reporter does not know what to ask.	"I'm not certain about this, but doesn't the school have a crisis plan to guide their actions?"
False	Purposely contain inaccuracies with the aim of retrieving information.	"Thirty students were injured?" An inexperienced communications representative may feel the need to correct the falsehood and accidentally reveal information: "No, only 15 students were hospitalized."
Know-it-all	Attempt to make the communications representative think the reporter already has the correct information.	"We already know what happened at the football game. Can you just tell me what you plan to do now?"
Silence	The reporter stops asking questions in the hopes you will keep talking and leak information in the process.	An awkward silence forces a nervous principal to utter the names of two students suspected of bringing firearms into the school.
Accusatory	Attempt to force you to place blame on another party.	"If you weren't the one who gave the OK for the police to leave, who was?"
Multiple-part	Bombard the speaker with confusing, multitiered questions.	"Mr. Maydak, how many threats does the school receive on average? Furthermore, are these threats usually violent in nature, how do you plan to trace them, and do you have a plan to stop them?"
Jargonistic	Use technical phrases or terms uncommon to the general public.	"Didn't this student have an IEP as per IDEA that should have addressed this problem?"
Chummy	The reporter acts in a friendly manner to elicit information from the speaker.	"C'mon Bob, just between you and me, the school wasn't prepared for this, was it?"
Labeling	Questions that ask to clarify an issue to cast them in a negative light.	"Would you say the district did not allocate enough resources in the school's budget to handle a flood of this magnitude?"
Good-bye	Come at the end of a news conference or interview. The equipment may be turned off, but the reporter is still listening.	"Thanks for the information. You did a great job. By the way, where is the kid's funeral?"

Source: From *Crisis Communications: A Casebook Approach* (2nd ed., pp. 71–72), by J. Fearn-Banks, 2002, Mahwah, NJ: Erlbaum. Adapted with permission.

Let's reflect . . .

As you review each of these sample inquiries, consider how you might respond without giving out confidential information or more detail than you wish. If possible, role-play with your colleagues posing as reporters. Try preparing key messages that are brief (20 to 30 seconds). Organize them as your speaking notes, making sure the most important messages are first (U.S. Department of Health and Human Services Substance Abuse and Mental Health Services Administration, 2002).

Media Interviews

If you are the spokesperson for your district, be sure you have practiced mock interviews and received feedback on your presentations. Such simulations can help you refine your content, vocal delivery, and body language. You may find volunteer "coaches" in your high school, university, or college communications departments. If you have practiced in such a safe situation, you will be less anxious when a real media appearance presents itself (Wallace, personal communication, 2006). Table 4.3 offers do's and don'ts for media appearances.

Table 4.3
Do's and Don'ts for Media Appearances

Do's	Don'ts
Listen to the entire question before giving your answer.	Appear frightened or nervous.
Use everyday language and avoid technical terms or jargon.	Guess the answer to a question if you do not know the facts.
Portray an image that is respectful, positive, calm, concerned, and, if the situation calls for it, apologetic.	Become too upset over being quoted out of context.
Return reporters' phone calls and understand the need for deadlines.	Play favorites with media representatives. Answer questions in a fair and unselective manner.
Be open and accessible.	Stick with a story if you are aware that the facts have changed.
Treat the reporter as a friend, not an enemy.	Predict what is going to happen in the future.
Maintain eye contact and address reporters by name.	Wear sunglasses, chew gum, or use tobacco.
Follow the guidelines set by your school's crisis communication plan.	Appear that you do not want to be answering questions about the event.

Source: From *Crisis Communications: A Casebook Approach* (2nd ed., pp. 69–71), by J. Fearn-Banks, 2002, Mahwah, NJ: Erlbaum. Adapted with permission.

SUMMARY

Planning for communications is an essential role in crisis responding. A crisis communications plan (CCP) directs how the school will convey and receive information from its employees, students, families, and the general public. By preparing ahead, school personnel not only can prevent or detect critical incidents, but they can mobilize the response, contain the crisis and prevent spinoff crises, restore the public's confidence, and inform future crisis responses.

CASE STUDY CONCLUSION

I picked up exactly where I left off with my lesson and continued to explain how and why the different decimal places were named. I explained the activity, and the students had just begun when there was another knock at the door. It was the guidance counselor. He motioned that he wished to speak to me outside. I stepped outside my door and he said, "Alex, you're from Pittsburgh, right?"

I said, "Yes, why?"

He responded, "There is a fourth hijacked plane circling around Pittsburgh; I just thought you should know," and he walked down the hall.

I know now that this plane was not meant for a Pittsburgh destination, but this false information struck me almost more immediately than the other news because my entire family lives there. As I was digesting all this, the music teacher was on her way to my class with her cart. I returned to my room and had my students start clearing their desks to prepare for music class. As soon as she assumed control of my class, I immediately went to the teacher's lounge and started making phone calls. I tried to use my cell phone three or four times but it kept saying that all circuits were busy, so I turned to the land line. I called my older brother at work and actually got through. He said he was very glad to hear my voice, that everyone was very concerned about me, and he would call around to my parents and other family members and assure them I was OK. When I asked him about the plane circling around Pittsburgh, he told me that it had crashed in a field outside of Somerset. With these immediate concerns of my own family lifted, I went down to the office to see if there had been any new developments. I spoke to my principal for only two minutes. Her first question was, "Are you holding up OK? Do you need anything?"

I assured her that I was fine. She then told me that recess was to be held inside. "Tell the students it is a red air quality day."

The secretary later explained to me that this air quality rating is in reference to a combination of heat index, humidity, and pollen count that causes breathing to be difficult, specifically for students with allergies and asthma. More importantly, it was a reason that the students recognized and needed no further explanation. All else was to remain as normal and it did, with one exception.

As I returned to my class, I held the door for the music teacher and her cart. I looked up at the class and noticed two children were missing. I asked the class, "Where are Chris and Luke?"

One of my students said, "Chris and Luke both had early dismissals during music." This continued on throughout the day.

After recess and lunch, I had only 18 students because six more had been taken during recess and lunch. I decided to fill the afternoon with hands-on science activities dealing with electrical circuits and reading aloud from the book *Where the Red Fern Grows* by Wilson Rawls.

When students asked why so many of their classmates had early dismissals, before I could answer, one of my students said, "They all live near each other. Maybe their neighborhood is having a block party." He then went on to explain that his street had just had a block party over Labor Day weekend. The remaining children seemed intrigued, and I was content to let the children think this was the reason their classmates were leaving early.

After this conversation, the day continued as normal. At dismissal, the students wrote in their agendas, gathered their things, and left when their buses were called. After dismissal was complete and all the students had exited the building, our principal announced over the public address system that there would be a brief staff meeting in the library. When we were all present, she thanked us for our professionalism and efforts throughout the day. She explained to us the latest news report that these attacks were most likely made by terrorists. She said, "I want you to go home and be with your families. It is a shame that sometimes it takes something like this to make us realize what is truly important. The superintendent has cancelled school for the next three days. We are to report next Monday at our normal time. If you need anything, please don't hesitate to call me. Take care and drive home safely."

Let's reflect . . .

Our case study illustrates a scene common to schools on September 11, 2001. School administrators, caught totally unprepared by this unprecedented disaster, used their best judgment to support employees, children, and families. As you continue reading this case, reflect on your own situation that day. Were you a teacher or school administrator? Were you a student or parent? How do you view the information you received or issued? What tough decisions might you have made differently, given what you now know?

DISCUSSION AND APPLICATION IDEAS

Consider the following scenarios.

Scenario A: Interpersonal Violence Witnessed by Students

A junior high student (John) is confronted by a teen (Don) after he steps off his bus. John pulls out a small pocketknife. While horrified students and the bus driver watch, Don collapses, wounded by the knife. Later, he dies in a local hospital.

Scenario B: Multiple Students at Risk

A seventh grader brings a syringe to school and assaults other students with it. Reporters are on the scene within minutes. About 20 students are taken to area hospitals. It is now 12:45 P.M.

Scenario C: Teacher Murdered

It is Wednesday night, and you have just heard on the television news that one of your experienced fourth-grade teachers has been murdered.

As you read each vignette, reflect on these questions:

1. "Who are our target internal and external audiences?"
2. "What information will we need to prepare messages, and how do we access that information during this emergency?"
3. "What is the best timing for this key message?"

4. "Who should be the spokesperson for a particular message?"
5. "What are the essential points we want to convey to our internal and external audiences?"

REFERENCES

Carlisle, V. (2005). Protecting vital records in a crisis. *School Administrator, 62* (11), 47.

Covello, V., Peters, R. G., Wojtecki, J. G., & Hyde, R. C. (2001). Risk communication, the West Nile virus epidemic, and bioterrorism: Responding to the communication challenges posed by the intentional or unintentional release of a pathogen in an urban setting. *Journal of Urban Health: Bulletin of the New York Academy of Medicine, 78,* 382-391.

Dorn, M. (2001). Are you prepared for the next crisis? *School Planning & Management, 40* (4), 35-36, 38. Retrieved September 7, 2006, from http://www.peterli.com/archive/spm/240.shtm

Fearn-Banks, K. (2002). *Crisis communications: A casebook approach* (2nd ed.). Mahwah, NJ: Erlbaum.

Hewitt, P. (2004). In a crisis, focus on the people. *The School Administrator, 9* (61), 44-45.

Kerr, M. M., Brent, D. A., McKain, B., & McCommons, P. S. (2006). *Postvention standards manual: A guide for a school's response in the aftermath of a sudden death* (5th ed.). Pittsburgh, PA: University of Pittsburgh, Services for Teens at Risk (STAR-Center).

Maxwell, R. (1999). The British government's handling of risk: Some reflections on the BSE/CJD crisis. In P. Bennett & K. Calman (Eds.), *Risk communication and public health* (pp. 95-107). London: Oxford University Press.

McDaniel, J. (n.d.) *Communicating about school safety: A how-to guide to help school board members and school administrators build support and understanding for public schools.* Washington State School Directors Association. Retrieved August 8, 1999, from http://www.keepschoolssafe.org/wssd.htm

Myers, F. (2001). *Communication: Key to controlling and responding to crisis.* Retrieved September 7, 2006, from http://www.peterli.com/archive/spm/240.shtm

National Education Association. (2002). *NEA crisis communications guide and toolkit.* Washington, DC: Author.

O'Toole, T. (2001). Emerging illness and bioterrorism: Implications for public health. *Journal of Urban Health: Bulletin of the New York Academy of Medicine, 78,* 396-402.

Polansky, H. B., & Montage, R. (2001). Handling an emergency: A defining moment. *School Business Affairs, 67* (7), 13-15.

U.S. Department of Education. (n.d.). *Family Educational Rights and Privacy Act (FERPA).* Retrieved October 29, 2007, from http://www.ed.gov/policy/gen/guid/fpco/ferpa/students.html

U.S. Department of Health and Human Services. (2003). *Summary of the HIPAA Privacy Rule.* Retrieved August 8, 2006, from http://www.hhs.gov/ocr/privacysummary.pdf

U.S. Department of Health and Human Services Substance Abuse and Mental Health Services Administration. (2002). *Communicating in a crisis: Risk communication guidelines for public officials.* Rockville, MD: Author.

CHAPTER 5

PREVENTION, MITIGATION, AND RESPONSE FOR ACCIDENTS AND ILLNESSES

CASE STUDY

At the end of the day at Los Alamos Middle School, the students were waiting to board the buses to go home. Manuel, a sixth grader, started talking to his friends about a new game that other kids were playing.

As Manuel boarded the bus he said to his friend Alejandro, "Hey, what are you doing after school today? I heard about this fun game from an eighth grader at lunchtime. It's called the Choking Game. Want to come over and play it?"

"Cool, a game . . . I'm always up for a game," replied Alejandro.

Later on that afternoon at Manuel's house, the boys talked about how this game was played. Unbeknownst to them, Manuel's younger 9-year-old brother Jaime was watching and listening from the hallway.

"So, how do we play this game?" asked Alejandro. Manuel explained, "OK, first, stand up against this wall. Then I'm gonna wrap this extension cord around your neck and hold it real tight, then the real fun will begin!"

"OK, I'm ready," responded Alejandro.

At his point, Manuel wrapped the extension cord from his stereo around Alejandro's neck and pulled it tight. The extension cord put pressure on the carotid arteries in the neck, which restricted blood flow and oxygen from reaching Alejandro's brain. Alejandro closed his eyes and slumped to the floor of Manuel's bedroom.

Manuel released the extension cord after Alejandro fell to the ground. Alejandro resumed consciousness and exclaimed, "That was the coolest feeling ever! I felt like I was floating in space and my legs felt tingly and numb."

Alejandro was experiencing the "high" created when the brain is deprived of oxygen. A secondary high is felt when the pressure on the carotid arteries is released and blood and oxygen are allowed once again to reach the brain.

At this point Jaime entered his older brother's bedroom. "Hey, that looks like fun. Let me play." Manuel replied, "No, get out of here; you're too little to play this game!" Jaime ran out of the room yelling, "I can do whatever you do, Manuel!"

Returning to the game, Manuel said to Alejandro, "See, I told you that was the coolest game ever. Those eighth graders weren't lying!"

"Yeah, it's so easy to play. I bet you can use a belt or a tie and play it by yourself too," observed Alejandro.

Later that evening, Manuel's younger brother Jaime was in his bedroom thinking about all the fun his brother and his friend were having. Since Jaime wanted to be a "big boy" like his brother, he decided to play the game himself.

A few hours later, Jaime's mother went upstairs to his room to see if he needed any help doing his homework. She found Jaime's lifeless body lying on the floor with a belt around his neck. As she began to shake Jaime, she screamed for Manuel to call 911.

INTRODUCTION

Anticipating and planning for common crises is one of the most important steps you can take in crisis prevention, as discussed in Chapter 2. Once you predict the medical emergencies most likely to happen in your school, you can focus your assessment, planning, and response efforts more effectively. Accordingly, this chapter begins by sharing data on the leading causes of childhood deaths, injuries, and hospitalizations.

In 2004 (the latest data available), among U.S. children aged 1 to 14, there were 11,619 deaths, with unintentional injuries (i.e., accidents) as the leading cause. Unintentional injuries accounted for 34.3% of all deaths among children aged 5 to 14. The leading cause of fatal injuries was motor vehicle crashes.

Among 15- to 19-year-olds, unintentional injury was also the primary cause of death, accounting for 49.8% of the 13,706 deaths in 2004. Of those deaths due to unintentional injury, motor vehicle crashes were the most common cause (48%); in nearly a third of these accidents, the teen was under the influence of alcohol.

The second leading cause of death in teens was homicide, accounting for 14.1%. Even when homicide could not be determined, deaths due to firearms were alarming: Firearms injuries constituted the second leading cause of deaths by injury (23%) (U.S. Department of Health and Human Services, 2006). The third leading cause of adolescent deaths was suicide (12.4%).

Hospitalization data such as those graphed in Figure 5.1 tell us about serious illness.

Examining the most recent available government data shown in Figure 5.1, we learn that diseases of the respiratory system (e.g., asthma) are primarily to blame for hospitalization for children aged 1 to 9. Asthma, one of the most common chronic childhood diseases, causes students to miss 15 million school days each year (American Association of School Administrators, n.d.). Mental disorders were the second leading cause of hospitalization for adolescents.

Studies indicate that school-age children are nine times more likely to sustain an *accidental injury* than to be the victim of an *intentional injury* while at school. Yet, schools too often focus their resources on the rare but highly publicized acts of terrorism and violence, overlooking these more common threats. As one frustrated teacher lamented, "My school is fully prepared for anthrax, but our everyday playground supervision is marginal. It just doesn't make sense."

Let's reflect . . .

How do these national statistics reflect your own experiences? Think about your school's crisis and safety plans. Would you say these incidents are addressed by your school's plans? What preventive measures do you have in place?

Getting ready for a crisis—or preventing one in the first place—necessitates a candid examination of your school's policies, procedures, facilities, and personnel. To aid you in this discovery of your school's vulnerabilities, we begin with a comprehensive assessment.

Figure 5.1

Major Causes of Hospitalization by Age: 2004.

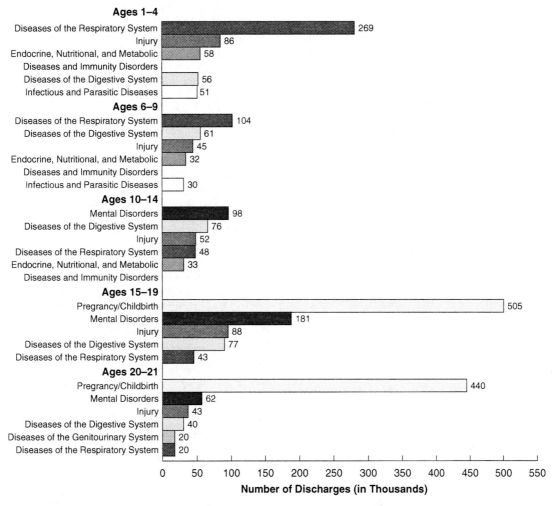

Source: From *Child Health USA 2006*, 2006, Rockville, MD: U.S. Department of Health and Human Services, Health Resources and Services Administration, Maternal and Child Health Bureau. Reprinted with permission.

ASSESSING SCHOOL HEALTH CONDITIONS

The *School Health Index (SHI) Self-Assessment & Planning Guide* is a free resource developed by the Centers for Disease Control and Prevention (CDC) in partnership with educators, school health experts, parents, and national nongovernmental health and education agencies. The SHI not only aids schools in the identification of risks to students as well as employees, but also offers schools an action plan for improving student health that can be incorporated into a School Improvement Plan. The SHI has eight different modules that correspond to the eight components of a Coordinated School Health Program (CSHP) as defined by the CDC:

1. School Health and Safety Policies and Environment
2. Health Education
3. Physical Education and Other Physical Activity Programs
4. Nutrition Services
5. Health Services
6. Counseling, Psychological, and Social Services
7. Health Promotion for Staff
8. Family and Community Involvement

A link to the School Health Index is on our companion website. At the SHI website you'll find the free online self-assessment, structured to enable teams to analyze their school objectively and efficiently while working toward an action plan with specific outcome measures. Additionally, training materials such as transparency masters are posted. You'll notice that the assessment and planning process encompasses not only student safety but employee well-being as well. After all, adults also are vulnerable to medical emergencies.

Next, we review ways to prevent particular accidents, respiratory crises, and behavioral/psychiatric emergencies.

PREVENTING ACCIDENTS ON THE WAY TO AND FROM SCHOOL

Children are at much greater risk traveling to and from school than at any other time in their school day (National Highway Traffic and Safety Administration, 2000). For example, during the 1998–1999 school year, more than 800 children aged between 5 and 18 were killed during normal school transportation hours while traveling by foot, passenger car, bicycle, public transportation, and school bus. Many others suffered serious injuries or narrowly escaped.

Let's reflect . . .

Consider these real-life cases as you anticipate the crises that can occur traveling to and from school:

- A kindergartner stepped to his death when he crossed in front of his bus as it pulled out. The driver never saw him.

- A fifth grader narrowly escaped death when his peers spotted him as their bus pulled away from the bus stop. The student had crept under the bus between the front and back axles in an impulsive attempt to end his life.

- A 12-year-old middle school student riding his bike near his home was struck by an ambulance. After a week in the hospital, he died of his injuries.

- Driving to pick up her granddaughter at the local elementary school, the grandmother made a left-hand turn toward the school without seeing the oncoming car. Seated beside her, a younger granddaughter was killed instantly.

In response to tragedies like these, the National Highway Traffic Safety Administration (NHTSA) launched its Getting to School Safely program, which offers free resources to help schools and communities improve the safety of students traveling to and from school (NHTSA, 2000). Table 5.1 offers an overview of the Getting to School Safely campaign. Note the emphasis on involving others to reduce the burden on school personnel and to increase public engagement. While this program is specific to protecting students traveling to and from school, *the prevention elements are applicable to many other risk situations.* For example, you could initiate a similar campaign for bicycle safety or pedestrian safety but also for childhood immunizations, sober and safe teen driving, or depression screening.

We turn next to the prevention of accidents that take place on school grounds.

Table 5.1
National Highway Traffic Safety Administration Prevention Program Steps

1. Involve partners	Before you begin developing your program, it is important to build partnerships with groups and individuals within your community that have a vested interest.
2. Identify the problem	Whether you are working as part of a coalition or on your own, the first step in developing an effective program is to identify the most prevalent school transportation safety problems in your community. To do that, you will have to gather various types of data from a number of sources.
3. Design your program	Once you have identified the major school transportation safety problems in your community, it's time to design your program. The first step is to review the list of problems you identified through your data collection and select a key target issue that your program will address, such as bicycle safety, pedestrian safety, illegal school bus passing, or seat belt use among school students.
4. Define the specific objectives through which you will achieve that goal	This step is critical, because the success of your program will be determined by how well you meet your stated objectives. Program objectives should be SMART (Specific, Measurable, Action-oriented, Reasonable, and Time-specific.) The following examples illustrate this concept: Sample objectives: *Not So Smart* • To encourage drivers to obey laws prohibiting the passing of school buses. • To encourage seat belt use among high school students. • To increase awareness of pedestrian safety issues among elementary school students and their parents. *Smart* • To increase citations issued for illegal passing of school buses by 15 percent in 6 months. • To increase the number of students using seat belts by 20 percent during this school year, as measured by observational surveys at the school parking lot. • To have at least 40 families participate in the school's first Walk to School Day

(continued)

Table 5.1 *(continued)*

5. Build program components	Now that you have established a strong foundation, you can begin to build your program. To a great extent, your target issue and objective will determine the nature and duration of your program. For example, if your issue is bicycle safety and your objective is to raise awareness of the need for students to use bicycle helmets, a bike rally for students and their families would be ideal.
6. Set the strategy, timeline, and sources of support	The final steps in the planning process are developing a strategy for implementing your program—including a timeline—and identifying sources for support and possible funding.
7. Measure success	Whether you are implementing a onetime event or a longer-term program, it's important to conduct some type of evaluation to measure the impact of your efforts. The evaluation process yields a wealth of information that can help you justify the program's existence and improve it in the future.

Source: National Highway and Traffic Safety Administration (NHTSA), 2000. Retrieved October 4, 2007, from http://www.nhtsa.dot.gov/people/injury/buses/GTSS/program.html

PREVENTING ACCIDENTS AT SCHOOL

Understanding how children interact with their school environment is one step in accident prevention. According to the CDC, each year *playground-related* injuries result in emergency room treatment for more than 200,000 children aged 14 and younger. About 45% of playground-related injuries are severe—fractures, internal injuries, concussions, dislocations, and amputations (Tinsworth & McDonald, 2001). Children aged 5 to 9, who have higher rates of hospital visits for playground injuries than any other age group, are usually injured at school (Phelan, Khoury, Kalkwarf, & Lanphear, 2001). On public playgrounds, more injuries occur on climbers than on any other equipment (Tinsworth & McDonald, 2001). To counteract this particular risk, the Consumer Product Safety Commission (CPSC, n.d.) offers the following prevention tips:

- Children's clothing should not have drawstrings because the strings catch on playground equipment.
- The ground around playground equipment should be covered with a 12-inch layer of nontoxic, shock-absorbing surface material, consisting of wood chips, mulch, sand, pea gravel, or mats made of safety-tested rubber or fiber material.
- There should be no exposed hardware to catch clothing and no free-hanging ropes attached to the equipment, which could cause strangulation.
- Make sure soccer goals are securely anchored when in use. At least 28 deaths have occurred when children climbed on soccer nets or played on the cross bar. Never allow children to climb on the soccer net or goal framework. When not in use, anchor goals or chain them to a nearby fence post or sturdy framework.

The CPSC also releases periodic reports on potential dangers associated with products commonly found inside and around schools. For example, *"Children cannot safely move mobile folding tables commonly found in school cafeterias and meeting rooms. The tall heavy tables can tip over and seriously injure or kill a child"* (CPSC, n.d., p. 1). Your school can sign up on the CPSC website (linked to our companion website) for e-mail product alerts.

Let's reflect . . .

How could your crisis team conduct a safety assessment of your school grounds? Who should receive the product alerts for your school? How should they share the alerts?

Accidents can also happen when large crowds gather, especially if alcohol and drugs are present. Safety at games, dances, festivals, concerts and other events should be reviewed in advance with an interagency advisory group (see Chapter 2). In response to injuries and deaths at rock concerts, for example, the U.S. National Fire Prevention Association passed a Life Safety Code regulation that defined festival seating (whereby the audience is allowed to stand) and banned it in certain public assembly buildings without a life safety evaluation (Wertheimer, n.d.).

ENVIRONMENTAL HAZARDS

The National Institute for Occupational Safety and Health (NIOSH) is the federal agency responsible for prevention research and guidance regarding work-related injury and illness, as illustrated in these cases:

- A first-grade teacher was pulling down the classroom map for a social studies lesson when the mounting became loose and fell onto her. She sustained a severe neck injury and was out of school for months.
- A school-based police officer required 10 stitches in his left arm when he cut it on a damaged locker door while breaking up a fight.

The NIOSH website also offers extensive resources for assessing and safeguarding your school, including workplace violence prevention. We recommend that your school facilities manager, with the help of appropriate staff, use pertinent NIOSH checklists to conduct a facilities safety audit at least annually. Here is an excerpt from the exhaustive list of safety checklists, available at no cost:

- Accident Prevention Signs and Tags
- Alarm Systems and Evacuation Plans
- Electrical—Temporary Wiring
- Fixed Stairs
- General Classroom Conditions
- Guarding Floors, Stairs, and Other Openings
- Portable Hand and Power Tools
- Career-Technical Safety Program

To see how schools can translate federal and state regulations and guidelines into user-friendly advice for school personnel, look at Figure 5.2, a safety fact sheet from the large online collection at the Fairfax, Virginia, County Schools (2002).

Now we shift our focus from accidents and injuries to other health emergencies.

SAFETY RULES FOR OUTDOOR RECESS

Safety & Security Fact Sheet

✔ Teachers on recess duty must be visible to children on the playground. They must position themselves around the playground and avoid standing in clusters.

✔ Follow the playground safety rules posted on the large blue sign posted near the playground equipment.

✔ Children may not wear backpacks while playing on equipment.

✔ Students should leave objects such as pencils, pens, and markers in the classroom.

✔ Shoelaces should be tied at all times.

✔ Equipment should be used only for the purpose it was designed.

✔ Once on the playground, children may not re-enter the building except when directed to do so by a teacher.

✔ Children should be encouraged to play actively without pushing, shoving, punching, pulling, or hitting other children.

✔ Children must not wear bicycle helmets while playing on equipment because their head could become entrapped in the equipment.

✔ "Gangs" of children are not permitted to march through play areas.

✔ Jump ropes may be used only for jumping, and not for playing tug-of-war and other games; they should not be taken on slides.

✔ Only soft balls are permitted on the playground during recess.

✔ Children shouldn't retrieve balls that are off the playground without permission from an adult.

✔ Snowballs are not allowed.

✔ Children may not climb trees.

✔ Children must stay away from dangerous areas, such as drains, trash receptacles, and streams.

✔ Contact sports are not permitted.

✔ Children on swings must sit in an upright position, and not twirl or jump off while a swing is in motion; they may not run in front or in back of the swings.

✔ Children must go down slides one at a time, sitting in an upright position, and not loiter at the top or bottom; they must not climb up or down the slide.

Adapted from the American Academy of Pediatrics

For more information, visit our web site, www.fcps.edu/fts/safety-security/factsheets/saf-2.pdf

If you need assistance, call the safety section at xxx-xxx-xxx

To place a work order for equipment repair call xxx-xxx-xxx

Figure 5.2

Safety Rules for Outdoor Recess.

Source: From *Safety Rules for Outdoor Recess (Fact Sheet) and Criminal Incidents in School (Fact Sheet)* (from website), 2002, Springfield, VA: Office of Safety & Security, Fairfax County Public Schools. Reprinted with permission.

RESPIRATORY EMERGENCIES

In this section we outline some common health emergencies and how to address them. Our companion website displays more extensive information about these and other risks. We begin with a look at respiratory illnesses, one of the leading causes of pediatric hospitalizations and school absenteeism.

Asthma

To address the widespread problem of asthma in school-age children, the CDC has funded an asthma project led by the American Association of School Administrators (see our companion website for more information). This project offers excellent guidance and links to other resources, including the student asthma action card shown in Figure 5.3.

Food Allergies

No doubt you have witnessed increased attention to allergies in schools, especially allergies to foods such as peanuts. When exposed to these allergens, sensitive students often experience severe respiratory distress, resulting in a medical crisis. Consider these guidelines in addressing the needs of a student with food allergies:

- Be knowledgeable about and follow applicable federal laws including the American with Disabilities Act (ADA), Individuals with Disabilities Education Act (IDEA), Section 504, and Family Educational Rights and Privacy Act (FERPA) and any state laws or district policies that apply.
- Review the health records submitted by parents and physicians.
- Include food-allergic students in school activities. Students should not be excluded from school activities solely based on their food allergy.
- Identify a core team of, but not limited to, these professionals: school nurse, teacher, principal, school food service and nutrition manager/director, and counselor (if available) to work with parents and the student (age appropriate) to establish a prevention plan. Changes to the prevention plan to promote food allergy management should be made with core team participation.
- Assure that all staff who interact with the student regularly understands food allergy, can recognize symptoms, knows what to do in an emergency, and works with other school staff to eliminate the use of food allergens in the allergic student's meals, educational tools, arts and crafts projects, or incentives.
- Practice the Food Allergy Action Plans before an allergic reaction occurs to assure the efficiency/effectiveness of the plans.
- Coordinate with the school nurse to be sure medications are appropriately stored, and be sure an emergency kit is available that contains a physician's standing order for epinephrine. In states where regulations permit, medications are kept in an easily accessible secure location central to designated school personnel, not in locked cupboards or drawers. Students should be allowed to carry their own epinephrine, if age appropriate, after approval from the student's physician/clinic, parent and school nurse, and allowed by state or local regulations.

Figure 5.3
Asthma Action Plan.

Asthma Action Plan

PATIENT'S NAME: _____   PARENT/GUARDIAN: _____

D. O. B.: _____   PHONE/PAGER NUMBER(S): _____

HEALTH PLAN NAME: _____   ADDRESS: _____

DOCTOR'S NAME: _____   _____

DOCTOR'S PHONE: _____   PARENT#2/RELATIVE: _____

MY PERSONAL BEST PEAK FLOW READING: _____   PHONE/PAGER NUMBER(S): _____

📷   EMERGENCY 911 OR _____

GREEN=GO

☐ BREATHING IS GOOD
☐ NO COUGH OR WHEEZE
☐ CAN WORK/PLAY
        OR
☐ PEAK FLOW NUMBER ABOVE _____
   (GREATER THAN 80% OF BEST)

NOTES   _____
_____
_____

USE THESE DAILY CONTROLLER MEDICINE(S)

MEDICINE	HOW MUCH TO TAKE	WHEN TO TAKE IT
_____	_____	_____
_____	_____	_____
_____	_____	_____
_____	_____	_____

BEFORE SPORTS OR PLAY, USE THIS MEDICINE
_____

YELLOW=CAUTION

☐ COUGH   **CALL DOCTOR**
☐ WHEEZE   ☐ YES
☐ TIGHT CHEST   ☐ NO
☐ WAKE UP AT NIGHT
☐ FIRST SIGN OF COLD
        OR
PEAK FLOW NUMBER
____ TO ____

TAKE THESE MEDICINES TO KEEP FROM GETTING WORSE

MEDICINE	HOW MUCH TO TAKE	WHEN TO TAKE IT
_____	_____	_____
_____	_____	_____

SPECIAL INSTRUCTIONS:

RED=STOP

☐ MEDICINE IS NOT HELPING
☐ HEART RATE OR PULSE IS VERY FAST
☐ NOSE OPEN WIDE WHEN BREATHING
☐ HARD TO WALK OR TALK IN SENTENCES
☐ RIBS OR NECK MUSCLES SHOW WHEN BREATHING
☐ LIPS OR FINGERNAILS TURN GRAY OR BLUE
        OR
PEAK FLOW NUMBER BELOW

GET HELP FROM A DOCTOR NOW!

MEDICINE	HOW MUCH TO TAKE	WHEN TO TAKE IT
_____	_____	_____
_____	_____	_____

SPECIAL INSTRUCTIONS:

Source: Rhode Island Department of Health. Retrieved October 4, 2007, from http://www.health.ri.gov/disease/asthma/aap100a.jpg. The RI Asthma Action Plan was adapted by the RI Department of Health from the NHLBI Asthma Action Plan with funding from the Centers for Disease Control and Prevention (CDC) under Grant No. U59/CCU123177-03.

- Designate school personnel who are properly trained to administer medications in accordance with the State Nursing and Good Samaritan Laws governing the administration of emergency medications.
- Be prepared to handle a reaction and ensure there is a staff member available who is properly trained to administer medications during the school day regardless of time or location.
- Review policies/prevention plan with the core team members, parents/guardians, student (age appropriate), and physician after a reaction has occurred.
- Work with the district transportation administrator to assure that school bus driver training includes symptom awareness and what to do if a reaction occurs.
- Recommend that all buses have communication devices in case of an emergency.
- Enforce a "no-eating" policy on school buses with exceptions made only to accommodate special needs under federal (or similar) laws or school district policy. Discuss appropriate management of food allergy with family.
- Discuss field trips with the family of the food-allergic child to decide appropriate strategies for managing the food allergy.
- Follow federal/state/district laws and regulations regarding sharing medical information about the student.
- Take threats or harassment against an allergic child seriously. (Food Allergy & Anaphylaxis Network, n.d.)

As you can see, child-specific planning can prevent respiratory emergencies, one of the most common reasons for pediatric hospitalizations. In adolescents, mental health crises are the second leading cause of hospitalization. Therefore, we address behavior emergencies in the next section.

RISKY BEHAVIORS

High-risk behaviors among your student body create ongoing risk, as illustrated in our opening case. Here are two other examples:

- An Illinois school district discovered too late the dangers of an elementary school game called "Chubby Bunny." The goal of the game is to jam marshmallows into one's mouth until one cannot say, "chubby bunny." A 12-year-old girl choked to death after stuffing four marshmallows in her mouth.
- Two high school students were found dead next to a natural gas line. Police reports indicated that they had been huffing the gas. The spot was well known for this activity and the area had been fenced to keep teenagers out.

To prevent others from being injured or killed, schools in such situations should join with community partners to protect their youth. For example, you might form an ad hoc task force of parents, pediatricians and other treatment providers, and law enforcement officials to gather information and disseminate information that would inform parents about the risks. Cases such as these also call to mind the steps in the NHTSA prevention program featured early in this chapter. You may recall that the program focused on child safety to and from school but offered an approach for engaging the community in public awareness and prevention.

SUICIDAL BEHAVIOR[1]

Suicide is the third leading cause of death for young people aged 10 to 14 and 15 to 19 years, killing 1,600 teenagers each year in the United States. The rapid increase of suicide deaths from the 1950s to the mid-1980s led to a national clarion call for more effective prevention. Thereafter, the general rate of youth suicide declined dramatically. Nevertheless, 5% to 8% of teenagers attempt suicide, and 1 in 5 teenagers seriously considers suicide each year (Gould, 2003).

In this section, we provide a general understanding of the risk factors for youth suicide completion and attempts, and we also highlight the implications of these risk factors for prevention efforts.

Age

The rates of completed youth suicides are low (1.5 per 100,000 among 10- to 14-year-olds and 8.2 per 100,000 among 15- to 19-year-olds). However, the Youth Risk Behavior Survey reported that 19% of high schoolers seriously considered a suicide attempt during the past year; 15% made a specific suicide plan, 8.8% reported a suicide attempt, and 2.6% made an attempt that required medical treatment (Grunbaum et al., 2002).

Completed suicide is rare in children under the age of 10 because children in this age group lack the access to, or information about, lethal methods. Accordingly, most prevention strategies focus on adolescents.

Gender, Race, and Sexual Orientation

Females experience suicidal ideation (thoughts about suicide) and make more suicide attempts than males, although completed suicide is more common among males (Grunbaum et al., 2002). In the United States, youth suicides are more common among whites than African Americans, highest among Native Americans, and lowest among Asian/Pacific Islanders (Anderson, 2002). A review of research on sexual orientation and youth suicide found higher rates of attempted suicide among homosexual youths compared to their heterosexual counterparts (Remafedi, 1999). More recent studies have identified "a two-to six-fold increased risk of non-lethal suicidal behavior for homosexual and bisexual youths" (Gould, Greenberg, Velting, & Shaffer, 2003, p. 390).

Method

Firearms, the leading cause of suicide completion in the United States, account for almost 60% of all suicides in both males and females. For those aged 15 to 19, suicide by firearms accounted for 63% of the increase in the overall rate from 1980 to 1996 (U.S. Public Health Service, 1999). Other methods include hanging and overdose. Some prevention approaches have as their goal the reduction of access to lethal means such as firearms.

---

[1]This section is based in part on Kerr, M. M. & Traupman, E. (2003). *Youth suicide prevention: Risks, implications, and strategies.* Publication Series. Harrisburg, PA: PA CASSP Training and Technical Assistance Institute.

RISK FACTORS AND PRECIPITANTS ASSOCIATED WITH YOUTH SUICIDE

Mental Illness

Without a doubt, mental illness is the most significant risk factor for suicidal behavior. Psychiatric diagnoses, often in combination, are present in about 90% of teen suicide completions. This dramatic link between mental illness and suicidal behavior explains why many prevention approaches have screening as a part of their program. For example, the *Columbia TeenScreen Program* uses a multistage screening program that (1) teaches teens about depression and treatment, to encourage them to identify and refer themselves, and (2) systematically screens each teen for anxiety, depression, substance abuse, and suicidality. The *SOS: Signs of Suicide Program* combines a curriculum for high school students with a brief screening. Help seeking is a goal of both programs.

Teens who do access psychiatric treatment usually find it effective. A combination of psychotherapy (e.g., cognitive behavior therapy) and medication treatment often works best. Sadly, however, in the month before suicidal behavior, many young people seek some medical care, but their need for psychiatric treatment goes unrecognized by their primary care providers.

Depression

Depression, with its accompanying hopelessness, anxiety, and cognitive distortions, is a major risk factor for suicide and suicide attempts. Consider this example:

> A teenager has experienced repeated episodes of depression and feels hopeless, despite some sessions with a school counselor. After encountering a former romantic partner on the street, she breaks down and isolates herself for days. Ultimately, she concludes that she has nothing to live for, and would be better off dead. She then overdoses.

Anxiety Disorders

Coexisting with a mood disorder, these conditions can interfere with a person's treatment and recovery. If not identified and treated, these disorders can increase the risk for suicidal thoughts and/or behaviors in depressed individuals. Consider this illustration:

> A gifted teenager experienced anxiety for several years. Despite help from his family and school counselors, he continued to be self-critical and overly concerned about his performance and others' approval of him. When he was caught parking his car on school campus without a student permit, he faced a suspension. Panicked, he drove the car to a bridge and jumped.

As illustrated in this case, a significant number of suicide completers faced a pending disciplinary crisis. Discipline should occur as soon as possible after misbehavior to decrease the feelings of anticipatory anxiety. If the student in trouble is highly anxious, school or law enforcement officials should take steps to reduce anxiety and get immediate assistance.

Drug or Alcohol Abuse

An increased prevalence of drugs or alcohol is a factor accounting for why older adolescents are more likely to attempt and complete suicide compared with younger adolescents. Some adolescents use drugs and alcohol to cope with depressive feelings. Alcohol acts as a disinhibitor to suicidal behavior.

A link seems to exist between alcohol abuse and suicide by firearms: *Adolescents who are depressed and use alcohol are more than five times more likely to use a firearm.* Consider this illustration:

> Diagnosed at age 8 with conduct disorder and attention-deficit/hyperactivity disorder, this 14-year-old struggled academically. He compensated for his poor academic status by being the class clown and taking risks to gain the attention of his friends. One night at a friend's house, he drank with the other kids and then played a fatal game of Russian roulette.

Because suicidal individuals are often impulsive, restricting access during critical times may reduce suicides. In addition, even if means substitution does occur, the chance of survival may be greater with less lethal methods. Educating parents of high-risk youth about injury prevention may also aid in reducing access to lethal means. We examine next family characteristics that place students at risk for suicide.

Family Mental Illness

A family history of suicidality significantly increases the likelihood that a teenager will take his own life (Gould et al., 2003). Children of depressed parents appear to be at substantially increased risk for completed suicide, as do children of parents with substance abuse problems (Brent et al., 1993).

Consider, for example, how a parent's own struggles might hinder attempts to help her child. A depressed parent might be overwhelmed by suggestions offered by professionals, feel anxious and guilty, lack confidence in parenting, have trouble setting limits for a teen's use of alcohol or other drugs, or lack the energy to follow through with treatment suggestions. Outreach to parents struggling with their own mental health challenges, including depression and substance abuse, is an important element of the prevention of youth suicide.

Family Discord

Child sexual or physical abuse is a significant risk factor for youth suicide. One study revealed that "discordant, hostile family interactions predisposed [youth] to suicidal thoughts" (Kosky, Silburn, & Zubrick, 1986, p. 527). Gould, Fisher, Parides, Flory, and Shaffer (1996) reported that suicide victims had less frequent and less satisfying communications with their parents. These findings support the need to incorporate the family in treatment efforts for a young person who is at risk for suicide.

Exposure to the Suicidality of Others

Research supports a contagion factor associated with suicidal behavior in adolescents. Exposure to TV programs and news stories on suicide may prompt suicidal behavior in vulnerable adolescents. Prevention involves educating reporters, editors, and producers about contagion to minimize harm and emphasize the media's positive role in educating and shaping attitudes about suicide.

Exposure to a classmate's suicide attempt may prompt suicidal behavior in other students. Young people most vulnerable to "contagion" immediately following a suicide generally are characterized as more isolated, not close to the suicide victims, and exhibiting the risk factors identified earlier. Chapter 9 reviews safeguards you should take if students are exposed to a suicide.

Behavioral Indicators

Suicidal teens may begin writing or talking about death and suicide. Clues may also appear in art and music projects, diaries, or journals. Occasionally, suicidal teens begin giving away prized possessions, writing "wills" or suicide notes or saying "goodbye" in an untimely way. Youth considering suicide also may:

- Begin listening to music about death or suicide.
- Complain they are feeling really hopeless or trapped in a bad situation.
- Become more aggressive or talk of wanting to harm others.
- Begin using or increase their use of drugs or alcohol.
- Suddenly become cheerful for no apparent reason after a period of depression.
- Have just had a bad fight with their parents, boyfriend, or girlfriend.
- Have recently lost someone they cared about.

Tragically, the stigma associated with mental health problems and substance abuse problems and their treatment prevents many youth (and their parents) from seeking help.

"Gatekeeper" community or school-based prevention approaches teach adults and peers to watch for and refer teens exhibiting these behaviors. Gatekeeper programs also attempt to minimize the stigma associated with seeking psychiatric treatment. For example, hotlines and crisis centers (which research indicates are used more often by females than males) train their staff to listen for warning signs and assist at-risk callers to access treatment. In many states, a Student Assistance Program trains school-based staff and faculty to serve as gatekeepers who meet to review their observations and concerns about students who may be at risk. The role of school gatekeepers is featured in the sample suicide prevention procedures shown earlier in Figure 2.1.

CRISIS INTERVENTION FOR A MEDICAL EMERGENCY

General Procedures

In the event of an accident or other medical emergency, you will first follow your school's emergency procedures, such as calling a code to summon help, dialing 911, and using first aid techniques. Figure 5.4 offers general guidelines for responding to a medical emergency.

Figure 5.4
Crisis Plan for Medical Emergency.

✔	Time	Serious Injury/Illness	"Clear the Halls" Date / /	
		Witness/Reported By	**Name of Contact**	**Contact No.**
		Notify School Administrator or designee who will call 911		
		Send someone to contact the nurse		
		Maintain open airway and administer CPR, if necessary		
		Immobilize victim if there is a potential for head, neck or back injury. Do not move victim unless immediate emergency situation dictates		
		Control bleeding by applying direct pressure and elevation		
✔	**Time**	**Priority Procedures**	**Name of Contact**	**Contact No.**
		Maintain open airway and administer CPR, if necessary		
		Immobilize victim if there is a potential for head, neck or back injury. Do not move victim unless immediate emergency situation dictates		
		Control bleeding by applying direct pressure and elevation		
		Treat for shock		
		Check for medical alert tags		
✔	**Time**	**School Administrator or Designee**	**Name of Contact**	**Contact No.**
		Contact parents		
		Contact superintendent		
		Work with counseling resources to initiate counseling plan as determined by need and severity of the situation		
		File incident report		
		Debrief Crisis Leadership Team and staff		

✔	Time	Crisis Leadership Team	Name of Contact	Contact No.
		Assist School Administrator or designee as needed		
✔	Time	Clinician	Name of Contact	Contact No.
		Coordinate counseling if needed		
✔	Time	Nurse	Name of Contact	Contact No.
		Collect first aid kit and proceed immediately to victim(s)		
		Coordinate first aid until emergency medical services arrive		

Note: These materials will help to make schools safer. However, in no way can a school district guarantee the safety of all students, all the time, using the VT School Crisis Guide.

Contributors include: Vermont State Police, Essex Police Department, Vermont Department of Education, Vermont School Boards Association, Montpelier Police Department, and Vermont Emergency Management.

Source: From *Vermont School Crisis Guide,* 2004, by Vermont School Crisis Planning Team. Adapted with permission.

Let's reflect . . .

> Student teachers, substitute teachers, and interns play a role in most schools as they supervise groups of students. How does your school prepare such interim personnel for medical emergencies?

Following the immediate response, you will enact your crisis communications plan (see Chapter 4) and provide individual psychological supports as described in Chapter 6. The concluding part of our chapter case study illustrates this process. Should the medical crisis result in a death, you would shift into the postvention protocol outlined in Chapter 9.

Although every medical crisis is unique and unnerving to students, parents, and staff members, some situations require special sensitivity because of an ongoing threat, legal actions, or witnesses. Our final section highlights these particular conditions.

SPECIAL CIRCUMSTANCES

Continuing Exposure to a Disease, Bacteria, or Virus

Some medical emergencies create a real or perceived risk for others in the school setting, as was the case in the following situations:

- A suburban high school informed parents of the discovery of several cases of infection caused by methicillin-resistant staphylococcus aureus (MRSA), a bacteria that is resistant to certain antibiotics such as methicillin. The health department determined that athletes playing soccer and football on a neighboring school's field contracted the infection and advised routine hygiene practices.
- Early one morning, a young secretary called into the administrative offices sick. By noon, she had died of meningitis. The entire office was put on alert for symptoms and told to see their physicians.
- Several students became ill and were diagnosed with salmonella poisoning. School officials were shocked to learn that the source of the poisoning was not cafeteria food but a Nature Center owl whose pellets the class had handled and dissected (Anderson, 2002).

In crises such as these, school officials bear the additional responsibility of informing and reassuring parents, students, and staff anxious about their own health. As you prepare for such an ongoing crisis, review the crisis communications guidelines in Chapter 4. In addition, here are some specific tips:

1. Ask the public health agency to prepare specific wording for any correspondence you send home to parents or distribute to staff. Write these letters with the "crisis continuum" from Chapter 4 in mind, choosing factual, up-to-date, and reassuring language.
2. Avoid language that unnecessarily raises the anxiety of your audience. (e.g., "We are really not sure whether we need to disinfect the playing field, but we will do our best.") Instead, show you are eager to provide good information. (e.g., "The school district will update our district hotline each day with new information and tell you the actions we are taking. Unless advised otherwise by the health department, we will play our games.")
3. Give your parents and staff as much specific factual information about risk reduction as possible. Here are some examples:
   - "We are asking that all athletes shower immediately after games and practice and launder uniforms after each wearing."
   - "Our custodians are using disinfectant products approved by the county health department. You can get a list of these products for home use from the school office or our district hotline."
   - "The Centers for Disease Control and Prevention reports that normal contact does not place others at any risk. Therefore, we do not anticipate seeing any additional cases."
4. Ask the involved public health officials to "share the stage" in press conferences and media interviews (unless your attorneys determine that this will undermine the school's reputation because the school was negligent).

Suicide Contagion

Suicide contagion is a special case of potential risk because a suicide attempt or death may elevate the likelihood of suicidal behavior in others. Chapter 9 offers specific guidelines about curbing contagion and assessing exposure and risk to those who experience such a tragedy; Chapter 4 explains how to reduce media contagion.

SUMMARY

Perhaps the most likely crisis facing school personnel is an accident or other medical emergency affecting a staff or student. Schools can use national and local data to predict some of these critical incidents, following that examination with a self-assessment such as the School Health Index, to determine risk on the school campus. Prevention initiatives reduce risk, especially if those involved follow a comprehensive process such as that outlined by the NHTSA for prevention of accidents to and from school. In addition, agencies such as the CDC, NIOSH, and CPSC distribute alerts, prevention advice, and training resources. Should a crisis occur, medical emergency procedures guide the initial actions, while special circumstances call for additional supports and safeguards.

CASE STUDY CONCLUSION

At 6 A.M. the next morning, the local police called our superintendent, Dr. Chitose, to share the news.

"We believe that one of your students died early this morning. I wanted to let you know. His mother said he attended your district. Do you have a student named Jaime Garcia in your fourth grade? He was found unconscious by his mother late last night. He was rushed to the emergency room and pronounced dead at 1 A.M. At that time, the details of his death were still under investigation, but it appears Jaime was asphyxiated while playing the choking game. His mother insisted that we call the school."

Dr. Chitose immediately contacted the principals of the middle, elementary, and high schools, relating her conversation with the local police chief. As the counselor in the elementary school, I got a call around 6:30 that morning from our principal. Horrified by the news, I could only imagine how the students would feel when they found out.

When the principals and the school crisis teams met that morning, we all agreed it was imperative for the students to receive correct information regarding this devastating event and that it be delivered in such a way to promote a supportive environment. Yet we did not want to offer inaccurate information or do anything to make the family's grief worse. We were discussing how to announce the death when we received a call from Jaime's mother.

"I told the police to call you because I don't want any other parent to go through this. Warn them about this game, so they won't lose a child like I did."

We held an emergency faculty meeting before school to alert our staff to the death. As soon as the students arrived school that day, we gave the announcement in small homeroom groups, so we could gauge student's reactions and see who might need support. For the time being, we decided to announce that Jaime had a terrible accident and had passed away. When students asked for details, we simply told them that the police were still investigating and that we did not know the cause of death. After all, the coroner had not ruled in the case, so we did not want to go on record as a district giving out inaccurate information. The homeroom teachers continued their announcements by encouraging any student or who needed to talk more about what they were feeling and experiencing to come to the counselor's office.

My first priority was making sure we had enough counselors to meet the students' needs effectively. I contacted our central office and requested the assistance of school psychologists for grief counseling. Realizing that students would need support in the weeks to come, I also called the local grief counseling center, which offered to work with us and with parents. Within the hour, we had a strong team of counselors and school psychologists ready to assist our school in any way they could.

I knew it would be extremely difficult for Jaime's close friends to get through the day after hearing such terrible news, so I invited them to meet with counselors in the library, which we closed for the day. While counselors met with students, I contacted their parents to let them know of the tragedy, to inform them about our support plan, and to invite them to join their children or take them home during this difficult time.

While we supported students throughout the day, the principal prepared a letter to be sent home with each student to inform parents of the tragic death that had occurred. Included in this letter were typical signs of stress that parents might want to monitor, as well as information about to contact the school's counseling office.

A few days later, the coroner did rule the death as resulting from the choking game. By then, Jaime's mother had spoken to reporters too. We responded to her request and subsequently notified parents of an informational meeting on this lethal activity, where we shared warning signs and resources.

I, too, found myself having a strong emotional reaction to this traumatic event, as I had known this student through a previous school counseling relationship. I was glad I had the opportunity to speak with my counselor colleagues about my feelings. A few of us got together and made a donation in Jaime's name to support the outreach efforts of a local professor and his students who were developing a presentation on the choking game for educators and youth workers.

DISCUSSION AND APPLICATION IDEAS

1. What would a review of accidents and illnesses during the past 3 years reveal about your school's vulnerabilities?
2. The School Health Index calls for a team approach to self-assessment. Who do you think should comprise such a team?
3. How does your school district's policy on suicide prevention compare with the one in Figure 5.4?
4. Reflect on steps you would take following these incidents:

   • You receive a call that one of the teacher-chaperones on your high schoolers' trip to London has suffered a fatal heart attack.
   • A primary school nurse calls a student's mother to come for her sick child. Two blocks from the school, the mother is in a serious car accident.

REFERENCES

American Association of School Administrators. (n.d.). *Building capacity among school district leaders to address childhood asthma*. Retrieved October 4, 2007, from http://www.aasa.org/focus/content.cfm?ItemNumber=1951&snItemNumber=1956

Anderson, T. (2002). Commentary: Owl pellets and crisis management. *Legacy: The Journal of the National Association for Interpretation, 13* (2), 22-24.

Brent, D. A., Perper, J. A., Moritz, G., Allman, C., Roth, C., Schweers, J., et al. (1993). Psychiatric risk for suicide: A case control study. *Journal of the American Academy of Child and Adolescent Psychiatry, 32*, 521-529.

Consumer Product Safety Commission (CPSC). (n.d.). *Children should not move or play with mobile folding tables*. Retrieved October 4, 2007, from http://www.cpsc.gov/CPSCPUB/PUBS5062.pdf

Consumer Product Safety Commission (CPSC). (n.d.). *Public playground safety checklist* (CPSC Document #327). Retrieved October 4, 2007 from http://www.cpsc.gov/cpscpub/pubs/327.html

Consumer Product Safety Commission (CPSC). (n.d.). *Safety on playgrounds and athletic fields*. Retrieved October 4, 2007, from http://www.cpsc.gov/cpscpub/prerel/prhtml05/05245.html

Fairfax, Virginia, County Schools. (2002). *Safety rules for outdoor recess: Safety & security fact sheet*. Retrieved October 9, 2007, from http://www.fcps.edu/fts/safety-security/publications/saf-2.pdf

Food Allergy & Anaphylaxis Network. (n.d.). *School guidelines for managing students with food allergies*. Retrieved October 4, 2007, from http://www.foodallergy.org/school/SchoolGuidelines.pdf

Gould, M. S. (2003, June). *Youth suicide epidemiology and risk factors*. Paper presented at the Youth Suicide Prevention Workshop, American Foundation for Suicide Prevention, New York, NY.

Gould, M. S., Fisher, P., Parides, M., Flory, M., & Shaffer, D. (1996). Psychosocial risk factors of child and adolescent completed suicide. *Archives of General Psychiatry, 53,* 1155-1162.

Gould, M. S., Greenberg, T., Velting, D. M., & Shaffer, D. (2003). Youth suicide risk and preventive interventions: A review of the past 10 years. *Journal of the American Academy of Child & Adolescent Psychiatry, 42* (4), 386-405.

Grunbaum, J. A., Kann, L., Kinchen, S. A., Ross, J., Hawkins, J., Lowry, R., et al. (2002). Youth risk behavior surveillance—United States, 2001. *MMWR CDC Surveillance Summary, 51* (SS4), 1-64.

Kosky, R., Silburn, S., & Zubrick, S. (1986). Symptomatic depression and suicidal ideation: A comparative study with 628 children. *Journal of Nervous and Mental Disease, 174,* 523-528.

National Highway and Traffic Safety Administration (NHTSA). (2000). Retrieved October 4, 2007, from http://www.nhtsa.dot.gov/people/injury/buses/GTSS/program.html

Phelan, K. J., Khoury, J., Kalkwarf, H. J., & Lanphear, B. P. (2001). Trends and patterns of playground injuries in United States children and adolescents. *Ambulatory Pediatrics, 1* (4), 227-233.

Remafedi, G. (1999). Sexual orientation and youth suicide. *Journal of the American Medical Association, 282* (13), 291.

Tinsworth, D., & McDonald, J. (2001). *Special study: Injuries and deaths associated with children's playground equipment*. Washington, DC: U.S. Consumer Product Safety Commission.

U.S. Department of Health and Human Services, Health Resources and Services Administration, Maternal and Child Health Bureau. (2006). *Child Health USA 2005*. Rockville, MD: Author.

U.S. Public Health Service. (1999). *The surgeon general's call to action to prevent suicide*. Washington, DC: Author.

Wertheimer, P. L. (n.d.). *The American experience: Rock concert safety*. Retrieved October 9, 2007, from http://www.crowdsafe.com/englishspeech.PDF

CHAPTER 6

PREVENTION, MITIGATION, AND RESPONSE FOR VIOLENCE

CASE STUDY

Ten years ago as the principal of a middle school, I was greeting students at the front door of our building during morning arrival when Linda, one of the school secretaries, appeared.

"Dr. Draft, you have to come now. There is an emergency," she said in a low voice.

"What is it?" I asked.

"There is a kid with a gun. He showed it to another kid as they were getting off the bus. It's the Pollock kid who just transferred last month." Linda responded.

"How do we know it's Kevin Pollock?"

"The kid he talked to is here …he came to see you."

I quickly turned to the frightened student standing behind me in the office.

"What did Kevin say and where did he go?"

"He didn't come into the building. He said he was waiting outside until Bus 82 came. He wanted some kid on that bus. The kid …" the student explained.

"What does Kevin have on …what's he wearing?" I interrupted.

"I'm not sure. I think his army jacket. He always wears that. And he has a gym bag . . . a black one. He never had that before. I'm scared. He sounded really mad," the student offered, his voice shaking.

"OK. You did the right thing. Now go into my office, pull down the shades, and sit on the floor. Stay there."

"Linda, radio Ron, our school resource officer ... channel 54 ... to the bus unloading area. Tell him to look for Kevin Pollock; we think he has a gun. Wearing an army jacket with a gym bag," I directed, trying to remain calm. "The kid is heavyset, about 5 feet 2 inches tall, long brown hair."

I could describe Kevin's appearance because he had just been in the office the day before to drop off his papers for the nurse. He was new in our building, so I had taken a few minutes to see how things were going.

Now I called over to the other secretary, anxiously listening.

"Annette, call 911 and tell them we have a Code G, and it's a student. We think he is at the bus unloading area around back. Tell them to radio me right away. Send police to stop the traffic into our driveway. But no sirens."

I then radioed to the teachers on duty at our bus unloading area.

"Teachers, listen carefully. We have a Code G. Move all kids into the building from the back driveway area. Watch for Kevin Pollock. We think he has a gun, so do this as calmly as you can … Tell the kids that the doors are stuck and they have to go around the building. I am sending our front door hall supervisors to help you. Ron (our police officer) is on the way. Leave Kevin to him."

By then, Ron was radioing me.

"I have the suspect in sight. He is standing alone, away from the building. Has a bag. Cannot see a gun. Advise sending all students into the building and locking down."

I grabbed the microphone and announced a lockdown.

"Attention, please, we are in a lockdown. Please move quickly to the classroom or office closest to you. Lock the door, turn off the lights, and stay low. Teacher, please take attendance.

Repeat. We are in lockdown; please move quickly into a room or office as you have practiced. No one should go near the bus unloading area. Repeat, stay away from the bus unloading area."

I ran through the school to the back of our building, to help the teachers moving students away from the back driveway.

"Good, no buses," I said to myself, seeing the empty driveway, where a line of buses would usually appear at this time of the morning. "The police must be at the top of the road. They got the word," I thought.

"Come on, come on. Hurry, kids. Go back into the kitchen. Sit along the back wall," I shouted as I ushered a group of confused teenagers into the safest part of the cafeteria.

INTRODUCTION

Preventing, and responding to, school violence and other crimes is the focus for this chapter. Unfortunately, we cannot reduce to one chapter the thousands of publications on school violence (though many are linked to our website). Therefore, we organize this chapter similarly to the last chapter, beginning with an overview of crises you might expect based on national school crimes data.

Keeping a school or group of schools safe is possible only when an interdisciplinary team works together. Such a team must include members with specialized training and experience. You may find yourself working alongside those in school administration or building maintenance, security, or psychology.

Let's reflect . . .

A crucial element of team planning and responding is communication. Take a little time to identify some of the specialized terms used by those in the security, emergency response, health, mental health, and education fields. How would you help a district team of interdisciplinary professionals and paraprofessionals learn one another's jargon? What problems might arise if you did not engage in this exercise?

Following our crisis model, we outline components of school safety for a school district safety team or building-level team to address: (1) prevention through a school safety assessment process; (2) mitigation, including threat assessment; (3) crisis response steps to take if a crisis is imminent; (4) best practices in the crisis phase to support those who have witnessed or experienced school violence; and (5) suggestions for safeguarding the school community when the threat continues or when other special circumstances arise.

Let's begin by learning about what crimes are most likely on school campuses.

SCHOOL SAFETY ASSESSMENT

"For parents, school staff, and policymakers to address school crime effectively, they must possess an accurate understanding of the extent and nature of the problem. However, it is difficult to gauge the scope of crime and violence in schools without collecting data, given the large amount of attention devoted to isolated incidents of extreme school violence." (DeVoe, Peter, Noonan, Snyder, & Baum, 2005, p. iii)

Despite media reports that might depict campuses as dangerous, students are less likely to be victims of a violent crime at school than away from school, according to the federal government's annual report on school crime, *Indicators of School Crime and Safety.* Derived from a variety of independent data sources, including national surveys of students, teachers, and principals, and data collection from federal departments and agencies, the report can initiate your assessment of crimes most likely to take place on your campus. You'll find the latest report on our website, but here are a few highlights to guide your thinking:

- Middle schools (42%) were twice as likely as high schools (21%) to report that student bullying occurs at least once a week at school.
- Of the responding schools, 81% reported having violent incidents.
- Only 18% of the schools reported *serious* violent incidents (rape, sexual battery other than rape, physical attack or fight with a weapon, threat of physical violence with a weapon, and robbery with or without a weapon).
- Vandalism was reported by 51% of all schools; 80% of schools with 1,000 or more students reported vandalism.
- Distribution of illegal drugs was reported by 44% of high schools and 27% of middle schools. (Guerino, Hurwitz, Noonan, & Kaffenberger, 2006)

These federal data, released each fall, can help direct your campus crime prevention and crisis intervention strategies. Naturally, you will rely primarily on local law enforcement data and school data as recommended here:

> There are a lot of different programs and procedures to reduce violence in schools, but I think the most important tool that teachers, principals, and students are missing is knowledge of exactly what is happening at their school site. How many fights are in their school? How many kids are affected by issues of sexual harassment? What grades are being impacted most? How are teachers responding? Very few schools know if they have 50 or 500 violent acts during the course of a month or a year. What people remember is what they heard or the most severe events. (Astor, cited in Belcher, 2003, p. 1)

Let's reflect . . .

How would you lead a discussion of national and local crime data with your district's crisis team? What questions might you pose? How would you help local responders to see the usefulness in this data review?

The national and local crime data focus on specific incidents. Now let's turn to *other* dimensions of school safety assessment: perception data, policies and procedures, and physical security. These comprise what we call a school safety audit (Peterson & Strassel, 2002).

Assessing Perceptions About School Safety

To protect students and staff, we must first be aware of the problem situations these individuals perceive. After all, as one urban police chief observed, "Safety is largely a matter of perception" (Earl Buford, personal communication). One simple tactic is to survey students and adults anonymously by asking them to respond in writing to the following question: "Is there any specific place on the way to school, at school, or on the way home from school where you do not feel comfortable and safe?" A further step is to ask students personally or through an essay to offer suggestions about what would make their school a safer place.

Ron Astor, whose groundbreaking work on predicting school violence highlighted the risk of "unowned spaces and times," offered this advice about surveying students and faculty:

> What we use in our surveys are maps of the school sites where we can identify the different territories where violence occurs. We ask the students to find the places that are "unowned" or dangerous in and around the schools. Why? Because students have a lot to say about those spaces. Students live and experience these spaces and they can articulate what is making those areas unsafe. Kids can tell you if they feel comfortable in the hallway, when, or why ...Asking about specific sub-spaces, specific times during the day, and specific school activities is much more helpful than asking about the school in general . . . Mapping areas with students and teachers really helps generate solutions to the problems. The areas that tend to be "unowned" tend to be the places that are the most unsafe. We're very careful that the mapping doesn't target people but places and times. Students and teachers feel a kind of a relief when you're talking about places and times, rather than people. (Astor, quoted in Belcher, 2003)

Astor and his colleagues found school violence to be predictably more frequent in the spaces and times in schools *when few or no teachers were present* (Astor, Meyer, & Behre, 1999). Moreover, they observed the importance of students being able to work alongside their teachers in identifying solutions to the problems they highlighted.

To supplement these periodic surveys, we strongly recommend that you implement a silent complaint procedure whereby students, employees, and parents have access to silent complaint forms or hotlines to report safety concerns (Kerr & Palmer, 2007). (Note: The procedure is called "silent" because reporters remain anonymous.) Silent reporting is especially important for adolescents, who tend to underreport their victimization:

> Despite being victimized more often than other age groups, teens are the least likely to report their victimization. Teens face many additional obstacles:
>
> - Lack of understanding that what they experienced was a crime
> - Fear that no one will believe them
> - Fear of being blamed or punished
> - Feelings of guilt, shame, and self-blame
> - Fear of retaliation
> - Mistrust of adults
> - Belief that nothing will be done
> - Lack of knowledge about available services

- Lack of access to services
- Perceived and real limits of confidentiality (National Crime Prevention Council and National Center for Victims of Crime, Office for Victims of Crime, 2005, p. 1)

Let's reflect . . .

Now that you have learned about different ways of gathering both objective data and subjective perception data about the safety of a district or school, what approaches will you adopt? How could you map the unowned spaces and times of your school's day?

Reviewing Policies and Procedures

In Chapter 2 we discussed the importance of policies that give the authority to implement safe schools procedures. Written guidelines are foundational in your prevention and response efforts, so we suggested that you schedule them for annual review. We also encourage you to examine your discipline policies because these may inadvertently contribute to a hostile school climate (see Skiba [2000] for a review of research on zero-tolerance policies). Resources for assessing and evaluating policies and procedures are available on our website.

Assessing Physical Security

Many surveys and checklists are available on our website for assessing the physical security of your campus. Your school crisis team, working with your facilities staff, can complete these assessments. In fact, such a walkthrough of your physical plant is an excellent crisis team training activity, as mentioned in Chapter 3. Security experts can provide you with a security audit that will identify vulnerable aspects of your school's physical environment, as well as suggest ways to protect yourself and your students.

In summary, assessing your school's safety begins with an examination not only of anticipated and actual critical incidents but of stakeholders' perceptions of the safety of the campus. In addition, policies, procedures, and physical security warrant at least an annual review. Once you have completed this assessment, you will understand the exposure of your school to acts of violence, harassment, and crimes. Our next section concentrates on risk reduction.

SCHOOL VIOLENCE PREVENTION

School safety generally encompasses several factors: (1) *school climate*, including individuals' perceptions about their school, its safety, and how they are treated by others; (2) *school organization, policies, and rules*; (3) *environmental design* of the school and campus, including how individuals use and move through spaces; (4) *security measures*, including interactions with potential perpetrators, surveillance equipment and personnel, locks, lighting, barriers, and alarms (National Crime Prevention Council, 2003) (5) competent and timely *threat assessment*, and (6) effective *crisis responses* to threatening situations.

Unfortunately, research has yet to be definitive about the best ways to make a school safe; indeed, much controversy characterizes the field (Skiba, 2000). For example, studies have not supported wholeheartedly the popular zero-tolerance policies promulgated by many lawmakers (Skiba & Peterson, 1999; Skiba, 2000). Instead, many experts prefer a model based on improving student–adult relations and school climate, identification of early warning signs, and using multiple approaches to reduce bullying and other problem behaviors (Kerr & Nelson, 2006; Skiba, 2000). Recognizing that violence prevention is complex and depends largely on factors that differ from school to school, we will review several approaches. We begin by examining the environmental aspects of school safety.

Crime Prevention Through Environmental Design

Crime prevention through environmental design (CPTED) improves school safety and security three ways: controlling access, improving natural surveillance, and increasing definition of school boundaries.

Controlling access includes such safeguards as limiting building access for visitors to one entrance, screening and identifying visitors, and monitoring loading docks and other potential entry points. *Natural surveillance* of buildings and grounds is achieved by removing anything that blocks one's vision and limiting hiding places. Examples would be removing the flyers posted on the office window that block the staff's surveillance of incoming visitors, trimming large shrubbery, and adding lighting to dark corridors and stairwells. *Enhancing school boundaries* means clearly defining the edges of the campus, posting school notices such as warnings about trespassing or drug-free school zone signs, and decreasing the "unowned spaces and times" in the school day. When you define areas of the school (e.g., posting signs that identify departments of the school), you not only promote boundaries or "ownership" but also make it easier to identify unauthorized individuals. Good maintenance also sends a message of ownership and reduces vandalism (National Crime Prevention Council, 2003).

Prevention Through Security Measures and Interactions

If your school or neighborhood has a history of crime or violence, you may adopt approaches to **target harden,** which means using physical barriers, security equipment, or changes in human behavior to reduce the opportunity for crime and to make completion of a crime more difficult (U.S. Department of Labor, 1998). For specific information on security technologies, consult *The Appropriate and Effective Use of Security Technologies in U.S. Schools: A Guide for Schools and Law Enforcement Agencies,* a research report from the National Institute of Justice. A link appears on our website.

Changing adult behavior requires some training and consultation, available through your local law enforcement agency. For example, consider the following suggestions from a school safety administrator to those working in high-risk school offices:

- Anticipate, anticipate, anticipate. Imagine a threatening scenario and how you could handle it. Enlist the advice of others. Practice your strategy.
- Plan your exit. Don't arrange your office furniture so that you can't get out quickly. In a heated public meeting, sit near the door.
- Don't advertise your whereabouts unnecessarily. Remove your name from your office door. Think twice about listing your name on the building directory; list the office instead. Paint over the name on your parking space.
- Consider security measures for your office, such as visitor and employee name tags, protective clothing for employees in high-risk situations, body alarm buttons that allow staff to call for help, undercounter buzzers that alert security, two-way mirrors, security cameras, and controlled entry systems.
- Require the reception desk to announce visitors before they may proceed to an office.
- Plan how you will communicate in an emergency. Ask yourself, where is the nearest phone? What's the access code to use it? Where is the fire alarm?
- Schedule a meeting that might be troublesome in a safer location (such as the school police office or a conference room with multiple exits and security nearby).
- Study your own office if that's where you must meet. Put away heavy paperweights, desk accessories, and photographs under glass; they could prove dangerous in the hands of an angry visitor. Hide your purse, keys, and personally identifiable information about your home or family. Offer your guest a cold beverage, never hot coffee or tea.
- Be alert to your surroundings—the parking lot, corridors, public meetings, and schoolyards. Pay attention to people and what they are doing. Don't be caught off guard.
- Most important, learn how to deescalate an agitated person. Practice effective strategies such as honoring personal space, monitoring your body language and gestures, and using active listening. (Kerr, 2000, p. 8. Reprinted with permission from the November 2000 issue of *The School Administrator*.)

Let's reflect . . .

Look around your office or classroom. Now reread the preceding checklist. How could you rearrange your space to make it safer for you and for students? What are the risky features of your workplace?

Next we turn to threat assessment, a methodology recently adapted for school settings.

THREAT ASSESSMENT

Threat assessment refers to how we assess a verbal or nonverbal declaration of intent to hurt another person. Essential to the success of a school-based threat assessment model are these factors:

1. A shared knowledge and conceptual framework regarding school violence and threat assessment, which reduces the likelihood that personnel will engage in reactionary behaviors.
2. A multidisciplinary, interagency team approach, to ensure not only multiple perspectives and objectivity in evaluating threats but to facilitate information sharing and actions necessitated by the conclusions.
3. Authority from the board and superintendent's office to conduct interagency threat assessments.
4. Understanding of the relevant laws and regulations.
5. Training that provides team members with the skills they require to conduct a threat assessment. (Cornell et al., 2004; Fein et al., 2002)

Table 6.1 lists the questions posed in the threat assessment model developed by the National Threat Assessment Center of the U.S. Secret Service, for specific use by school personnel. *Keep in mind that threat assessment requires considerable experience and training.* Even though school personnel may be asked to respond to questions such as those posed in Table 6.1, they should not profile students based on these questions. Every situation should be weighed individually with the help of trained individuals.

Not all threats are delivered in person, as we know from experiences with e-mail threats, telephoned bomb threats, or messages left at school. Consider these case illustrations:

- The morning after Columbine, in our high school there was a buzz. By 8 A.M. talk was circulating about whether there was going to be a shooting. By third period, the kids were pouring in with their rumors. We immediately reacted. We were able to trace it to three kids who had sent messages to one another threatening to do something in the building. They had IM'd everyone in their buddy list. In a period of an evening, this conversation among three kids got passed around 200 to 300 kids, all as a result of the Internet. The story morphed with embellishments. In our building that day, a climate of near terror was created. We put an administrator on every floor. For seven hours, we went door-to-door and met with every class. We asked the police to put an officer in the parking lot. We got through the day and completed our investigation as a team (J. G., high school administrator, personal communication).
- In our elementary school, a student received several threatening letters. Her parents demanded action, so we interviewed many classmates and teachers, but we still couldn't determine who had written the letters. The entire grade was in turmoil. Weeks later, the student admitted that she had written the letters herself. Until that time, we had not recognized just how much she was struggling emotionally and interpersonally.

We close this section with a perspective from the leading experts in school threat assessment.

Threat assessment should be looked upon as one component in an overall strategy to reduce school violence. The threat assessment process by itself is unlikely to have a lasting

Table 6.1
Threat Assessment: Factors to Consider

	Factors to Consider
1. **What are the student's motive(s) and goals?**	• What motivated the student to make the statements or take the actions that caused him or her to come to attention? • Does the situation or circumstance that led to these statements or actions still exist? • Does the student have a major grievance or grudge? Against whom? • What efforts have been made to resolve the problem and what has been the result? Does the potential attacker feel that any part of the problem is resolved or see any alternatives?
2. **Have there been any communications suggesting ideas or intent to attack?**	• What, if anything, has the student communicated to someone else (targets, friends, other students, teachers, family, others) or written in a diary, journal, or website concerning his or her ideas and/or intentions? • Have friends been alerted or "warned away"?
3. **Has the subject shown inappropriate interest in any of the following:**	• School attacks or attackers; • Weapons (including recent, acquisition of any relevant weapon); • Incidents of mass violence (terrorism, workplace violence, mass murderers).
4. **Has the student engaged in attack-related behaviors? These behaviors might include:**	• Developing an attack idea or plan; • Making efforts to acquire or practice with weapons; • Casing, or checking out, possible sites and areas for attack; • Rehearsing attacks or ambushes.
5. **Does the student have the intent and capacity to carry out an act of targeted violence?**	• How organized is the student's thinking and behavior? • Does the student have the means, e.g., access to weapon, to carry out an attack?
6. **Is the student experiencing hopelessness, desperation, and/or despair?**	• Is there information to suggest that the student is experiencing desperation and/or despair? • Has the student experienced a recent failure, loss, and/or loss of status? • Is the student known to be having difficulty coping with a stressful event? • Is the student now, or has the student ever been, suicidal or "accident prone"? • Has the student engaged in behavior that suggests that he or she has considered ending their life?

Table 6.1 *(continued)*

	Factors to Consider
7. **Does the student have a trusting relationship with at least one responsible adult?**	• Does the student have at least one relationship with an adult where the student feels that he or she can confide in the adult and believes that the adult will listen without judging or jumping to conclusions? (Students with trusting relationships with adults may be directed away from violence and despair and toward hope.) • Is the student emotionally connected to—or disconnected from—other students? • Has the student previously come to someone's attention or raised concern in a way that suggested he or she needs intervention or supportive services?
8. **Does the student see violence as an acceptable—or desirable—or the only way to solve problems?**	• Does the setting around the student (friends, fellow students, parents, teachers, adults) explicitly or implicitly support or endorse violence as a way of resolving problems or disputes? • Has the student been "dared" by others to engage in an act of violence?
9. **Is the student's conversation and "story" consistent with his or her actions?**	• Does information from collateral interviews and from the student's own behavior confirm or dispute what the student says is going on?
10. **Are other people concerned about the student's potential for violence?**	• Are those who know the student concerned that he or she might take action based on violent ideas or plans? • Are those who know the student concerned about a specific target? • Have those who know the student witnessed recent changes or escalations in mood and behavior?
11. **What circumstances might affect the likelihood of an attack?**	• What factors in the student's life and/or environment might increase or decrease the likelihood that the student will attempt to mount an attack at school? • What is the response of other persons who know about the student's ideas or plan to mount an attack? (Do those who know about the student's ideas actively discourage the student from acting violently, encourage the student to attack, deny the possibility of violence, passively collude with an attack, etc.?)

Source: From *Threat Assessment in Schools: A Guide to Managing Threatening Situations and to Creating Safe School Climates*, by R. Fein, B. Vossekuil, W. Pollack, R. Borum, W. Modzeleski, and M. Reddy, 2002, Washington, DC: U.S. Department of Education, Office of Elementary and Secondary Education, Safe and Drug-Free Schools Program and U.S. Secret Service, National Threat Assessment Center. Adapted with permission.

effect on the problem of targeted school violence unless that process is implemented in the larger context of strategies to ensure that schools offer their students safe and secure learning environments. The principal objective of school violence-reduction strategies should be to create cultures and climates of safety, respect, and emotional support within educational institutions. (Fein et al., 2002, p. 11)

School Climate and Staff Supervision

As experts have noted, how people perceive their school's climate and their individual connections and support is absolutely essential to crime reduction. Outfitting a campus with security equipment does not make it safe; human supervision, surveillance, and supports do. Studies have shown that merely assigning an adult or placing a camera in a school corridor, however, does not alter students' behavior (Astor, quoted in Belcher, 2003).

Schools become safer when adults supervise by paying close attention to students, speaking to them and showing an interest in them, and engendering trust so they share their concerns (Astor et al., 1999; Colvin, Sugai, Good, & Lee, 1997; Kerr, 2001). As one administrator observed about his staff and students,

> They want to be safe. They want the health and safety in the building not in the hands of four administrators but in the hands of all of the eyes and ears of the faculty and staff and students. Kids and adults knew we would never violate that trust . . . that if they passed it on, their name wasn't going to be involved in it. It takes about a year or two to get them to believe that you can be confidential. We never discussed these situations out in the office or in halls where others could overhear us. And as a result, we had so much intelligence in that school. (J. G., personal communication)

Note the emphasis on creating safe and caring school environments where students can trust adults. Countless studies tell us that safe schools are created when students and adults are connected in an environment of respect, comfort, trust, and tolerance. Specifically, research on resilience tells us that students thrive personally and academically when they experience *connections with caring adults, high expectations, and opportunities to belong* (Benard, 1991). Our website offers you resources for fostering resilience in schools.

Unfortunately, many students, feeling alienated from adults and peers at school, are bullies or their victims. In the next section, we study the widespread problem of peer harassment and how to prevent it.

BULLYING OR PEER HARASSMENT

Bullying can be defined as repeated physical or psychological intimidation that creates, over time, a pattern of abuse and harassment (Banks, 1997). We recognize three types of bullies:

- Physical bullies hurt people and/or property. Physical bullies as well as their victims are usually males.
- Verbal bullies, often females, use humiliating, insulting comments. Their actions often go undetected, especially when they use the Internet (cyberbullying) or cell phones to harass others.

- Relational bullies, often girls, influence their peers to reject or exclude another child. (Bully B'Ware Productions, 1999)

One in six children in the sixth through tenth grades is bullied (NCES, 2005). Physical harassment begins in elementary schools, peaks during the middle school period, and seems to decline through high school. However, verbal harassment remains constant through the upper grades, as illustrated in this case:

- Twenty-one students were suspended after what high school officials called racially motivated fights. The fights were believed to be triggered by graffiti written by white students Thursday night in the boys' bathrooms. The graffiti contained racial epithets and the letters KKK.

Let's reflect . . .

Re-read the statistics about how many students are involved in bullying. Now consider the students under your supervision. Do you feel that your school is identifying all those at risk?

An *imbalance of power* is a key factor in bullying. The bully's intent is to create fear or distress in the victim (National Safe Schools Center, 1993). This imbalance of power is one way you can determine whether students are "just messing around" or whether threatening behavior is taking place. Another criterion of bullying and harassment is an *imbalance in emotional reaction* to the incident (Olweus, 1996). When two students are engaged in horseplay or friendly teasing, they seem equally emotionally involved and affected; this is different with bullying, where the victim feels more emotional than the bully.

Identifying Those at Risk for Involvement as Bullies or Victims

The key to identifying bullying or any potentially dangerous behavior is to know the inhabitants (and visitors) to the building. For example, we recommend that an administrator and student support staff interview any new transfer students or students with a significant disciplinary history. Asking a potentially aggressive student (or parent) some questions can reveal prevention tactics. For example, you might ask, "What kinds of things bothered you in your last school? We want to avoid those situations, but we need for you to tell us about them." Or, "What 'sets you off' or makes you mad? We can help you with your anger, but we first need to know when it is happening." One principal described his approach as follows:

I began interviews after we began to get an influx of troubled students. I figured I could be reactive or I could be proactive. So, I started interviewing every new child and parent, regardless of background. "What are they coming from? Why are they coming? What are their hopes or dreams for their children?" The interviews took about 20 minutes.

It allowed up to us to put up a support framework from day one. If a child were troubled, we already were connecting him with counseling and support services. The family began a connection that day.

During this interview, I would get the sense that I could *feel* this child. I was being honest. I said the same things to everybody, regardless of SES [socioeconomic status], race, or background. People need to know that you are consistent, interested, and not prejudging them. Every day-to-day decision defines that climate in your building that leads to safety.

In summary, successful peer harassment programs have relied on these components:

1. Assessment of unsafe and potentially unsafe situations.
2. Case finding based on a personal knowledge of each student and an understanding of the prevalence of bullying.
3. Staff development on bullying (including its origins and consequences).
4. Family awareness activities, including policies and an overview of what students and parents can do if they suspect bullying.
5. Enlisting the 85% caring majority of students who are not involved in bullying by teaching them how to use proximity and verbal interventions to aid a peer who is a potential victim and how to get adult intervention. (Atlas & Pepler, 1998; Craig & Pepler, 1997)
6. Enforcement of a strict policy against harassment and intimidation.
7. Ongoing review of student and adult perceptions of how to improve the safety of the school.

Thus far, we have focused on how to create a safe and responsive school environment where students will not feel alienated or alone, and where caring bystanders will speak up about what they see. Moreover, we have emphasized the importance of a team threat assessment process that you can mobilize rapidly. When these efforts fail, however, you will need to protect yourself and others, using individual or schoolwide crisis responses.

INDIVIDUAL CRISIS RESPONSES

The first step in assessing a situation is to determine *whether you and others are in immediate danger.* Remember that some individuals pose a grave threat but never verbalize their intentions. We recommend that all school personnel have training in how to deescalate angry individuals (Kerr & Nelson, 2006). Here are some general tips on how to deescalate an individual who is getting out of control.

- Try to listen actively to the individual's complaints. Nodding, repeating back to the individual what he or she has said, and listening without interrupting can convey that you are interested in what the person is saying. Many angry individuals just want to be heard.
- Don't threaten. The individual might interpret this as a power play, become more fearful, and respond with assaultive behavior.

- Do use a normal voice level. Don't shout (unless distance or hearing loss prevents the individual from hearing your normal speaking voice).
- Do speak slowly and calmly, but avoid a tone that sounds condescending or treats an adult or teen as if they were a child.
- If you can offer the individual a choice that is reasonable, try this. For example, you might ask, "Would you be more comfortable sitting here or at the table?" "Would you like some water or a soft drink?" "Would you like for me to call someone for you?"
- Call the individual by his or her name, if appropriate and known. Refer to adults by title (e.g., "Mr." or "Ms.") if you think that gesture will convey respect.
- Don't criticize. It will only make matters worse. It cannot possibly make things better.
- Don't squabble with others over "best strategies" or allocations of blame. This is no time to prove a point.
- Don't bait the individual into acting out wild threats. The consequences could be tragic.
- Don't stand over the individual if he or she is seated. Instead, seat yourself.
- Do avoid direct, continuous eye contact.
- Do give the individual at least 3 feet of "personal space."
- Don't touch the individual.
- Do comply with requests that are neither endangering nor beyond reason. This provides the individual with an opportunity to feel somewhat "in control."
- Don't block the doorway. (Adapted from the National Alliance on Mental Illness (NAMI), Southwestern Pennsylvania, 1996).

Let's reflect . . .

As you recall an experience with an individual who was losing control or very angry, can you recall what you did to alleviate the situation? Were there words or actions you tried that made the situation worse?

If someone approaches you with a weapon, you must do whatever possible to be safe. The U.S. Immigration and Customs Enforcement, Federal Protective Service (n.d.) advises that you take these steps if threatened with a weapon:

- Stay calm. Quietly signal for help. (Use a duress alarm or code words.)
- Maintain eye contact.
- Stall for time.
- Keep talking, but follow instructions from the person who has the weapon.
- Don't risk harm to yourself or others.
- Never try to grab a weapon.
- Watch for a possible chance to escape to a safe area (U.S. Immigration and Customs Enforcement, Federal Protective Services, n.d.).

SCHOOLWIDE CRISIS RESPONSES

Although violence is a relatively rare event in schools, your school's crisis plan should include preparation and practice for such an event. Chapters 2 and 3 offer guidance for preparing staff and students to communicate and act calmly and quickly. The exact steps to take will depend on the layout of the school, who and where the violent individual(s) are, what their weapons and intentions are, your communications strategy, and what help you can mobilize. Figure 6.1 exemplifies how a school might respond to a violent individual. Other schoolwide plans are available on our website.

Figure 6.1
Crisis Response Plan for Weapon in School.

Weapons			"Clear the Halls" "Secure the School" "Evacuate the Building" Date / /
A dangerous or deadly weapon as defined by state and federal law includes, but is not limited to a gun, knife, metal knuckles, straight razor, noxious or irritating or poisonous gas, poison, other items used with the intent to harm, threaten or harass students, staff, parents or school visitors			
✔ Time	Witness/Reported By	Name of Contact	Contact No.
	Take safety measures to protect yourself and others		
✔ Time	Priority Procedures	Name of Contact	Contact No.
	Call 911		
	Stay calm and avoid confrontation if possible		
	Obtain good description of individual and the type of weapon he/she has		
	Notify the principal or designee as soon as possible		
	Take safety measures to protect yourself and others		
	Inform police of your observation and be prepared to write a statement		

✔	Time	Principal or Designee	Name of Contact	Contact No.
		Direct students and staff to "Clear the Halls," "Secure the Building," or "Evacuate the School"		
		In the event that the incident requires that you "Secure the Building," direct staff to lock all hallway and exterior doors		
		Meet with law enforcement upon arrival		
		Attend to the safety of students and staff at all times		
		Assess situation in regard to location of person with weapon and potential for injuries		
		Direct wrecker(s) to remove vehicles blocking emergency routes		
		Convene school crisis team and decide how the school will respond		
		Contact parent(s), guardian(s), or other close relative(s) of victims		
		Contact superintendent		
		Issue a press release or assign this task to the Communication Coordinator as deemed appropriate		
		Complete an incident report and file		
		Debrief with school crisis team and staff		
✔	Time	School Crisis Team	Name of Contact	Contact No.
		Convene school crisis team at the school and decide what additional resources and support will be needed		
		Provide victim assistance services		
✔	Time	School Counselor	Name of Contact	Contact No.
		Assist principal or designee with notifying parents of victims		
		Work with the counseling coordinator to initiate grief counseling plan as determined by need and severity of the situation		

✓	Time	School Nurse	Name of Contact	Contact No.
		Be prepared to treat injuries and assist EMS as needed		
		Assess the degree of injuries and report back to principal or designee		
		Establish triage area in safe location		
✓	Time	Communication Coordinator	Name of Contact	Contact No.
		After consultation with Law Enforcement, prepare a written statement for staff to read to students and send to parent(s)/ guardian(s) describing the known facts		
		Refer all media questions to law enforcement officials		
✓	Time	Teacher/Staff	Name of Contact	Contact No.
		Direct students who are in bathrooms or halls to join closest class and to inform the office about their location		
		Direct students to use alternate evacuation routes away from the incident if the fire alarm is activated, During a gun incident, instruct students to "drop to the floor/ground" or "run into the building quickly"		
		Lock all hallway and exterior doors; however, no doors should be barricaded or locked in a manner that would prevent rapid evacuation		
		Ask teachers, staff, visitors and students to remain quiet in designated area, on the floor away from windows and doors, and with all lights turned off		
		Remain in "Secure the Building" mode until the principal or law enforcement commander gives the "all clear" command		

Note: These material will help to make schools safer. However, in no way can a school district guarantee the safety of all students, all the time, using the VT School Crisis Guide.

Contributors include: Vermont State Police, Essex Police Department, Vermont Department of Education, Vermont School Boards Association, Montpelier Police Department, and Vermont Emergency management.

Source: From *Vermont School Crisis Guide* (pp. 65–66), 2004, by Vermont School Crisis Planning Team. Reprinted with permission.

Because we cannot possibly describe exactly how each school should respond, we instead highlight some lessons learned from addressing school violence.

1. **Practice responding to different scenarios.** For example, conduct drills where an intruder enters from different areas of the campus and at different times of day. Whether these are tabletop simulations or actual drills, be sure your staff is mentally prepared for several possibilities.

2. **Do not assume potential harm comes only from youth perpetrators.** After all, research shows that adults are more often engaged in violent behavior in our society than are children and youth. An elementary school principal shared a personal experience that taught us this lesson in crisis team preparation:

> Be sure you practice as if an adult intruder were the perpetrator. When I left my husband after enduring years of physical abuse, I made a difficult decision to share my situation with a few colleagues at school. Something just told me that he might show up there. Three weeks later, he appeared in the very early morning at our front counter, asking my secretary to see me. Thankfully, I had shown her his photograph and we had practiced what we would do if he ever showed up. She stalled while offering that I was in another part of the building. As he went down the hall to locate me, she called the police and signaled me. I crawled out my office window to the safety of my car and drove away. When the police arrived minutes later, they discovered that my husband was armed. That day has haunted me for years.

3. **Have a good crisis response plan that involves but does not rely totally on law enforcement.** The research on targeted school shootings uncovered that the first responses to violence had to come solely from school personnel, with law enforcement arriving later.

4. **Use crisis communications that are straightforward and will be understood by those unfamiliar with the building (e.g., substitute teachers, emergency responders, visitors, volunteers, and new students).** If your codes are too cumbersome or cryptic, individuals will not understand how to respond or will forget them.

5. **Spend time getting to know the communities that send students to your building as well as the neighborhood surrounding the building.** A school is only as safe as its community. If a feud breaks out between two groups in the neighborhood, the hostility may come into the school, as evidenced in this case:

> I was completely unprepared that day. Tyrone, a new transfer on whom we had almost no information, went after another art student and shattered a glass door. There was blood everywhere. I screamed to the student teacher to run for help while I tried to stop the bleeding. We found out later that they were members of rival gangs that had lost members to a shooting over the weekend.

6. **Monitor websites where students may be posting information that could inform you about a threatening situation (and advise parents to do the same).** If you are concerned about an individual, do an Internet search for that person's publicly available information to see what's going on. You may not be able to take any action to

remove what you read or see, but you will be able to add this information to your threat assessment or investigation. Here's an example from a retired school administrator:

> The new student denied any drug or weapons involvement, but my instincts said he was lying. When he left my office, I checked My Space only to find that he was bragging about his drug and gun deals all over his page. So, we just kept a watchful eye on him during that summer, tried to get him involved in decent activities, and alerted his case worker and probation officer. Sure enough, the first day of school, he had our youngest at-risk kids following him like the pied piper. In the ninth-grade meeting, he challenged me from the middle of the assembly, with 500 kids present. We put the team together, talked to him again, met with his parent, and got his probation officer into the building. Unfortunately, our efforts came too late in his troubled life. He is now in prison.

Let's reflect . . .

How does your school learn about new students or those who transfer from other districts with a discipline history? What information is shared with classroom teachers or counselors?

SUPPORTING STUDENTS AFTER A VIOLENT INCIDENT

Students and staff who witness, directly experience, or indirectly experience a violent incident will have many needs for safety and psychological support from adults at school and at home. Reflect on what students and adults in these cases might require:

- A man was charged with fatally shooting his estranged wife and her cousin as the two women waited outside the city elementary school for pupils to be dismissed. Kindergartners were in the schoolyard and witnessed the shooting.
- A 6-year-old was abducted from her rural school's playground during the first day of school. Her abductor, a middle-age woman, impersonated the child's mother when she called to the new playground aide. Many children witnessed the event, later learning that their playmate had been kidnapped.

In some instances, many are in need of psychological support, so you must **triage,** or set priorities on whom to help first. Understanding who is at high risk is one way to triage those in need. Here are the risk factors for the long-term consequences of posttraumatic stress disorder):

1. Exposure/contact (in order of greatest risk):

    Direct exposure—victims/witnesses/perpetrators/suspects

    - Onsite—students, faculty, staff, parents
    - Off-campus—students/staff absent on day of incident
    - Out-of-vicinity—ex: friends at other nearby schools

2. Other risk factors:

- Familiarity with victims
- Previous trauma or loss, especially during the past year
- Worry about safety of family member or significant other
- Family response psychopathology—family dysfunction
- Individual psychopathology—history of previous dysfunction or exposure to violence

Already at-risk students, such as those in special education or foster care, may be more likely than other students to suffer psychological trauma after school-related violence. They may need more assistance than other students, and those who conduct triage assessments should be aware of this fact. (Wong, Fink, Stein, Kataoka, & Steiger, 2003)

Acknowledging the extraordinary needs of affected students and staff, the federal government has developed Project School Emergency Response to Violence (SERV). This project has produced a report on supporting schools after a violent incident, available with other project documents on our website. A major finding of the project's expert panel was that mental health services be available for an extended period following the incident, given the incidence of posttraumatic stress disorder and stress-related impairment. As one teacher on the panel observed, "There were some teachers who, three years later, were just exhibiting signs now, and this is right when they wanted to cut off services . . . You can't put a timeline on when people are going to manifest symptoms" (Wong et al., 2003).

The panel also advised that teachers not be put in the role of therapists while acknowledging that they provide invaluable reassurance to children. Teachers, the panel advised, should learn to recognize acute stress reactions but should have trauma specialists to whom they can refer those children in their care. Many observed that these mental health services were more effective when provided on the school campus.

McGlenn and Jimerson (2004), veteran crisis responders who shared their experience of the Santana school shooting, echoed the observations of others that victims (like school institutions) respond to and recover from a school shooting in different ways and along different timetables. Violence reawakens reactions to previous traumas and exacerbates prior mental health challenges. Subsequent threats, fights, and even fire drills can retraumatize particular individuals. As an expert panel noted, exposure to school violence often requires *long-term* follow-up (Wong et al., 2003). Provision of such long-term services raises the question of where to locate mental health services. McGlenn and Jimerson (2004) found that school-based mental health services made support more accessible to survivors. Others have concurred, although cautioning that long-term provision of support services on campus (past the first year) can also serve as traumatic reminders of the event, prolonging and exacerbating stress in individuals attempting to return to normal routines (Wong et al., 2003).

Should your school experience an act of terrorism or violence affecting large numbers of individuals or resulting in severe trauma, you will need the expertise of those who have worked under such circumstances. Other suggestions for supporting those who have experienced trauma related to school violence appear in Chapter 8. Chapter 9 outlines postvention procedures that have been used in conjunction with other expert consultation after many violent incidents, including the Breslan school massacre in 2004. Another excellent resource is the National Education Association Health Information Network's "Stress Reduction Guide" for educators whose schools have experienced violence-related crises (2000). This guide includes a primer on stress for school employees, facts about school violence, recommendations for reducing violence-related stress, and resources.

Crisis Responding After a Crime Has Been Committed

If a crime has been committed (as is often the case in school violence), school officials have yet another set of issues to consider. For example, consider these cases:

- Yvonda, a middle school student, was found murdered in an alley near her home. Detectives got their first break in the case when a peer offered that Yvonda had confided recently that her stepfather had molested her. Her stepfather was found guilty in the subsequent trial.
- A student was found guilty of premeditated murder, after a classmate reported to the school counselor that the defendant had talked about his plans to hurt the teen.
- A crisis response team member was leading a group session following a fatal car crash when a participant spoke up, acknowledging that the driver's parents had supplied alcohol to those in the car for several hours before the crash.

Such situations place school personnel in a challenging position. To prepare for such eventualities, we recommend that you confer in advance with your school district's legal adviser to write a procedure for building-level staff. Figure 6.2 illustrates how one school district advises its administrators to respond when a crime has been committed at school.

Safeguarding the School Community When the Threat Continues

Frightening those in the school community, the threat of harm continues after some initial incidents. Try to identify the ongoing threats in these cases:

- An elementary school bus on the way home stops at an intersection, where students looking out of the bus witness a male pedestrian step off a public bus only to be shot repeatedly by another adult on the street. The shooter escapes on foot.
- A small urban elementary school receives a bomb threat over the phone. Nothing is found after the school is evacuated by the police. However, the school continues to receive telephone bomb threats for months.
- A school custodian discovers a threat written across a rest-room mirror in a suburban high school. Days later, the school receives a faxed threat naming students and teachers.

Another example of an ongoing threat to staff and students was the 20-day period during which two snipers killed 10 adults and wounded a school child along the I-95 corridor from Maryland to Virginia in the fall of 2002. Although extremely rare, this kind of incident provides your crisis team members with a complex case study for reflection and "what-if" planning. One of the superintendents whose district was affected has written about his

CRIMINAL INCIDENTS IN SCHOOLS

Safety & Security Fact Sheet

✔ Call the police immediately. Studies have shown that an immediate notification of the police significantly increases the chances of solving a crime.

✔ The scene of the incident should be preserved. Once it has been confirmed that the scene is cleared of all persons, no one should be allowed to enter the area or touch anything. The crime scene generally includes the location of the actual offense as well as the points and routes of entry and exit. Total isolation of these areas may not be possible in all cases, but every effort should be made to preserve this important evidence. The first police officer to arrive will help school officials to define and secure the scene.

✔ Questioning of any victims should be limited in scope and conducted by only one person until the police arrive. A description of the suspect should be obtained as soon as possible and relayed to the police. Do not delay reporting because of sketchy information; additional information can always be relayed to responding police officers.

✔ Victims should be isolated from other activities relating to the incident, and appropriate adult companionship should be provided. The victim should not be discouraged from discussing the incident, but direct questioning regarding the incident should be avoided. The companion should be attentive to any statements made, but written notes should not be made while the victim is present. Specific details will be obtained by a trained police investigator.

✔ A victim should not be shown any photographs or composite drawings of possible suspects, nor should a victim be brought into direct contact with any persons who may be involved. Suspect identification must meet strict legal standards and should not be attempted by school officials.

✔ School officials should recognize that a victim may provide conflicting or contradictory details of the incident. This does occur in cases and may or may not be indicative of deception. Under no circumstances should school officials confront the victim on these discrepancies, but they should note them and privately inform the police investigator of them at the earliest opportunity.

For more information, visit our web site, www.fcps.edu/fts/safety-security/factsheets/sec-4.pdf. If you need assistance, call the security section at xxx-xxx-xxx

Figure 6.2

Criminal Incidents in School.

Source: From *Safety Rules for Outdoor Recess (Fact Sheet) and Criminal Incidents in School (Fact Sheet)* (from website), 2002, Springfield, VA: Office of Safety & Security, Fairfax County Public Schools. Reprinted with permission.

experience, so you could use this diary as a basis for crisis team discussion (see Roberson, 2004). Superintendent Roberson highlighted the importance of crisis leadership: "Unwittingly, but willingly, Richmond-area superintendents found themselves as players in the law enforcement strategy and in the efforts to bring calm to a terrorized population" (p. 26).

Of course, these situations require ongoing threat assessment and investigation by law enforcement officials, who will recommend safeguards that protect witnesses (as in the first case) and those potentially targeted (as in the other cases). Parents (as well as employees and their families) will look to the school for reassurance and information. In such cases, your communications are scrutinized, so you may want to reread the advice provided in Chapter 4. Here are some additional tips:

- Try to reestablish normal routines, although with heightened supervision and surveillance. For example, in the case cited earlier involving child witnesses to a shooting, the principal sat with children on the bus to and from school for several days following the incident. The bus route was altered to avoid the scene of the crime, and a school police car accompanied the bus along its route.
- Do not overlook the needs of employees and their families; they, too, need to know that their safety is valued.
- Heighten the visibility of security measures, including police or security staff, until the threats cease.
- Provide families and staff with regular factual updates. Let the information regarding the investigation come from the experts (e.g., the police).
- Pay close attention to those who attend any public informational meetings or contact the school with questions about the incidents; log these names because they may be of interest to the police. Sometimes a perpetrator seeking attention will observe the school's reactions.
- Keep in mind that threats may come from within the school district. In the bomb threat case described here, the perpetrator was an angry employee.

SUMMARY

Using data to anticipate school violence and crimes is a sensible approach facilitated by federal, state, and local reports such as those referenced in this chapter. However, incident data cannot replace the "real-time" reports of those within the school and community, whose voices are overlooked sometimes. Periodic canvassing of students, staff, and community members is essential in establishing a safe and caring school environment. Experts agree that the school climate is key to violence prevention. Other prevention tactics include CPTED, target hardening, and threat assessment. Individual deescalation of hostile individuals can reduce the risk of serious harm to persons or property, as can schoolwide approaches such as bullying prevention. Should your school experience violence, psychological supports such as those prescribed by Project SERV will be necessary. Special circumstances such as ongoing threats or witnessing of a crime add to the school's crisis response agenda.

CASE STUDY CONCLUSION

I'll never forget Kevin's face as he sat in the back of the police car. Crying, he looked up at me and said, "I didn't mean to scare everybody. I just couldn't take it anymore, Dr. Draft. He wouldn't leave me alone. He was even calling my house and asking for my little sister. I had to stop him. Nobody else would."

The rest of that week is now a kaleidoscope of flashbacks: the faces of teachers earnestly trying to reassure kids that they were safe . . . the harrowing stories staff told among themselves of being in lockdown with frightened children calling parents on their cell phones . . . the sound of Kevin's gun going off when he shot it into the air before he finally dropped it on the ground . . . the huge TV cameras mounted in front of our school . . . the reporters who seemed to camp out there every day . . . the parents whose questions never stopped . . . the half-empty buses, with seats abandoned by kids whose parents insisted on driving them that first week.

We later discovered that Kevin had been harassed—well, bullied is more like it—when he was in a neighboring elementary school. His parents had reported it, but I guess not much happened. Maybe his elementary staff didn't believe a big kid like Kevin could be on the receiving end of a bully. When Kevin's parents moved to a new apartment, they entered our school district.

"We had such high hopes. Kevin was really getting to like this school and had even made a few friends. Then one day, he spotted LaVon on that bus and realized LaVon was an eighth grader here," Kevin's mother shared with me when we met before Kevin's hearing. "LaVon wouldn't let up. The last straw was when Kevin's little sister found a dead bird from LaVon in her doll stroller in front of our apartment."

LaVon was also new to our district, and I frankly had not spent much time getting to know him. But all that changed, after I heard this story. We called in LaVon and his parents and confronted them with the accusations. To my amazement, LaVon admitted what he had done. He almost seemed proud of it.

Our crisis team met with the police days afterward and reviewed the steps we had taken. We were pleased that a student had trusted us with critical information. Connecting with kids, and "owning" the unowned spaces and times of the school day had been an emphasis of our back-to-school professional development. Our school safety committee met a few weeks after the incident to talk about what we could do to prevent this from ever happening again. Once we fit together the pieces about the bullying, we knew we had to renew our efforts to prevent kids from ganging up on one another. We made bullying a priority in our school professional development plan and asked the local community to support us in launching an antibullying campaign.

DISCUSSION AND APPLICATION IDEAS

1. Check the data from the most recent year's *Indicators of School Crime and Safety* as well as local crime data. Discuss their implications with your colleagues. Do you believe your school's crisis plans are focused appropriately?
2. Review how your school or district assesses safety and risk for violence, bullying, and other problems. Do you think your approach meets the needs of students (especially teens) reluctant to report threats and victimization?
3. If you were to adopt the mapping strategy put forth by Astor and his colleagues, how would you go about it?

4. Search your community for resources to train your staff to deescalate hostile individuals.

5. Using the case studies in this chapter, lead a crisis team refresher session. Plan how you would respond to each scenario.

REFERENCES

Astor, R. A., Meyer, H. A., & Behre, W. J. (1999). Unowned places and times: Maps and interviews about violence in high schools. *American Educational Research Journal, 36* (1), 3-42.

Atlas, R. S., & Pepler, D. J. (1998). Observations of bullying in the classroom. *Journal of Educational Research, 92,* 86-97.

Banks, R. (1997). Bullying in schools. *ERIC Review, 7*(1), 12-14. Champaign, IL: ERIC Clearinghouse on Elementary and Early Childhood Education. (ERIC Document Reproduction Service No. ED4 07154)

Belcher, S. C. (2003). Tools for reducing school violence: An interview with school violence expert professor Ron Avi Astor. *Teaching to Change LA, 3* (1-7), 2002-2003.

Benard, B. (1991, August). *Fostering resiliency in kids: Protective factors in the family, school, and community.* Portland, OR: Northwest Regional Educational Laboratory.

Bully B'Ware Productions. (1999). *More information on bullying.* Retrieved November 24, 2006, from http://www.bullybeware.com

Colvin, G., Sugai, G., Good, R. H. III, & Lee, Y. Y. (1997). Using active supervision and pre-correction to improve transition behaviors in an elementary school. *School Psychology Quarterly, 12* (4), 344-363.

Cornell, D. G., Sheras, P. L., Kaplan, S., McConville, D., Douglass, J., Elkon, A., et al. (2004). Guidelines for student threat assessment: Field-test findings. *School Psychology Review, 33,* 527-546.

Craig, W., & Pepler, D. J. (1997). Observations of bullying and victimization on the schoolyard. *Canadian Journal of School Psychology, 2,* 41-60.

DeVoe, J. F., Peter, K., Noonan, M., Snyder, T. D., and Baum, K. (2005). *Indicators of school crime and safety: 2005.* U.S. Departments of Education and Justice (NCES 2006-001/NCJ 210697). Washington, DC: U.S. Government Printing Office.

Fein, R., Vossekuil, B., Pollack, W., Borum, R., Modzeleski, W., & Reddy, M. (2002). *Threat assessment in schools: A guide to managing threatening situations and to creating safe school climates.* Washington, DC: U.S. Department of Education, Office of Elementary and Secondary Education, Safe and Drug-Free Schools Program and U.S. Secret Service, National Threat Assessment Center.

Guerino, P., Hurwitz, M. D., Noonan, M. E., and Kaffenberger, S. M. (2006). *Crime, violence, discipline, and safety in U.S. public schools: Findings from the school survey on crime and safety: 2003–04.* U.S. Department of Education, National Center for Education Statistics. Washington, DC: U.S. Government Printing Office. (NCES 2007-302)

Kerr, M. M. (2000, November). When duty calls, you can't run away. *The School Administrator, 57* (10), 6. American Association of School Administrators.

Kerr, M. M. (2001, February). *Workplace violence prevention for educators.* Paper presented at the American Association of School Administrators, Orlando, FL.

Kerr, M. M., & Nelson, C. M. (2006). *Strategies for addressing behavior problems in the classroom* (5th ed.). Columbus, OH: Merrill.

Kerr, M. M., & Palmer, C. D. (2007, January). Bullying: What you don't know can hurt them. *Middle Matters, 15* (3). n.p. Retrieved July 11, 2007, from http://www.naesp.org/ContentLoad.do?contentId=2149

McGlenn, R. L., & Jimerson, S. R. (2004). Support services following a shooting at school: Lessons earned regarding response and recovery. In E. R. Gerler, Jr. (Ed.), *Handbook of school violence* (pp. 333-343). Binghamton, NY: Haworth Press.

National Alliance on Mental Illness (NAMI) of Southwestern Pennsylvania. (1996). The crisis. *Voice, 3,* 6.

National Center for Educational Statistics. (2005). *Indicators of school crime and safety: 2005.* Retrieved November 11, 2006, from http://nces.ed.gov/programs/crimeindicators/Indicators. asp?PubPageNumber=12&ShowTablePage=TablesHTML/table_12.1.asp

National Crime Prevention Council. (2003). *School safety and security toolkit a guide for parents, schools, and communities.* Washington, DC: Author.

National Crime Prevention Council and National Center for Victims of Crime Office for Victims of Crime. (2005). *Reaching and serving teen victims: A practical handbook.* Washington, DC: Author.

National Education Association, Health Information Network (2000). *Violence in Communities and Schools: A Stress Reduction Guide for Teachers and Other School Staff.* Washington, DC: Author.

National Safe Schools Center. (1993). *School bullying and victimization: NSSC resource paper.* Available from http://www.nsscl.org

Olweus, D. (1996). Bully/victim problems in school: Facts and effective intervention. *Reclaiming Children and Youth, 5* (1), 15-22.

Peterson, R., & Strassel, A. (2002). *Security audits and inspections.* Retrieved November 26, 2006, from http://education.indiana.edu/~safeschl/security_audits_and_inspections.pdf

Roberson, S. D. (2004). Three weeks in October: Managing widespread fear in a school community during the final days of the Beltway sniper crisis. *School Administrator, 61* (6), 26-32.

Skiba, R. (2000). *Zero tolerance, zero evidence: An analysis of school disciplinary practice.* Bloomington, IN: Indiana Education Policy Center. (Policy Research Report #SRS2)

Skiba, R., & Peterson, R. (1999). The dark side of zero tolerance: Can punishment lead to safer schools? *Phi Delta Kappa, 80,* 372-382.

Skiba, R., & Peterson, R. (2000). School discipline: From zero tolerance to early response. *Exceptional Children, 66,* 335-347.

U.S. Department of Labor. (1998). *Recommendations for workplace violence prevention programs in late-night retail establishments.* Washington, DC: Occupational Safety and Health Administration. (OSHA 3153)

U.S. Immigration and Customs Enforcement, Federal Protective Service. (n.d.). *Making buildings safe.* Retrieved December 14, 2006, from http://www.gsa.gov/gsa/cm_attachments/GSA_DOCUMENT/ fps_making_buildings_safe_R25Z74_0Z5RDZ-i34K-pR. pdf

Wong, M., Fink, A., Stein, B. D., Kataoka, S., & Steiger, E. M. (2003). *A guide for intermediate and long-term mental health services after school-related violent events.* Retrieved November 18, 2006, from http://mentalhealth.samhsa.gov/publications/allpubs/NMH03-0151/page7.asp

CHAPTER 7

PREVENTION, MITIGATION, AND RESPONSE FOR DISASTERS

CASE STUDY

I used to work as a school social worker in a large K–5 elementary school that occupied a flat, low-lying area not far from a creek. On this particular morning I had listened to the weather forecast while drinking my coffee. News bulletins warned of heavy rain and thunderstorms in our suburb, so I grabbed my raincoat on the way to my car.

Also alerted to the impending storms, our elementary school principal and vice principal listened to the weather reports throughout the morning. During lunch, I noticed the children were startled and frightened by the lightning and thunder that raged outside and rumbled through the hallways of the school. To help calm their fears, the principal spoke to groups of students in the lunchrooms, reassuring them they would be safe inside the building.

Torrential rains continued through the afternoon. Around 1 P.M., our principal received a call from the central office: "The township has closed several roads near the creek. Twenty families have orders to evacuate their homes. We will give you updates as soon as we have them."

The rain never stopped; nor did the communications between the central office and our school. The local police, the county emergency management office, and the Red Cross had already contacted us when we heard the radio news: "Mudslides have forced the closure of roads in the area."

Realizing that school buses would not be able to navigate the area and reach their destinations, we made announcements to the students in the classrooms that they would be staying until roads were passable. To reassure them, we explained that although the roads were impassable, there were no reports of any injuries. Then we mobilized our staff to tackle the many logistics necessary for keeping the students at school during the long hours ahead.

INTRODUCTION

This chapter addresses how schools can prepare for disasters and community-wide events that have a major impact on the school. First, let's examine how a disaster might differ from other school-level crises. A **disaster** is an event or series of events that cause widespread, severe damage, injury, death, or loss of property. In a disaster, a local community cannot cope successfully *without* outside aid (Perez & Thompson, 1996). Therefore, the school is but one partner in the disaster prevention, mitigation, preparation, response, and recovery processes. While schools may take specific steps to ready themselves, they will rely largely on the expertise of other disaster prevention and response agencies.

PREPARATION, PREVENTION, AND MITIGATION

Most disasters are beyond the control of the school or the community, so prevention is not always realistic. Nevertheless, you can become familiar with the federal and state models

The author of this chapter is Dr. Mark Lepore, Assistant Professor of Counseling Psychology at Chatham University. Dr. Lepore is also a mental health trainer for the American Red Cross, and a supervisor for National Disaster Response.

for response so that you will be more prepared in a large-scale incident. Perhaps you have heard of the National Incident Management System (NIMS), developed in 2003 to coordinate the responses of all levels of government in the United States as well as private-sector and nongovernmental organizations. NIMS provides protocols for such agencies to coordinate their efforts in prevention, preparation, response, and recovery. The focus is on domestic incidents and terrorism.

Schools can prepare for large-scale events by using the many resources available through the U.S. Department of Education and the Federal Emergency Management Agency (FEMA). For example, the Department of Education has posted many resources for pandemic planning on its website. FEMA offers a face-to face one-week course, "Multi-Hazard Safety Program for Schools," which helps school personnel learn how to reduce risk, hold drills, practice crisis responses, and engage in postdisaster recovery and mitigation. Alternatively, several free online courses are available on emergency planning for schools that cover emergency management operations; the NIMS procedures, roles and duties; how to assess potential hazards that schools may face; and how to develop and test an emergency operations plan that addresses potential hazards. Consider using one or more of these courses as crisis team refreshers or offering them for continuing education credits to all staff.

Awareness and Assessment

The first step in disaster preparedness is to be aware of the disasters that could occur in your community. FEMA's website has local and national maps that offer risk information about the disasters and hazards listed in Figure 7.1.

For each of these potential disasters, FEMA offers planning and preparation guides.

Preparation Activities for Students

In addition to these adult aids, schools in high-risk areas (e.g., areas susceptible to tornadoes, hurricanes, floods, or neighborhood violence) can prepare their students by using some of the curricula now available. FEMA provides free publications and materials of

Figure 7.1
Hazards and Disasters.

Chemical emergencies	Nuclear power plant emergency
Dam failure	Terrorism
Earthquake	Thunderstorm
Fire or wildfire	Tornado
Flood	Tsunami
Hazardous material	Volcano
Heat	Wildfire
Hurricane	Winter storm
Landslide	

interest to parents concerned with their children's readiness in the event of a disaster or crisis situation. FEMA offers curricula and activities for students through its children's interactive website, which is very well developed and provides a fun and informative experience for children. Clearly much thought and preparation has gone into its development; as a result, this website provides a good way for parents and educators to approach the topic with a positive, can-do approach.

The American Red Cross has developed a ready-to-go curriculum kit called "Masters of Disaster" to help teachers integrate disaster safety instruction into their regular core subjects such as language arts, math, science, and social studies. These have been designed specifically to meet national education standards. These are available in printed form from your local chapter of the American Red Cross or on our companion website.

Ready Kids is a US Department of Homeland Security website offering cheerful interactive games and planning tools that elementary school-aged children can use. These resources help schools in their disaster preparation by giving educators a curriculum-based head start in this daunting task.

DISASTER RESPONSE: HOW EXTERNAL AGENCIES ARE INVOLVED

Perhaps you have wondered how external resources are mobilized in a disaster. Let's review the chain of events in a disaster:

Local government responds, supplemented by neighboring communities and volunteer agencies. If overwhelmed, turn to the state for assistance.

The state responds with state resources, such as the National Guard and state agencies.

Damage assessment by local, state, federal, and volunteer organizations determines losses and recovery needs.

A major disaster declaration is requested by the governor, based on the damage assessment and an agreement to commit state funds and resources to the long-term recovery.

FEMA evaluates the request and recommends action to the White House based on the disaster and the local community and the state's ability to recover.

The president approves the request or FEMA informs the governor it has been denied. This decision process could take a few hours or several weeks depending on the nature of the disaster (FEMA, 2007).

Next, let's explore the resources that schools may access through these external agencies.

Partnered with the National Institute for Mental Health, American Red Cross chapters have the ability to provide each U.S. county with crisis counseling and to assist individuals and families with psychological first aid. This early intervention counseling is defined as any psychological intervention delivered within the first four weeks following mass violence or disasters (NIMH, 2002). Disaster mental health services are provided at the disaster site and consist of (a) an assessment of the individual, (b) provision of basic environmental supports, (c) provision of psychological first aid, and (d) connecting them with appropriate local resources for medication, shelter, additional mental health services, or physical health services.

The Red Cross works in what is termed a disaster action team, or DAT team. This team consists of individuals specifically trained in a variety of disaster relief and crisis mitigation modalities. Disaster mental health specialists for DAT teams provide psychological first aid and counseling. Like all mental health specialists they must have a master's degree in counseling, social work, or psychology and hold a license to practice in the mental health field. Additionally, they receive specific disaster and disaster mental health training directly from the American Red Cross. The American Red Cross maintains up-to-date personnel records for all members of a DAT team. Here's a personal reflection offered by the author of this chapter, a DAT disaster mental health specialist:

> When I go to a disaster site, the first thing I do is to engage those persons affected in a conversation and to ascertain some information about their current coping mechanisms, what types of essentials they may need to help them recover, and to have them articulate how they are feeling and doing. This initial intervention usually lasts from one to three hours, depending on what's needed. During that conversation, I can provide them with environmental supports such as access to a telephone, water, food, children's activity packets, and a disaster relief packet with toiletries and other essentials. The benefit of providing these supplies is that while we are talking about their needs, I can gauge both their level of distress and their natural coping strategies. This time also allows the victim to tell me about other concerns they have such as the whereabouts of their family members or a medical condition for which they need medication urgently.
>
> Depending on the severity of the disaster, I've seen victims with a great deal of disorientation—to the point where they could not remember phone numbers or the names of friends and family members. When that happens, we have to do more to help the victim. We have to take that first step for them. We might have to help them find the information in a wallet or in their home somewhere. I've seen people with milder disorientation, where we were able to work out a plan together. Other times, people appear to be coping well, so we provide psychological first aid and they are able to move out on their own.
>
> Psychological first aid might be listening and having them feel comfortable with you. We always offer affirmations, when we can, about how they are showing control. For example, we might help them make a list of things they need help with. Losing control is very frightening to adults.
>
> We always let victims know that they can reconnect with us, and many times they do. After all, the last thing a disaster victim needs is to be repeatedly prompted to tell their story over and over to new people.

In addition to crisis counseling, the Red Cross has persons to support schools and communities including client assistance, providing shelter, food, clothing, and at times financial support, disaster health-related services serving the needs of people with disabilities, disaster assessment, disaster preparedness training, including cardiopulmonary resuscitation (CPR), first aid, automated external defibrillator (AED), and others.

If the American Red Cross DAT teams need more assistance, FEMA may call in another resource, the Emergency Services and Disaster Relief Branch of the Center for Mental Health Services. This agency also is responsible for meeting the mental health needs of disaster survivors and responders. The branch works with FEMA to implement the Crisis Counseling Assistance and Training Program when a state has applied for a Crisis Counseling Program grant after a federally declared disaster.

Another resource often called in after a disaster involving schools is the National Organization for Victims Assistance (NOVA), a private, nonprofit organization of victim and witness assistance programs and practitioners, criminal justice agencies and professionals, mental health professionals, researchers, former victims and survivors, and others committed to the recognition and implementation of victim rights and services. NOVA's role in a disaster is to arrive in the immediate aftermath and to provide mental health crisis consultation and coordination for 72 hours. A school might contact NOVA through their website, for example, if its community experienced a disaster or tragedy that overtaxes its ability to respond and recover. NOVA's four goals for their short-term assistance include crisis planning, responder training at the crisis site, direct victim assistance (restitution of basic needs, aiding in death notification, and supportive counseling), and victim advocacy (financial assistance, managing media, ensuring legal rights, and getting correct information for families of victims) (Young, 1998).

The National Association of School Psychologists (NASP) provides materials free of charge that help children and youth cope with traumatic or unsettling events. Topics include school safety/violence prevention, crisis response resources, and suicide prevention/intervention. In a disaster, NASP materials (many of which are available on the website) might be useful to your school team. NASP also has an on-call assistance program accessed through their website.

DISASTER RECOVERY: ACKNOWLEDGMENT, EXPRESSION, AND REENGAGEMENT

The overriding goal for school personnel responding to a disaster is to provide safety for the students and staff and minimize any further danger or harm. The next task is that of stability, to return the school to a point of precrisis functioning. According to grief and trauma counseling specialists, most people will return to a state of normal functioning, although they will be changed by the event in some way (Worden, 2002). Let's explore how school personnel can facilitate psychological recovery during the weeks and months after a disaster.

Students and staff need acknowledgment that a crisis has occurred, an opportunity to express and have their feelings validated, and a process for reengagement into the school environment and its routines. The quality and extent of support for these three processes has a significant impact on how individuals react following a trauma and how they move forward (Spiers, 2001).

Acknowledgment

Although it may seem unnecessary to acknowledge something as high profile as a community disaster, crisis responders recommend that you not overlook this step. Many of us have

Let's reflect...

Return to the opening case study about a community experiencing a flood. If you were teaching in that elementary school during a heavy rain, would you assume a flood had taken place? How might you find out that the flood was affecting your workplace or the neighborhood? How would your school share that information with all staff?

experienced situations in which the school staff either did not know about an event or did not understand how the event might affect the school.

Acknowledging a disaster may also entail convincing others to take some action while they can. For example, if you are a school principal told to evacuate your building because of a chemical spill or threatening weather, you need to convince your staff to leave immediately, even though some staff may not take the threat seriously.

Expression of Feelings

One of the major goals in helping the school community to recover is to provide an environment that is inclusive and supportive as individuals begin to explore their feelings and reactions to the disaster. Schools have been creative in developing outlets for students and staff to express their feelings, sometimes while expressing their need to help as well.

After September 11, 2001, one elementary school provided opportunities for the students to send drawings and letters of encouragement to the New York Police Department (NYPD) and the New York Fire Department (FDNY). Several weeks later, the school and students were surprised by a visit from four members of the NYPD who wished to thank them personally for their support. The act of writing the letters was a curative activity, and the power of the visit from the NYPD officers could not be overestimated.

Many students show an innate ability to be tuned in to the emotional dimensions of a crisis and its aftermath. They are often the best persons to develop ways to memorialize those who have been lost. Of course, any type of memorializing ceremony or activity should be monitored by school officials for appropriateness. When educators and school officials model expression of feelings for students, they also informally give students per-

Let's reflect...

In the aftermath of an incident involving the death of a student, how would you, as a teacher or school administrator, deal with the emotional reactions of your students? Would you openly express your own feelings about the incident? What would you choose to share or not to share? How might you to encourage the expression of feelings of your students?

mission to verbalize what the youth are experiencing, which is a very powerful and normalizing activity (Thompson, 2004).

Educators can facilitate discussion about the disaster that occurred, calling on school counselors, psychologists, or social workers for assistance in facilitating these discussions. We recommend that you be as factual as possible when explaining the events that took place. Teachers can structure activities in their classrooms to allow student expression of their feelings, including writing poems or stories, listening to music for expression, creating art, reading stories that deal with relevant themes, developing memorials that include a ceremony at the school, or raising money for donated library books for the library.

During discussion with students, try to remain nonjudgmental and show unconditional acceptance of youths' feelings. Students need your reassurance that their emotional response to a traumatic event is normal.

Reengagement with School

Disaster victims may experience feelings of grief and loss similar to the feelings of those who have lost a friend or a loved one in death. "It is not just the loss of another that leads to bereavement following a disaster. Often it is what is felt to have been lost" (Spiers, 2001, p. 13). For example, the loss experienced may be the loss of one's sense of security and safety, the loss of the disaster victim, the loss of one's lifestyle and routines before the disaster, or a sense of loss about what he or she could have done differently during the incident (Spiers, 2001; Thompson, 2004).

Because the ability for students to work through the grieving process is partly a *social* phenomenon, perceived emotional and social support from others at school can be invaluable to children and adolescents (Worden, 2002). To provide support, we pay attention to the day-to-day routines and procedures while attending to the psychological needs of students and staff. Vulnerable to sudden changes in their environment, children do well in a stable environment with structure. To bring about this stability, routines should be reestablished while adults reassure students they are doing everything in their power to keep them safe.

Some of us working in schools following the September 11 disaster observed the importance of supported reengagement with school routines. Many students believed strongly that things were going to be safe because they had resumed their normal school routines such as saying the pledge of allegiance and resuming schoolwork (Hooker & Friedman, 2005).

Students and parents may struggle with being separated from one another with the reopening of schools after a crisis (U.S. Department of Education, Office of Safe and Drug Free Schools, 2003). Yet students should return to school as soon as this becomes possible after a disaster. It has been our experience that when anxious children and adolescents stay at home, their fears continue to magnify, making a return more and more difficult. Their fears about returning to school may become far more debilitating than the dreaded experience of returning.

Children and adolescents take their lead in recovery from the cues and emotional responses from adults around them. At times parents who are overly concerned with their child's safety may have difficulty allowing them return to school. In past situations we have allowed parents to bring their son or daughter to the school following a traumatic event, then encouraged them to join other parents either in a parent drop-in center or in volunteer work. You may also try these strategies:

- Allow parents to ride the bus for the first couple of days.
- Greet parents and allow them to remain at school the first days.
- Get parents and students involved in reconstructing a school that has to be relocated.
- Get parents and students involved in a memorial project in honor of a deceased student or a faculty member.
- Sponsor parent gatherings.
- Send letters home to parents providing reassurance and pertinent information and resources to help them cope in the aftermath.

In general, when school personnel can communicate with parents in the community following a disaster, the transition will go more smoothly. This dialogue also gives parents an opportunity to voice their thoughts and concerns.

Educators are among the most important adults in the transition and recovery of students impacted by a natural disaster or other crisis. Your efforts will begin to give students a sense of stability, security, and belonging (U.S. Department of Education, 2005).

TYPICAL REACTIONS TO DISASTERS

How a child or an adolescent reacts to a disaster depends on many variables. However, immediate reactions to crisis often involve shock or numbness, denial or the inability to acknowledge what has occurred, dissociative behavior (appearing dazed, apathetic), confusion, disorganization, and difficulty making decisions (Thompson, 2004). Children and adolescents may experience increased fears and anxiety, show a decrease in academic performance or poor concentration, increased aggression and decreased frustration tolerance, and increased irritability and depressive feelings (Lerner & Shelton, 2001). These symptoms are, for the most part, normal responses to an abnormal event. Many persons who are exposed to a traumatic event experience some symptoms in the immediate aftermath of the event. Most symptoms eventually remit and, therefore, do not always necessitate long-term follow-up (NIMH, 2002). However, if symptoms of severe stress should persist beyond several weeks, parents and teachers should seek evaluation and possible treatment.

Remember that a sensible working principle in the immediate postincident phase is to expect *normal* recovery (NIMH, 2002). Individuals who may be at risk include those who have an acute stress disorder or preexisting psychiatric disorder, those who require medical or surgical attention, and those who have had particularly intense exposure to the incident or exposure of long duration (NIMH, 2002).

Children may need support as they work through their thoughts and emotions resulting from the trauma. Parents and teachers can help children by modeling effective coping strategies and monitoring their own, as well as the children's emotional state (National Association of School Psychologists, 2002). Students often look to adults' responses to the crisis and allow this to direct their own actions and responses. Teachers and staff need help and a plan of action in understanding and handling young people's normal, yet often inappropriate, responses to trauma to provide an environment that fosters the healing process and prevents developmental crises (Thompson, 2004).

School officials may look to staff members such as school counselors and school psychologists and other support staff to help assess the emotional needs of all students and staff and determine who may need additional counseling. Let's examine some typical reactions that your students may experience.

Young Children's Reactions

Very young children are primarily concerned with becoming autonomous; thus the critical factors for them are those related to independent functioning. This age group, unable to verbalize their emotions, may display more generalized fears. They may be fearful of reminders of the incident and appear confused about its location, sequence of events, and meaning. Nervousness, anxiety, and irritability, loss of appetite, fear of the dark, regression in behavior, and withdrawal from friends and routines are symptoms of severe stress in young children. They may lose an acquired developmental skill, such as toilet training, or revert to thumb sucking or clinging to parents. Their attention spans become shorter and they may become aggressive and disobey adults. They may engage in repetitive play, acting out themes of the trauma. Psychological first aid for this group should focus on reestablishing trust and security, self-control, and autonomy (Johnson, 2000; National Association of School Psychologists, 2002).

Figure 7.2
Suggestions for those Helping Children Displaced by the Hurricane and Floods.

1. **Physical needs are of priority:**
   Water, food, warmth, medical care, a way to get clean. Sometimes overlooked: protection from aggressive people (adults or children). Also often overlooked: a quiet, dim place to sleep and enough time to sleep, with regular sleeping hours if possible. Please don't make children wait to pee or poop: Scared kids sometimes need to go in a hurry.

2. **Keep this important psychological goal in mind:**
   That the child's memories of this experience will help the child know there are trustworthy and kind people, and it is possible, with help, to handle hardship.

3. **Be honest with the child:**
   Many people are tempted to lie to children to keep them from feeling bad. What's at stake: If the child hears reassurance that turns out to be false, the child may develop trouble trusting anyone who says that anything is OK. If there is uncertainty about what has happened to a child's loved ones, "I don't know; I wish I could tell you for sure," is better than "They are doing fine." If there is bad news for the child, it should not be put off too long.

4. **Tones of voice are important:**
   A kind and caring tone of voice is probably more important than the specific words that are spoken. If you are helping to calm a child, speak with low pitch, soft volume, and slow tempo. Sad children need to hear some enthusiastic and positive tones of voice at least some of the time.

---

5. Help people make friends:
The best defense against fear and grief is having friends. See if you can get children talking with each other and playing with each other. See if the older ones can take younger ones under their wing. If you suggest to kids that they take on the mission of supporting each other, they just might come through. Let them have time away from television. Let the young ones have toy animals and toy people to do pretend play with. Try some cooperative games that give them a common goal.

6. Listen:
When children talk with you about what has gone on, don't feel that you need to give them advice or solve all their problems. It's easier to be kind if you don't feel your job is to make everything right. Sometimes "I'm glad you're talking about this; tell me more" is the best message to give. Sometimes the kindest thing to do is just to nod and keep listening.

Source: Available from http://www.projectreassure.org, by J. M. Strayhorn, Jr., MD (Child and Adolescent Psychiatrist, University of Pittsburgh). Reprinted with permission.

To help young children displaced by Hurricane Katrina, a child and adolescent psychiatrist offered the advice shown in Figure 7.2.

Elementary School Children's Reactions

Elementary school students' important developmental tasks are taking initiative and establishing productivity. Therefore, psychological first aid for this age group should focus on bolstering self-esteem, relieving guilt, reestablishing productivity, and providing assurances of safety. Signs of significant stress in elementary children are clinging to parents, irritability, aggressiveness, school avoidance, poor concentration, withdrawal from activities and friends, disobedience, drop in school performance, repetitive reenactment of the incident, and overconcern for family safety (Johnson, 2000).

Elementary school children may benefit from small skits and plays in which they "triumph" over the imaginary disaster. Writing can help children express feelings. Finally, remember the curriculum resources mentioned in the beginning of the chapter.

Adolescents' Reactions

Identity and peer status are the chief concerns at this developmental stage. Important objectives for psychological first aid for adolescents are preventing isolation, depression, and impaired identity development. Signs of posttrauma stress in adolescents include problems concentrating, overt concern regarding health, depression, and anxiety. The adolescent may revert to earlier coping styles, have difficulty meeting responsibilities, withdraw socially, and drop in school performance. Teens may experience survival guilt, display antisocial behavior, or suddenly change attitude, lifestyle, or relationships. Physical symptoms include headaches, loss of appetite, or overeating (Johnson, 2000). Adolescents are more likely than younger children or adults to exhibit impulsive and aggressive behaviors (National Association of School Psychologists, 2002).

Adolescents seek others for support and typically discuss experiences to help them vent and normalize their powerful emotional reactions (see guidelines for group interventions in Chapter 9). Students can develop a disaster plan for home, school, or community to increase a sense of mastery and security. The initiation of such a project can help the community in a constructive way to aid teens in overcoming feelings of helplessness or survivor guilt (Thompson, 2004). Chapter 8 offers additional strategies offered by Project Reassure to help adolescents cope.

Adult Reactions

Adults who work with children and families at school are often survivors of the disaster as well. They must deal with students' emotional stress as well as their own. These professionals can become overwhelmed, so they benefit by becoming aware of self-care needs and strategies. Chapter 10 describes such secondary reactions to trauma and accompanying self-help strategies in detail.

SUPPORTING DISASTER VICTIMS THROUGH SCHOOL-BASED COUNSELING

School is a stabilizing factor in the lives of students. The school's response can be more important than the response of any one individual (Johnson, 2000). When a disaster affects the school environment, staff can assess who might benefit from ongoing counseling. Written parent consent for students to receive ongoing counseling, both individually and as a group, is a prerequisite in many locales.

Mental health specialists within the school or from approved outside providers can offer individual or groups supports. Individual counseling provides a safe place for students to express feelings and release stress, following an assessment to gauge the anxiety and stress of an individual. Information about the normal process of grieving can be provided (James & Gilliland, 2001). Group interventions can help students receive support from their peers and realize they are not alone in their feelings. Opportunities exist in groups to work through stages of grief and to construct new meanings for one's experience. Groups can work on projects that may memorialize or commemorate those who have been lost.

School-based health centers are growing in popularity in schools. Students are much more likely to access mental health services when a school-based health center is available. Delivering expanded disaster mental health services through a school-based health center integrates health and mental health services and improves screening for mental health services. These centers allow for collaboration among school counselors, community counselors, psychiatrists, substance abuse counselors, and others, making them potentially valuable resources for students (Brown, 2006).

SUMMARY

Although most disasters are beyond the control of the school or the community, schools can prepare for disasters and successfully cope with them by using the many resources discussed and understanding their role in such events. Awareness is the first step to preparedness; and effective planning and implementation for immediate and postdisaster response can be facilitated.

The school community can restore a sense of safety and stability by openly communicating with students, families, and with the community at large regarding the event and the steps taken to restore safety; by reestablishing school routines; by encouraging openness in the expression of feelings about the incident; and, by understanding and responding to typical and atypical emotional responses and behaviors of those experiencing disaster.

CASE STUDY CONCLUSION

Our first task was to recruit volunteers to remain after school to help supervise the children. Many offered to help. Some staff members opened the cafeteria and figured out how to feed the students; others began planning games and other activities to keep the students busy and distracted from their fears. Still others began communicating with parents in the community.

Meanwhile, many parents with sport utility vehicles made their way to school to pick up their children. With parents and vehicles converging on the school campus all at once, we needed a system to manage the traffic coming to the building. School faculty members quickly organized an orderly plan for releasing students. Volunteers helped the parents to form a line, set up tables where parents could sign their students out, and facilitated communication with the classrooms to call down the children.

Many remaining children were afraid and worried about their parents and other family members. The weather conditions and the change in routine were unsettling for them. To allay their fears, we provided ongoing reports on the safety of their families and community members. By midafternoon, additional counselors had reached the school, coming to our aid from the community and from other schools in the district. These counselors were able to help provide individual psychological first aid to the students, targeting first those who seemed the most frightened.

To speed up the safe reunification of children with the families, we called the American Red Cross local chapter, which dispatched emergency response vehicles (ERVs) to the community. The Red Cross also provided shelter for families in hotels for several days and offered ongoing support for families, including emergency financial assistance to families affected by the floods.

The local township contacted FEMA for property and damage assessments and community recovery plans. FEMA's partner agency, the Center for Mental Health Services, provided psychological support to the community.

At 9:30 that night, the last students left the building. The remaining two young children were picked up by their parents, who were excited about seeing their children but obviously distraught and exhausted by the events of the disaster. Although the hour was late, we gave these adults an opportunity to share their stories, to have something to eat, and to relax before heading out on the roads. We later arranged ongoing crisis counseling for them and for many other community members.

In the days that immediately followed the flood, we recognized that the needs still were more than our local community could address. So many families were stranded without homes or were facing major damage to their homes. NOVA (National Organization for Victims Assistance) joined the effort, providing victim advocacy in obtaining the necessary resources that were available on a federal level to help affected households.

To support parents, the school counselors and principal composed a parent letter with the details of events at the school, including the altered school schedule for the days following the flood. To further assist families, we sent a second letter, based on guidance from the National Association of School Psychologists, to explain some common reactions to the disaster. We invited parents to come into the school with their children for a doughnuts and conversation session to review the events, ask questions, and share concerns. When we saw 400 parents and children in the auditorium, we realized we were meeting a real need.

The community's recovery continued. Looking back, our team attributes this recovery, at least in part, to the extraordinary collaboration among the school, the local responders, and the national agencies that came to our aid.

DISCUSSION AND APPLICATION IDEAS

1. Research and read a school district's mission statement and determine how helping a school community recover from a traumatic event could be a component of the district's mission.
2. Within a school district, how and why could a group discussion process in response to trauma be superior to an individual one?
3. Could you name an instance when (a) intervention from inside the school might be more effective than outside intervention, and (b) outside intervention from an agency might be beneficial?
4. Perform a website review of the governmental and agency resources cited in this chapter. Select one resource, write a one-page summary of the site, and describe how you could use this resource to help a school community recover from a disaster.
5. List in order of priority the steps to take in response to an impending flood affecting a school dismissal.
6. Research and compile a guidance lesson to be used in classrooms helping fourth-, fifth-, and sixth-grade students recover from the stress of a community/school traumatic event such as a flood, hurricane, or tornado.
7. Describe one basic difference between teens' and children's processing of traumatic stress.
8. How would interventions with individuals showing extreme disorientation differ from an intervention with an individual who is alert and demonstrating good problem-solving skills?

REFERENCES

Brown, M. B. (2006). School based health centers: Implications for counselors. *Journal of Counseling & Development, 84* (2), 187–191.

FEMA. (2007). *The disaster process and disaster aid programs: Response and recovery.* Retrieved October 16, 2007, from http://www.fema.gov/hazard/dproc.shtm

Hooker, K. E., & Friedman, H. (2005). *Responding to the psychological needs of children after 9/11: A review of the literature.* Retrieved October 16, 2007, from http://wf21a3.webfeat.org/nWSDH1134/url=http://search.ebscohost.com/login.aspx?direct=true&db=eric&AN=ED490449&site=ehost-live

James, R. K., & Gilliland, B. E. (2001). *Crisis intervention strategies* (4th ed.). Belmont, CA: Brooks/Cole.

Johnson, K. (2000). *School crisis management: A hands-on guide to training crisis response teams* (2nd ed.). Alameda, CA: Hunter House.

Lerner, M. D., & Shelton, R. D. (2001). *How do people respond during traumatic exposure?* Commack, NY: American Academy of Experts in Trauma Stress.

National Association of School Psychologists. (2002). *Managing strong emotional reactions to traumatic events: Tips for parents and teachers.* Retrieved October 16, 2007, from http://www. nasponline.org/resources/crisis_safety/angermgmt_general.aspx

National Institute of Mental Health. (2002). *Mental health and mass violence: Evidence-based early psychological intervention for victims/survivors of mass violence. A workshop to reach consensus on best practices* (NIH Publication No. 02-5138). Washington, DC: U.S. Government Printing Office.

Perez, E., & Thompson, P. (1996). Natural hazards: Causes and effects. Lesson 8: Desertification. *Prehospital Disaster Medicine, 11,* 147–159.

Spiers, T. (Ed.). (2001). *Trauma: A practitioner's guide to counseling.* New York: Brunner-Routledge.

Thompson, R. A. (2004). *Crisis intervention and management: Strategies that work in schools and communities.* New York: Brunner-Routledge.

U.S. Department of Education, Office of Safe and Drug Free Schools. (2003). *Practical information on crisis planning: A guide for schools and communities.* Washington, DC: Author.

U.S. Department of Education. (2005). *Tips for helping students recovering from traumatic events.* Washington, DC: Author.

Worden, J. W. (2002). *Grief counseling and grief therapy: A handbook for the mental health practitioner* (3rd ed.). New York: Springer.

Young, M. (1998). *The community crisis response team training manual* (2nd ed.). Washington, DC: National Organization for Victm Assistance.

CHAPTER 8

RECOVERY: PSYCHOLOGICAL SUPPORTS IN A CRISIS

CASE STUDY

"I'll be back in 20 minutes. I just have to get a couple of things from the market. Maria is ready for day care. Just keep an eye on her," Rosella's grandmother called to her early one morning.

"Okay, Nana. We'll play hide-and-seek while you're gone. But hurry, because I don't want to be late for school."

Ten-year-old Rosella was accustomed to watching her little sister Maria before she went to school. The girls lived with their grandmother in an apartment on the third floor of a house. Nana often ran quick errands early in the morning before dropping Maria at day care.

To pass the time, the girls played their customary hide-and-seek. Little Maria hid upstairs in their apartment while one floor below, Rosella closed her eyes and counted. Suddenly, Rosella smelled smoke. As Rosella turned to see what was creating the smoke, she was pushed aside by a man dashing out of his apartment. Smoke poured out of his apartment doorway, causing Rosella to cough and choke. Panicked, she dashed up the staircase two steps at a time to find Maria. Her heart beat wildly as she tried to picture where the toddler would be hiding. As she arrived on her grandmother's floor, she could hear Maria screaming. In seconds, Rosella heard loud crackling noises and watched in horror as a fiery ceiling collapsed above her.

Miles away, Mrs. Valenti, Rosella's principal, was at home pouring coffee into her travel mug when the phone rang.

"Is this Michelle Valenti, the principal for Ross Elementary School?" the caller asked.

"Yes, I am Mrs. Valenti."

"There is a house fire a couple of blocks from your school, at 1407 West Crescent Avenue. It's pretty bad. We have it under control, but the area is cordoned off, and there's a lot of smoke. We have to close off the 1400 and 1500 blocks of West Crescent in both directions. You'll need to cancel school or reroute your buses and do something about students who walk," explained the 911 dispatcher at the local police department.

"1407 . . . 1407 . . . I think we have a child at that address. Wait a minute! That is where Rosella Garcia lives with her grandmother. I just took them some clothes last week. Was anyone hurt?"

"They took one child to Children's Hospital. Smoke inhalation. They found a younger girl under a bed. She didn't make it. I'm sorry, but that's about all I can tell you. The fire company commander is Roberts . . . Jay Roberts. You can reach him at 374–9500," the dispatcher advised.

INTRODUCTION

Tragedies like the one just described can occur any time, despite our best crisis planning. This chapter will help you answer some questions about how a critical incident affects individuals cognitively, emotionally, and behaviorally. For example, you may have wondered about the answers to these questions:

This chapter is based in part on Kerr, M. M. (2001). *Helping youth cope with traumatic events*. Retrieved October 16, 2007, from www.projecttreasure.org

- How does trauma affect people?
- What's the difference between acute stress disorder, and posttraumatic stress disorder (PTSD)?
- What's the difference between "normal" grief and traumatic grief?
- How long do stress reactions last?
- What is a teacher supposed to do after a traumatic event?
- How do we respond to students without adding to the hype?

UNDERSTANDING THE TRAUMATIC EXPERIENCE

We say that people have been exposed to trauma when they have experienced, witnessed, or been confronted an event that seriously threatened, injured, or killed someone *and* when they have experienced intense fear, horror, and/or helplessness (American Psychiatric Association, 2000). Children may also experience disorganized or agitated behavior (American Academy of Child and Adolescent Psychiatry, 1998). Keep in mind that the individual does not have to be a *direct* victim but may be a witness or have only learned about the stressful event (e.g., through the media). Moreover, what is traumatic (i.e., creates horror, fear, and helplessness) for one person may not be perceived as traumatic by another.

We recognize two kinds of trauma. Event trauma, or trauma type I is a sudden unexpected occurrence of a stressor limited in time and space (Terr, 1991). The house fire illustrates this type of trauma. Process trauma (type II) is a continuing and unrelenting exposure to an enduring stressor such as ongoing abuse or living in a war zone (Shaw, 2000).

How distressing an event is for a young person depends on the event, the individual, and on the supports available to the individual (see American Academy of Child and Adolescent Psychiatry, 1998; Perry, 1999). For example, type II events likely increase acute stress reactions because of their longer duration and exposure. Damage to a school or home can increase a student's risk for prolonged reactions (Perry, 1999). We reviewed other event-specific factors in our discussion of the effects of school violence in Chapter 6.

Individual factors that may indicate greater risk include previous traumatic experiences, limited intellectual capacity, preexisting anxiety disorder, and being alone during the event (Perry, 1999). For example, young children often experience events as highly stressful because they do not yet have the information and experience to anticipate or understand those events. Consider the apprehension with which many children face injections, blood tests, or X-rays. Over time, most children overcome their fear as these medical procedures become more familiar and they recognize that they are not being injured. Put another way, maturity prepares us for many situations that might otherwise surprise us. But an extreme stressor can overwhelm even the most mature individual because it is too shocking and frightening to manage.

The third factor affecting how one responds to a traumatic experience is the support provided by one's social network. Fortunately, most individuals who experience typical stress reactions can be helped significantly by their social support systems—those who know and care about them at home and at school (Gray & Litz, 2005). Lyons (1987) postulated that the single best predictor of positive outcome for children surviving a traumatic event is the ability of parents and other significant adults to cope with the trauma.

Typical Indicators of Helplessness, Fear, and Horror

Helplessness is a defining aspect of a traumatic event. Understanding this helps you recognize that trauma victims need to regain control. Empowering victims of trauma to regain some control of their situation is one of our most important goals (Herman, 1997). For example, pediatric nurses talk through procedures with their young patients and offer them choices whenever possible: "You can look or close your eyes. It is OK to cry. You can keep your stuffed animal with you, if you want. Would you rather have your medicine in a pill or syrup?" Children who feel helpless often become irritable unless they are given choices. You may notice that they are "bossy," critical of others, judgmental, argumentative, stubborn, or attention-seeking.

Fear is a natural reaction to the *horror* a child experiences during a trauma. Again, each child responds according to past experiences, age, cognitive abilities, and emotional maturity. Remember that the experience of trauma is individual; what may terrify one child may be manageable for another. These disparities often confuse parents attempting to console siblings whose behavioral and emotional reactions require different supports. Children respond to fear by being frightened by darkness, monsters, strangers, "bad guys," and reminders of the event. They may have worries and fears about their own health and that of loved ones. Teens may try to calm their fears with alcohol and other drugs. Other reactions to trauma include general anxiety, guilt, withdrawal from others, and not wanting to engage in one's favorite activities (known as **anhedonia**).

Let's reflect...

> Return to the opening case study about a fifth grader whose little sister died in a house fire. As you reread this story, ask yourself what aspects of the tragedy would cause fear, helplessness, and horror. How might the girl react to each of these aspects?

In the next section, we describe how school personnel help children regain control over their immediate world through the restoration of routines and activities, reassuring messages, and reliance on healthy coping strategies.

SCHOOL-BASED SUPPORTS FOR STUDENTS

You may feel inadequate to support students, especially if you, too, have witnessed a traumatic event. Consider the comments of a security guard whose school experienced tragedy when students and staff perished in an accident: "I know it sounds weird, but I can't stop worrying about what I am going to say to the kids when they return to school. How can I help them? They are so young to deal with death. Their friends and teacher are gone. Please tell me what to say. I want to be there for them."

Your students will draw from your strength during a scary time in their lives. As Nader and Pynoos (1991) reported, "[T]eachers' recovery is important to the welfare of the students. Children often carefully observe their teachers' responses to an event." Even those who have not had specialized training in trauma counseling can provide basic reassurance to the youngsters in their care, as we see in the next section.

Reassurance Provided by Teachers, Parents, and Paraprofessionals

This section provides information for those of you who may not have a background in counseling or psychology. Do not underestimate your importance in children's recovery from a crisis. After all, you may have a good understanding of developmental needs, the basis for many of the suggestions in this section. Children exhibit their reactions to stress somewhat differently across the developmental span. For example, young children may express more generalized anxiety and fear (Hamblen, n.d.).

Table 8.1 offers typical reactions in children and teenagers. These reactions derive from the elements of a traumatic experience that we explained in the opening section. Each set of reactions is paired with strategies that teachers, parents, and paraprofessionals might employ.

Let's reflect...

As you study these responses to trauma, ask yourself:

- Which element of trauma does this response echo?

- Why is the strategy helpful? In other words, what trauma reaction does it alleviate?

As Table 8.1 suggests, even those not training in crisis counseling have many ways to support students who have experienced a traumatic incident. If you are a classroom teacher, you may want to look at a program that Marlene Wong and her colleagues developed: *Listen, Protect, Connect—Model & Teach: Psychological First Aid (PFA) for Students and Teachers*, which is available on the U.S. Department of Education website.

When adequately reassured by those closest to them, most students do not have prolonged stress unless they were victimized or had preexisting vulnerabilities (Gray & Litz, 2005). However, some youngsters need more than we can provide through reassurance and comforting routines. Now let's turn to more specialized supports for trauma victims.

Psychological First Aid Provided by Trained Responders

What most of us need immediately after a traumatic event is "psychological first aid": emotional support, psychoeducation about our experience and what to expect, information about what we can do or how our routines may change, safety, medical care, shelter,

Table 8.1
Typical Child and Adolescent Stress Reactions and Adult Supportive Strategies

Age	Type of Reaction	Stress Reaction	Supportive Strategies
1–5	**Behavioral Responses**	• Increased clinging to parents or familiar adults • Helplessness and passive behavior • Temporary loss of previously acquired milestones (e.g., bedwetting or thumb sucking may return) • Tattling on peers and siblings • Fears of the dark and sleeping alone • Increased crying	• Provide verbal reassurance and physical comfort. • Make sure child has familiar, comforting objects/sources of comfort available (blanket, favorite toy, picture). • Maintain daily family routines as well as bedtime routines. • Avoid unnecessary separations from loved ones. • Encourage expression of feelings regarding losses (deaths, pets, toys).
	Physical Responses	• Loss of appetite • Stomachaches or nausea • Sleep problems including nightmares • Speech difficulties • Tics	• Monitor/limit media exposure. • Encourage expression of feelings through play activities and "magical thinking." • Permit child to sleep in parents' room temporarily.
	Emotional Responses	• Anxiety (expressed by clinging often) • Generalized fear • Irritability; tantrums • Sadness (increased crying or withdrawal) • Withdrawal from people or events • Angry outbursts	
6–11	**Behavioral Responses**	• Inability to concentrate; distractibility • School avoidance • Aggressive behavior at school and home • Hyperactive or silly behavior • Whining, clinging, behaving as a younger child • Increased competition with younger siblings for parental attention • Play that involves reenactments of the trauma	• Encourage verbal and play expression of thoughts and feelings. • Listen to child's repeated retelling of traumatic event. • Clarify child's distortions and misconceptions if these are not helpful. • Identify and provide supports when there are reminders of event. • Help children identify and understand acute stress reactions and coping skills.

Table 8.1 *(continued)*

Age	Type of Reaction	Stress Reaction	Supportive Strategies
	Physical Responses	• Changes in appetite • Headaches • Stomachaches • Sleep disturbances, nightmares • Other somatic complaints: limb pain, vague physical discomforts	• Avoid exposure to adult conversations about the events. • Maintain rules and routines, especially around sleeping, eating, and extracurricular activities.
	Emotional Responses	• Fear • Withdrawal from friends, familiar activities • Reminders of event trigger fear • Angry outbursts • Preoccupation with crime, criminals, safety, and death • Self-blame • Guilt	• Avoid high-pressure academic or sports activities temporarily. • Avoid unnecessary separations from important caregivers, including teachers. • Avoid exposing the child to reminders of the trauma; limit exposure to the news and other television programs about the tragedy. • Maintain family routines as much as possible, particularly around sleeping, eating, and extracurricular activities. • Avoid unnecessary separations from important caregivers. • Expect temporary regression in child's behaviors (e.g., baby talk, bedwetting). • Provide soothing activities such as art, physical games, or singing. • Remind children that there are adults to help them. • Encourage verbal and play expression of thoughts and feelings. • Listen to child's repeated retelling of traumatic event. • Clarify child's distortions and misconceptions if these are not helpful. • Identify and provide supports when there are reminders of event. • Help children identify and understand acute stress reactions and coping skills.

(continued)

Table 8.1 *(continued)*

Age	Type of Reaction	Stress Reaction	Supportive Strategies
			• Avoid exposure to adult conversations about the events. • Maintain rules and routines, especially around sleeping, eating, and extracurricular activities. • Avoid high-pressure academic or sports activities temporarily. • Avoid unnecessary separations from important caregivers.
Adolescents	Behavioral Responses	• Irritability; bossiness • Decline in academic performance • Distractibility; difficulty concentrating • Decline in previous responsible behavior for self and others • Agitation or decrease in energy level, apathy • Memory loss • Risk-taking behavior • Testing limits and rules • Desire for revenge • Altruism • Social withdrawal	• Provide additional supervision. • Protect from reexposure to event on news, Internet, conversations. • Encourage teens to seek factual information if it is manageable. • Relax expectations for performance at home and school temporarily. • Encourage discussion of experience of trauma with significant adults • Be sure teens are nurtured at home and at school.
	Physical Responses	• Appetite changes • Headaches • Gastrointestinal problems • Skin problems • Complaints of vague aches and pains • Sleep difficulties	• Educate teens about the dangers of self-medication (alcohol and other drugs) • Educate about acute stress and the link between trauma and reactions. • Help teens identify coping skills. • Encourage physical activities.
	Emotional Responses	• Fear of foreshortened future • Loss of interest in peer social activities, hobbies, recreation • Sadness or depression • Anxiety and fearfulness about personal safety • Feelings of inadequacy and helplessness • Guilt, self-blame, shame, and self-consciousness	• Encourage teens to seek help for their peers. • Provide information in advance about changes in routines. • Ask teens how they are doing, every day.

Note: Because the supportive strategies may alleviate more than one child response, they are not listed in any particular order.

and food (Gray & Litz, 2005). The National Organization for Victim Assistance has outlined its model for providing immediate crisis support as follows:

Safety and security (S and S)
- Address physical safety and medical needs
- Ensure warmth, food, clothing, and other basic needs
- Provide a sense of connection with others in a secure setting
- Help find privacy to express emotions
- Ensure confidentiality of communication
- Reassure survivors that their reactions are acceptable
- Help survivors take control of events going on around them
- Enable survivors to achieve efforts toward emotional safety

Ventilation and validation (V and V)
- Listen and let survivors 'tell their story'
- Help victims understand that their reactions are not abnormal

Prediction and preparation (P and P)
- Make practical predictions about what survivors will face, such as relocation, financial issues, medical conditions, and identification of loved ones
- Make predictions about future emotional reactions
- Discuss preparation for future events; for example, planning for future protection, discussing additional counseling resources, informing victims of rights in the legal system, and planning for memorial services[1]

Perhaps your school or community has NOVA volunteers or can arrange the NOVA training for your school counselors, social workers, or psychologists. NOVA offers a 40-hour Basic Crisis Response Team Training Institute as well as advanced training. The training equips responders to aid the survivors of a disaster and to help communities coordinate resources for long-term recovery.

Group Interventions

Group interventions for those who have shared a traumatic experience differ widely across schools and communities. Some of these interventions are for students who share a common experience. Other interventions target those most at risk.

One group intervention, **psychological debriefing**, has been the source of some controversy in the crisis response field. Because you may have heard about this debate, we offer some perspectives on using debriefing interventions immediately following a traumatic event.

Psychological Debriefing

Researchers have raised questions about the efficacy of so-called debriefing sessions for those who have experienced trauma (McNally, Bryant, & Ehlers, 2003; Raphael & Wilson, 2000). Debriefing began as a support for emergency responders; its popularity led to its use in schools with students.

---

[1]From "An Integrated Model of School Crisis Preparedness and Intervention: A Shared Foundation to Facilitate International Crisis Intervention," by S. Jimerson, S. Brock, and S. Pletcher, 2005, *School Psychology International*, *26* (3), p. 283. Copyright 2005 by SAGE Publications. Reproduced with permission.

Some researchers maintain that there is no empirical evidence that conducting a debriefing group after a tragic loss prevents posttraumatic stress disorder among children and adolescents. These critics of debriefing contend that encouraging individuals to discuss their thoughts and feelings immediately after a tragedy may retraumatize and overwhelm the survivors as well as impede their natural recovery process, thus doing more harm than good (McNally et al., 2003).

Unfortunately, the definition of debriefing is not consistent, so the term does not connote a specific protocol that lends itself to comparisons across studies. Moreover, many studies of one particular protocol, critical incident stress debriefing (CISD), reveal misapplication of the intended procedures. CISD is "a specific, 7-step group crisis intervention tool designed to assist a homogeneous group of people after an exposure to the same significant traumatic event" (Mitchell, 2004, p. 4). Its developers warn that CISD should not be considered a standalone intervention but should be considered as one of an array of crisis stress management offerings. As the developer of CISD and Critical Incident Stress Management contends,

> One of the primary reasons mental health professionals who are trained in CISM are rejecting or ignoring the negative outcome studies is that, as they review them, they see clearly that those studies have misapplied the crisis interventions, particularly the small group CISD process. (Mitchell, 2005, p. 48)

Originally designed as a postincident support for emergency responders, CISD became popular in schools, where its use did not always comply with the intentions of its developers. CISD was not intended to support primary victims but to support their responders (Mitchell, 2004).

But even those who argue against some forms of psychological debriefing agree that structured *educational groups* can provide several benefits for specific individuals. Educational support groups give trained professionals the opportunity to provide participants with information about the traumatic event as well as to educate students on common reactions to trauma, thus normalizing some of their reactions. This process may help students feel less alone and regain a sense of hope (Brock, Lazarus, & Jimerson, 2002). For example, students who participated in a class, club, musical, or sports team with the victim may need this type of additional support. Jimerson et al. (2005) have developed a group crisis intervention, as outlined in Table 8.2.

As Jimerson et al. (2005) caution, this group should not include those students or staff who have been physically injured or are at high risk for severe traumatic stress. These highly vulnerable individuals may experience undue distress in a group situation as they listen to accounts of the incident. Rather, they should be seen by a credentialed professional.

Even when supported through school efforts, some students and adults may experience significant stress reactions within the first 30 days, exhibiting what is called *acute stress disorder* or *acute stress reaction*. Understanding the manifestations of acute stress can help you take care of your students as well as yourself. The next section offers descriptions of these stress reactions.

Table 8.2
Classroom Group Crisis Intervention (GCI) Summary

GCI Step	Facilitative Statements	Goal(s)	Goal Attainment Signs
Introduction	"I'm sorry this happened to your (our) school. When bad things like this happen, it is often helpful to talk about it. So we are going to spend some time today talking. From our discussion we will have a better understanding of what happened, how it has affected us and what we can do to help each other cope."	• Explain GCI purpose • Identify facilitators • Review GCI steps • Review rules	Questions about GCI stop
Providing facts and dispelling rumors	"We have experienced an event that was so unusual we might find it hard to understand. I would like to share with you what we know about this tragedy. Feel free to ask questions. It's important that you understand what happened."	• Assist students to come to a reality-based under-standing of the event	Questions about the traumatic event stop
Sharing stories	"Each person who gets through an event, such as the one we have just experienced, has a story. We are going to tell as many of these stories as we can today. Who wants to start?"	• Get students to talk about their experiences • Help students feel less alone and more con-nected to classmates	Everyone has had a chance to share crisis stories
Sharing reactions	"Following a trauma, such as the one we've just experienced, it is not unusual for people to feel and behave differently for a while. Some common reactions are ... These are normal reactions to abnormal circumstances. Who has had some of these reactions?"	• Get students to talk about trauma reactions • Help students feel more connected to classmates • Normalize trauma reactions	Everyone had had a chance to share trauma reactions
Empowerment	"Traumatic events can make us feel helpless. I would like to see us take action or make plans to repair trauma-related damage or prevent trauma reoccurrence."	• Help students regain a sense of control over their lives	Concrete action is taken or planned
Closing	"What can we do to begin to place this event behind us and move on with out lives?"	• Help students begin to think about placing the trauma behind them	Completion of activ-ities that enable students to begin the process of say-ing good-bye to that which was lost

Source: From *Best Practices in School Crisis Prevention and Intervention,* by S. E. Brock, P. J. Lazarus, and S. R. Jimerson, 2002, Bethesda, MD: National Association of School Psychologists. Copyright 2002 by the National Association of School Psychologists, Bethesda, MD. Reprinted with permission of the publisher. www.nasponline.org

ACUTE STRESS REACTION DISORDER

When individuals experience multiple stress reactions *within 30 days* of a traumatic event, including at least three symptoms of dissociation (e.g., numbing, reduced awareness), we say they are experiencing acute stress disorder (American Psychiatric Association, 2000; Bryant & Harvey, 2000; Gibson, n.d.). Acute stress disorder is relatively common in children; a recent study revealed that one in four children involved in automobile crashes experienced symptoms (Winston, Baxt, Kassam-Adams, Elliott, & Kallan, 2005). Consider this example:

> Stasha was in a minor bus accident during her fifth-grade year at our elementary school. The bus hit a car that was parked illegally. There was a little noise, but no one was injured. We assumed that all the kids on that bus were fine. Then we got a call from Stasha's mother. Stasha was having nightmares and even insisted on walking to school. Her mother reported that Stasha was "jumpy" every time she got into a car. When we checked with Stasha's teacher, we discovered that she had failed her last three quizzes and seemed to be daydreaming in class.

Children exhibiting the symptoms of acute stress disorder listed in Figure 8.1 should be referred for an evaluation by a school mental health specialist or an outside provider and be monitored by their parents and educators. If your school has counselors, school psychologists, or social workers on staff or available through a school-based mental health clinic, they may use a school-based intervention such as the *Brief Recovery Program (BRP) for Trauma Survivors* (Foa & Riggs, 2001), which is available free of charge. This program requires skills in cognitive behavior therapy.

Acute stress disorder has characteristics that overlap but do not always lead to post-traumatic stress disorder (PTSD). PTSD, the topic of our next section, may call on resources beyond what the school can offer, as illustrated in this account from a high school teacher:

> I will always remember Orlando, a student I had when he was a freshman. Three years later, Orlando was the sole survivor of a prom-night car crash that killed two of his friends. After being released from the hospital a few weeks after the accident, he returned to our small high school. Just before the last class of the day, I was standing in the hall when he passed by, moving almost as if sleepwalking. His expression was blank, and he jumped when I called his name and invited him into my classroom during my planning period. I offered him a cup of coffee and attempted to start a conversation with him.
>
> "I want to help, Orlando. I am here to listen."
>
> After a long silence, he responded in a quiet, strange voice that did not even sound like his.
>
> "I feel like I am in a nightmare. I feel like a robot. Mr. Garcia, tell me I am going to wake up and this will be over. I will be back in ninth grade and everything will be okay again. You remember ... Josh was my best friend. And Olivia ..."
>
> His sobs took over. I moved near him and put my hand on his shoulder. We sat that way for over an hour. And that was my introduction to PTSD.

Figure 8.1
Diagnostic Criteria for 308.3 Acute Stress Disorder.

A. The person has been exposed to a traumatic event in which both of the following were present:
    1. the person experienced, witnessed, or was confronted with an event or events that involved actual or threatened death or serious injury, or a threat to the physical integrity of self or others
    2. the person's response involved intense fear, helplessness, or horror
B. Either while experiencing or after experiencing the distressing event, the individual has three (or more) of the following dissociative symptoms:
    1. a subjective sense of numbing, detachment, or absence of emotional responsiveness
    2. a reduction in awareness of his or her surroundings (e.g., "being in a daze")
    3. derealization
    4. depersonalization
    5. dissociative amnesia (i.e., inability to recall an important aspect of the trauma)
C. The traumatic event is persistently reexperienced in at least one of the following ways: recurrent images, thoughts, dreams, illusions, flashback episodes, or a sense of reliving the experience; or distress on exposure to reminders of the traumatic event.
D. Marked avoidance of stimuli that arouse recollections of the trauma (e.g., thoughts, feelings, conversations, activities, places, people).
E. Marked symptoms of anxiety or increased arousal (e.g., difficulty sleeping, irritability, poor concentration, hypervigilance, exaggerated startle response, motor restlessness).
F. The disturbance causes clinically significant distress or impairment in social, occupational, or other important areas of functioning or impairs the individual's ability to pursue some necessary task, such as obtaining necessary assistance or mobilizing personal resources by telling family members about the traumatic experience.
G. The disturbance lasts for a minimum of 2 days and a maximum of 4 weeks and occurs within 4 weeks of the traumatic event.
H. The disturbance is not due to the direct physiological effects of a substance (e.g., a drug of abuse, a medication) or a general medical condition, is not better accounted for by Brief Psychotic Disorder, and is not merely an exacerbation of a preexisting Axis I or Axis II disorder.

Source: From *Diagnostic and Statistical Manual of Mental Disorders* (4th ed.) (text revision), 2000, Washington, DC: American Psychiatric Association. Copyright 2000 by American Psychiatric Association. Reprinted with permission.

POSTTRAUMATIC STRESS DISORDER

Posttraumatic stress disorder (PTSD) describes long-term reactions to a traumatic experience such as the fatal car accident that Orlando experienced. Figure 8.2 describes the warning signs for PTSD.

Let's reflect...

Can you identify Orlando's PTSD symptoms? Can you recall students who have experienced PTSD? How did you recognize their impairment?

Figure 8.2
Diagnostic Criteria for Posttraumatic Stress Disorder.

A. The person has been exposed to a traumatic event in which both of the following were present:
   1. the person experienced, witnessed, or was confronted with an event or events that involved actual or threatened death or serious injury, or a threat to the physical integrity of self or others
   2. the person's response involved intense fear, helplessness, or horror. **Note:** In children, this may be expressed instead by disorganized or agitated behavior
B. The traumatic event is persistently reexperienced in one (or more) of the following ways:
   1. recurrent and intrusive distressing recollections of the event, including images, thoughts, or perceptions. **Note:** In young children, repetitive play may occur in which themes or aspects of the trauma are expressed.
   2. recurrent distressing dreams of the event. **Note:** In children, there may be frightening dreams without recognizable content.
   3. acting or feeling as if the traumatic event were recurring (includes a sense of reliving the experience, illusions, hallucinations, and dissociative flashback episodes, including those that occur on awakening or when intoxicated). **Note:** In young children, trauma-specific reenactment may occur.
   4. intense psychological distress at exposure to internal or external cues that symbolize or resemble an aspect of the traumatic event
   5. physiological reactivity on exposure to internal or external cues that symbolize or resemble an aspect of the traumatic event
C. Persistent avoidance of stimuli associated with the trauma and numbing of general responsiveness (not present before the trauma), as indicated by three (or more) of the following:
   1. efforts to avoid thoughts, feelings, or conversations associated with the trauma
   2. efforts to avoid activities, places, or people that arouse recollections of the trauma
   3. inability to recall an important aspect of the trauma
   4. markedly diminished interest or participation in significant activities
   5. feeling of detachment or estrangement from others
   6. restricted range of affect (e.g., unable to have loving feelings)
   7. sense of a foreshortened future (e.g., does not expect to have a career, marriage, children, or a normal life span)
D. Persistent symptoms of increased arousal (not present before the trauma), as indicated by two (or more) of the following:
   1. difficulty falling or staying asleep
   2. irritability or outbursts of anger
   3. difficulty concentrating
   4. hypervigilance
   5. exaggerated startle response
E. Duration of the disturbance (symptoms in Criteria B, C, and D) is more than 1 month.
F. The disturbance causes clinically significant distress or impairment in social, occupational, or other important areas of functioning.

Source: From *Diagnostic and Statistical Manual of Mental Disorders* (4th ed.) (text revision), 2000, Washington, DC: American Psychiatric Association. Copyright 2000 by American Psychiatric Association. Reprinted with permission.

The most frequent stressor associated with PTSD is sudden and unexpected death of a loved person (Breslau et al., 1998). Three additional factors help us predict which children are at highest risk for developing PTSD:

1. The severity of the traumatic event
2. How close the child was to the event
3. How well the family responds and supports the child (Hamblen, n.d.)

Always recommend specialized help if a child's symptoms do not improve within 30 days or if the child has been exposed to prolonged violence, loss, or serious injury (trauma type II).

Specialists who assess a child for possible PTSD first assure the child that he or she is safe (Herman, 1997). Children may feel safer when they are in the company of familiar adults in a comfortable and private setting such as their home. An interview can identify the child's experience of what happened as well as help the therapist inventory stressors and losses from the youth's point of view. Next, the therapist wants to learn about feelings, cognitive distortions, reminders, perceived worries, and problems in functioning, as well as coexisting psychiatric symptoms. Of course, the therapist also evaluates the social supports available to the child. Treatment allows the child to reexplore the event carefully at the child's pace while identifying explicating feelings, misattributions, cognitive distortions, fantasies, and changed attitudes and view of his [or her] world. The goal is to help the child integrate the experience into his sense of his world. Treatment may include medication for specific symptoms and school-based interventions, including consultation models in which parents and teachers provide supports (American Academy of Child and Adolescent Psychiatry, 1998).

Faced with a traumatic death, most individuals experience sadness for a time. Yet some students do not seem to feel better after a period of time. These students may be experiencing what is called *traumatic grief*. Let's examine how traumatic grief is different from normal bereavement.

TRAUMATIC GRIEF

You may have heard the term **traumatic grief,** which refers to the experience of the sudden loss of a significant and close attachment. Here is a description from the Center for Traumatic Stress in Children and Adolescents (n.d.):

> Children with traumatic grief get "stuck" on the traumatic way their loved one died, such that whenever they try to remember happy times with their loved one, their memories veer off into thoughts about the terrible way the person died. Since these thoughts are not happy or comforting but instead frightening and upsetting, these children usually avoid thinking about the person who died. Alternatively, they cannot stop thinking about the person who died, but instead of these thoughts becoming comforting and healing, the thoughts continue to be hurtful, upsetting and even terrifying. As a result of being "stuck" on the traumatic aspects of their loved one's death, these children are not able to remember their loved ones in comforting, healing ways. Children with traumatic grief may develop sleep problems, difficulties with school, irritability, ongoing anger, sadness, or avoidance of friends, family and memories of the loved one. If these difficulties do not get better over

Figure 8.3

Letter After a Neighbor's Suicide.

Bruce,

First, let me say how very sorry I am for your neighborhood's tragic loss. Death in a community is always painful; a young adult's death by suicide is especially sad. Here are some suggestions to support the neighborhood children.

When children and teens return from school today, there should be familiar adults awaiting them. Children may or may not know of the event by that time. Generally, families will gather as families and not feel much like neighborhood gatherings right away, but that could be different if neighbors are very close. If there are any neighbors not aware of the situation, I would suggest that you notify them at work. Parents may also want to alert their children's school and bus driver of the event, so that they can be on the look out for symptoms of stress.

I would anticipate acute stress reactions for the next couple of weeks. Here are some specific responses you can anticipate and for which parents may want to be prepared:

The location of the death will take on great importance. Children and adults may avoid the area where this happened. This can take several forms. Younger children can be scared and/or "spooked" by the area. Teens, through their humor and conversations, can even make jokes about the area or find other ways to try to deal with it. Adults will have to help them (despite their own discomfort) identify very concrete ways to cope with the area. I trust that the area has been cleaned. If not, there will be more intense reactions. Families may want to plan other walking paths, if the alley is directly next to their house, leads to their bus stop, etc. The deceased's family may not want any children in the area, as they view it as a kind of shrine to their loved one. Neighbors may assist in maintaining this area—putting flowers, etc. This memorializing has to be balanced with the needs of the neighbors and of the family of the deceased. Of course, much of this depends on who owns the property where the suicide took place. If there is a police investigation, then police will have jurisdiction.

People will focus on the deceased. Everyone will have questions; most will voice them. People tend to blame themselves, and we have seen this in children. If they were unfriendly, if they failed to greet the individual last week—even the smallest oversight can become the focus of self-blame. It is important to reassure everyone that they did not cause this individual's death. Rather he was struggling with a psychological condition that led to his suicide. This may be difficult if—for any reason—the family does not accept suicide as a cause of death.

Children may have concerns about their own parents' mortality at this time. Reassurance and time together are good antidotes.

People will feel a need to take some action. Adults, children, and teens will take comfort in being able to do something. Young children can write or draw cards for the family. Older children and teens can write a note, help their families prepare food, fruit baskets, or select flowers. Attendance at memorial services is a private family decision.

Older children and teens may need help on what to say when they see the family of the deceased. A simple, "I am really sorry about your son" is fine for them to express. They may need advice on what not to do. (e.g., "Don't talk about it on the bus with other kids who are not part of the neighborhood and don't participate in gossip.") They may need advice about how to act in the alley (depending on how the site is handled).

Children will have different individual reactions. Nightmares about the area and the event can result in sleep disturbances. Parents can be distressed when their child does not want to eat. Parents often cook special foods as a caring gesture. Children may have fears (spoken or not) about the side of the house that faces the site of the death. They may want to change sleeping arrangements and eating spots. These are temporary changes.

Limiting further exposure is important. Try to protect children and teens from print and electronic media. The local print media usually avoid suicide coverage, but I cannot predict what the radio and television will do. The media may come to the neighborhood if they choose to cover it. In this case, warn children and teens that they are not to talk to anyone. Televisions in children's bedrooms can be a special problem at a time like this, if they stay up watching the news. Visual images are hard to erase, so people should try to avoid any of the visuals related to the event. Parents tend to talk with other adults, and this often happens within earshot of their children. This is not a good idea.

Bruce, I hope that these ideas are helpful. Feel free to call if you have any questions.

Madelyn

time, they may interfere with important things that children need to do like school work, extracurricular activities, making and keeping friends, and spending time with family members. These children may also develop a psychiatric condition related to childhood traumatic grief called Posttraumatic Stress Disorder, which can be associated with more serious problems if left untreated. (Retrieved September 22, 2006, from http://pittsburghchildtrauma.com/articles_1.html)

For more information on traumatic grief, see Cohen, Mannarino, Greenberg, Padlo, and Shipley (2002).

SUPPORTING STUDENTS AND THEIR FAMILIES

Families who experience a traumatic death in the community may turn to the school for advice. If the event took place at school, you may choose to hold a parent meeting to share some of the information in this chapter. For parents whose first language is not English, consider the *Facts for Families* handouts developed by the American Academy of Child and Adolescent Psychiatry, available from their website in several languages.

As an illustration, families turned to the school when a young adult committed suicide near his home one morning, a case described in Figure 8.3. As you read this case, you'll see how trauma might affect daily life for children and their caregivers. In addition, you'll see how simple suggestions help families anticipate reactions and take care of their children.

SUMMARY

Children's reactions to traumatic events vary somewhat by age and by individual, as do the reactions of adults who may witness the incident alongside them. Nevertheless, school personnel who understand typical reactions to stress can reassure one another and those in their care. Specific interventions, including individual and group interventions, may be implemented by credentialed staff. Studies have shown that such social supports are helpful in reducing distress and long-term impairment. When individuals have prolonged or more severe reactions, such as traumatic grief, acute stress disorder, or post-traumatic stress disorder, we recommend they be evaluated by a specialist.

CASE STUDY CONCLUSION

Stunned by the news of the house fire, I quickly gathered my things and left for school. I knew it was too late to cancel school because our buses would already be on the roads. We had no way to reach families, and most parents would have left for work already. I called several members of our staff who always arrived at school first.

"Try to contact the transportation department to reroute the buses. I will call the superintendent to send someone over to the hospital. Alert the custodian to pull down all blinds and close all windows—our children don't need more exposure to this. See if you can reach the crossing guard supervisor. We need to reroute our walkers away from that area. Get Arlene to meet teachers at the door to let them know what's going on. Get them to station themselves along the block as we have practiced. I will be there in 15 minutes."

We got through the day, but it was hectic during the first hour as we checked and double-checked to make sure no kids were outside. Listening to Rosella's classmates talk about the tragedy, our art teacher wisely suggested that the class make cards for Rosella; that helped the kids feel less helpless. Many of them were neighbors and voiced their fears about their own houses. Several wept.

Although she escaped with only minor injuries, Rosella's psychological recovery was long and painful. With help from the mental health specialist at the hospital, we tried to make school as comfortable as we could. Before she returned, we made a list of anything that might remind her of the fire. Thank goodness we did because she returned days before we were scheduled to have an assembly on fire safety. We postponed it for a few weeks. Every time she heard a siren, Rosella looked startled. We told her about fire drills in advance and made sure a counselor was with her.

Months later, the news broke the story that the apartment building had no smoke alarms. The newspapers jumped on the story, and it was all over the evening news. We sent a letter out to parents, suggesting they shield their children from the coverage, but the entire school was upset all over again. Rosella missed a week of school. Her therapist said she just couldn't concentrate because of all the flashbacks.

Out of the tragedy something good did happen. A few parents got together and called on local companies to help them purchase smoke alarms for families who needed them.

DISCUSSION AND APPLICATION IDEAS

1. Write a short presentation for a school faculty entitled, "What is trauma and what does it have to do with schools?"
2. How does trauma affect children and adolescents at different ages?
3. How might you know that a teenager is experiencing acute stress disorder?
4. Check out websites such as the National Institute of Mental Health, Project Reassure, and the National Center for Posttraumatic Stress Disorder for parent-friendly publications that you might include in your crisis kit.

5. Why is it important to teach parents about traumatic events and their effects? What happens if you don't?
6. How would you describe the difference between normal grief and bereavement and traumatic grief?
7. What would you advise an elementary school teacher to do to reassure her students after a traumatic event?

REFERENCES

American Academy of Child and Adolescent Psychiatry (Judith A. Cohen, principal author). (1998). Practice parameters for the assessment and treatment of children and adolescents with posttraumatic stress disorder. *Journal of the American Academy of Child and Adolescent Psychiatry, 37* (Suppl. 10).

American Psychiatric Association. (2000). *Diagnostic and statistical manual of mental disorders* (4th ed.) (text revision). Washington, DC: Author.

Breslau, N., Kessler, R. C., Chilcoat, H. D., Schultz, L. R., Davis, G. C., & Andreski, P. (1998). Trauma and posttraumatic stress disorder in the community: The 1996 Detroit area survey of trauma. *Archives of General Psychiatry, 55,* 626-632.

Brock, S. E., Lazarus, P. J., & Jimerson, S. (2002). *Best practices in school crisis prevention and intervention.* Bethesda, MD: National Association of School Psychologists.

Bryant, R. A., & Harvey, A. G. (2000). *Acute stress disorder: A handbook of theory, assessment, and treatment.* Washington, DC: American Psychological Association.

Foa, E., & Riggs, D. S. (2001). *Brief recovery program (BRP) for trauma survivors.* Retrieved October 17, 2007, from http://www.ptsd.factsforhealth.org/treatment/brp.pdf

Center for Traumatic Stress in Children and Adolescents. (n.d.). *Information on childhood traumatic grief (CTG).* Retrieved September 22, 2006, from http://pittsburghchildtrauma.com/articles_1.html

Cohen, J. A., Mannarino, A. P., Greenberg, T. A., Padlo S., & Shipley, C. (2002). Childhood traumatic grief: Concepts and controversies. *Trauma, Violence and Abuse, 3* (4), 307-327.

Gibson, L. (n.d.). *Acute stress disorder: A brief description: A National Center for PTSD fact sheet.* Retrieved October 17, 2007, from http://www.ncptsd.va.gov/ncmain/ncdocs/fact_shts/fs_asd_public.html

Gray, M. J., & Litz, B. T. (2005). Behavioral interventions for recent trauma: Empirically informed practice guidelines. *Behavior Modification, 29* (1), 189-215.

Hamblen, J. (n.d.). *PTSD in children and adolescents.* Retrieved October 17, 2007, from http://www.ncptsd.va.gov/ncmain/nc_archives/rsch_qtly/V4N4.pdf?opm=1&rr=rr174&srt=d&echorr=true/

Herman, J. (1997). *Trauma and recovery.* New York: Basic Books.

Jimerson, S., Brock, S., & Pletcher, S. (2005). An integrated model of school crisis preparedness and intervention: A shared foundation to facilitate international crisis intervention. *School Psychology International, 26* (3), 275-296.

Lyons, J. A. (1987). Posttraumatic stress disorder in children and adolescent: A review of the literature, *Journal of Developmental and Behavioral Pediatrics, 8,* 349-356.

McNally, R. J., Bryant, R. A. & Ehlers, A. (2003). Does early psychological intervention promote recovery from posttraumatic stress? *Psychological Science in the Public Interest, 4* (2), 45.

Mitchell, J. (2004). *Crisis intervention and critical incident stress management: A defense of the field.* Retrieved October 17, 2007, from http://www.tema.ca/lib/CISM_Defense%20or%20the%20field.pdf

Nader, K., & Pynoos, R. (1991). School disaster: Planning and initial interventions. *Journal of Social Behavior and Personality 8*, 1993. Retrieved October 17, 2007, from http://www.giftfromwithin.org/html/nader.html

Perry, B. D. (1999). Stress, trauma and post-traumatic stress disorders in children: An introduction. *Child Trauma Academy, Interdisciplinary Education Series, 2*, 9.

Raphael, B., & Wilson, J. P. (2000) (Eds.). *Psychological debriefing. Theory, practice and evidence.* Cambridge: Cambridge University Press.

Shaw, J. A. (2000). Children, adolescents, and trauma. *Psychiatric Quarterly, 71* (3), 227-243.

Terr, L. (1991). Childhood trauma: An outline and overview. *American Journal of Psychiatry, 148*, 10-20.

Winston, F., Baxt, C., Kassam-Adams, Elliott, M., & Kallan, M. (2005). Acute traumatic stress symptoms in child occupants and their parent drivers after crash involvement. *Archives of Pediatric and Adolescent Medicine, 159*, 1074-1079.

Young, M. (1998). *The community crisis response team training manual* (2nd ed.). Washington, DC: National Organization for Victim Assistance.

CHAPTER 9

RECOVERY: POSTVENTION FOLLOWING A DEATH

CASE STUDY

The state police called me at work that Friday afternoon in January to tell me that Jerell, one of our 12th-grader basketball players, had died from a self-inflicted gunshot wound. Anne, his mother, found him when she returned home from working in our school cafeteria. He was lying on the kitchen floor, next to his father's hunting rifle.

Anne and I had met 7 years earlier when I became principal of the high school. A beloved employee, she had often supported other staff members through their own tragedies by delivering meals and being an attentive listener. Now it was our turn to pull together and support her through this unspeakable tragedy. After activating our school crisis telephone tree and calling a faculty meeting for Saturday morning, I drove over to Anne's house to offer my help.

Anne's sister explained, "Jerell had been really struggling, but he told only his closest friends. Do you remember the basketball game at West High last Tuesday when the recruiters came? Well, his father started screaming at the West High team before that game even started. Everyone knew his dad was drinking again. Security had to remove his father from the stands before the game even started. Jerell was humiliated. Then on Thursday night, Jerell and his father had a fight about his father's most recent DUI. His father ended the argument by speeding out of the driveway and refusing to come home. Anne called me that night. She was beside herself. And now this. I don't know how she will ever recover."

Let's reflect...

Can you identify those who will need ongoing support in this school? Given that the death was a suicide, what safeguards against suicide contagion must be in place to prevent other suicidal behavior?

Postvention is the set of services provided to a school or community following a death. Shneidman (1981) first used the term **postvention**, in contrast to *prevention*, to describe these supports after a suicide. For purposes of this chapter, however, we use the term to describe supports offered after *any* death affecting the school community. The goals of postvention are (1) to support those grieving the loss, (2) to assist the school in returning to its normal routines, (3) to identify and support those most at risk for severe reactions to the death, and (4) in the case of a death by suicide, to prevent contagion (Kerr, Brent,

---

Sections of this chapter were based on Kerr, M. M., Brent, D. A., McKain, B., & McCommons, P. S. (2006). *Postvention standards manual: A guide for a school's response in the aftermath of a sudden death* (5th ed.). Pittsburgh, PA: Services for Teens at Risk. Used with permission.

Figure 9.1

Factors to Be Considered When Planning a Postvention.

- Previous tragedies affecting the school
- How the school has dealt with those losses
- How long the victim (adult or student) was at the school
- How well known and well liked the victim was
- How much information about the death has been reported in the media
- How many students witnessed the tragedy or death and what was their exposure
- How many students are thought to be at risk
- The ages of the students affected
- Whether the victim has other family members in the school district
- Whether school is in session or not

McKain, & McCommons, 2006). Research on postventions is sparse, in large part because it is awkward or impossible to obtain institutional approvals, individual consents, and multiple assessments required in a study (see Besançon, 2003; Callahan, 1996; Commission on Adolescent Suicide Prevention, 2005).

Put yourself in the place of the principal in our opening case study, and think about the factors we consider in setting up postvention activities and estimating needs for support. Do not overlook the perspectives of students in considering what they need. For example, the death of a little-known student can be devastating to his or her friends, or the death of a high school student who babysat for children can have an effect at their elementary school. Figure 9.1 presents some factors to consider. These are not factors that determine whether a postvention will take place or not; after a student or staff death, we assume postvention will be offered.

Our opening case dealt with a suicide, which can increase the risk for others to engage in suicidal behaviors. Our next section explains the rationale for preventing suicide contagion and outlines how to identify those most in need of support.

POSTVENTION FOLLOWING SUICIDE: PREVENTING CONTAGION

Suicide creates a unique postvention condition. Postvention following a suicide attempts to arrest or reduce contagion in other youth, as well as the incidence of youth depression and posttraumatic stress disorder (PTSD) among friends of the suicide victim. The Centers for Disease Control and Prevention in Atlanta have called for a community response in the aftermath of suicide to prevent further suicidal behavior and deaths (O'Carroll, Mercy, & Steward, 1988). However, researchers have warned schools to plan and implement such responses carefully, so the suicide is not in any way romanticized (Callahan, 1996). The guidelines in this chapter take into account the best clinical research in suicide prevention while recognizing that studies on postvention as a whole are few.

Research on suicidal behavior among young people has shown that exposure to suicide can trigger suicidal behaviors in others. We call this phenomenon *contagion. Exposure* to suicide refers to witnessing the death, hearing about it, or learning of it through the media. Current evidence supports the theory that adolescents, in particular, are highly vulnerable to suicide contagion (Gould, Jamieson, & Romer, 2003).

Fortunately, most youth exposed to a suicide do not become suicidal. However, there is a small vulnerable group of teens, along with the grieving friends of the victim, we most need to identify and assist. Teens identified as close friends are understandably distressed but generally resolve never to attempt suicide because of the pain it has inflicted (see Brent, Perper, Moritz, Baugher, & Allman, 1993). In effect, they experience a kind of psychological inoculation against suicide as an option for themselves. Nevertheless, this group should receive ongoing support with their grief because they *are* at high risk for major depressive disorder (29%) or PTSD (5%) (Brent et al., 1993) within the first 6 months to 1 year. Risk factors for the development of depression include a previous depression, being a close friend of the victim, having a conversation with the victim within 24 hours of the death, and/or being aware of the victim's plan before the suicide. Symptoms of PTSD may emerge when an individual witnesses the death, discovers the body, or sees the scene of death (Brent et al., 1993).

Among the school community at large, those at increased risk for suicide would include but not be limited to individuals with these characteristics:

- Have a personal or family history of mental health problems, most notably depression, anxiety disorders including PTSD, and substance abuse
- Have a past history of suicide attempts
- Are currently in mental health or drug and alcohol treatment
- Are not in treatment but have been a concern for parents, teachers, or peers.

The school's mental health specialists (counselors, social workers, and psychologists) should create a tracking system to monitor individuals they deem to be at risk for suicide contagion or related problems, keeping in mind that this monitoring must extend over time.

AN OVERVIEW OF THE POSTVENTION PROCESS

The checklist in Table 9.1 outlines the postvention process. However, every tragedy has its own timetable. For that reason, we cannot offer a step-by-step sequence in which activities should take place. Rather, we have tried to include the elements of postvention you need to consider. We begin with a verification of the death.

VERIFYING THE DEATH

Upon hearing of a death, the postvention coordinator or senior school official should contact the coroner's office or law enforcement officials to obtain accurate information about the deceased student's death. Although this information generally is public record, do not release it unless perhaps parents and public health officials believe disclosure would protect others from harm. Parents of a child who dies from the choking game, for example, may want the community to be aware of the risks of this activity.

Table 9.1
Postvention Implementation Plan

Date	Time	Initials	Responsibility
			1. The school is informed of the death
_____	_____	_____	• Postvention coordinator is notified
_____	_____	_____	• Superintendent is notified
_____	_____	_____	• Building administration is notified
			2. Factual information is gathered
_____	_____	_____	• Postvention coordinator or school official contacts Coroner or law enforcement agency and confirms death and identity of the victim
_____	_____	_____	• Postvention coordinator completes the Coroner's/Law Enforcement Agency's Report
			3. Postvention coordinator contacts the victim's family
_____	_____	_____	• Conveys the school's condolences
_____	_____	_____	• Asks parents/guardians about funeral arrangements
_____	_____	_____	• Determines how the parents/guardians would like the school to participate in the funeral
_____	_____	_____	• Reassures parents/guardians that school will safeguard and return victim's personal belongings
			4. Informs parents that the school is providing counselors for students and staff
			5. Postvention coordinator contacts district crisis team or mental health agency for on-site support and/or consultation
_____	_____	_____	• Mental health agency states what services will be provided
_____	_____	_____	• Superintendent approves use of mental health services
_____	_____	_____	• Postvention coordinator reviews District's policy regarding outside school personnel who screen students and the need for signed consent
			6. Meeting is scheduled for Postvention/Crisis/SAP team and building administration
_____	_____	_____	• Crisis team prepares the announcement that is to be read by teachers
_____	_____	_____	• Principal prepares letter to inform parents of the death as well as the postvention services
_____	_____	_____	• Postvention coordinator locates victim's personal belongings and puts them into safekeeping
_____	_____	_____	• Postvention coordinator removes victim's name from individual class rosters, school mailing lists, and automated attendance call lists
_____	_____	_____	• Crisis Team identifies rooms for screening students
_____	_____	_____	• Crisis Team confirms designated media spokesperson with the Superintendent

Table 9.1 *(continued)*

Date	Time	Initials	Responsibility
			7. If death was a suicide, Crisis Team assesses the risk for contagion
_____	_____	_____	• Postvention coordinator identifies and contacts feeder schools and/or adjacent school districts where students may be affected
_____	_____	_____	• Mental health consultant contacts neighboring mental health providers
			8. Faculty and school staff are informed of the death through phone chain
_____	_____	_____	• Teachers are informed of faculty and staff meeting to take place as soon as possible (e.g., an early morning meeting)
			9. Crisis team begins to compile a list of at-risk students to be individually screened
_____	_____	_____	• Friends of the victim
_____	_____	_____	• Siblings of the victim
_____	_____	_____	• Students with a personal or family history of mental health problems
_____	_____	_____	• Students with a past history of suicide attempts
_____	_____	_____	• Students who are currently in mental health or drug and alcohol abuse treatment
_____	_____	_____	• Students who have been a concern for parents and/or teachers
_____	_____	_____	• Classmates/teammates/fellow club members of the victim
			10. Postvention coordinator or principal holds faculty meeting before school or as soon as possible
_____	_____	_____	• Expresses condolences to the staff
_____	_____	_____	• Acknowledges the efforts of the Postvention/Crisis/SAP team
_____	_____	_____	• Reviews the facts of the death as known
_____	_____	_____	• Announces funeral arrangements if known
_____	_____	_____	• Makes sure that staff members will attend funeral
_____	_____	_____	• Introduces all outside professionals
_____	_____	_____	• Gives an overview of the postvention services
_____	_____	_____	• Advises teachers to send visibly distressed students to the guidance office or designated area with a hall monitor or escort
_____	_____	_____	• Encourages teachers to monitor behaviors that may indicate that a student is grieving (e.g., journal entries, comments written in margins, off-handed comments, etc.)
_____	_____	_____	• Describes the school's policy on what to do with gifts/memorials that students leave for the victim

(continued)

Table 9.1 *(continued)*

Date	Time	Initials	Responsibility
_____	_____	_____	• Distributes the announcement that is to be read to the students
_____	_____	_____	• Encourages any teacher who needs assistance reading the announcement to contact the postvention coordinator
_____	_____	_____	• Announces follow-up meeting to be held ideally at the end of the school day
			11. Postvention coordinator contacts the funeral home
_____	_____	_____	• Reviews specific funeral arrangements and family's wishes
_____	_____	_____	• Informs the funeral director that students might visit the funeral home
			12. Superintendent approves letter to be mailed to parents
_____	_____	_____	• Letter describing the tragedy and the postvention service is distributed to students at the end of the day and mailed to parents
			13. The schedule of the victim is followed by a school counselor or postvention team member
_____	_____	_____	• Expresses condolences
_____	_____	_____	• Responds to students' questions about the death
_____	_____	_____	• Explains funeral arrangements and procedures if any are known
_____	_____	_____	• Discusses the subject of memorials
_____	_____	_____	• Explains that counselors are available to see students
_____	_____	_____	• Reviews various stress reactions and the necessity of exhibiting tolerance and understanding
			14. Trained classroom teacher or counselor may conduct grief presentation for their classroom
_____	_____	_____	• Asks how each student learned about the death
_____	_____	_____	• Explores each student's reaction to the death
_____	_____	_____	• Reviews aspects of grief
_____	_____	_____	• Discusses ways to deal with tragic loss
_____	_____	_____	• Encourages student discussion and questions
_____	_____	_____	• Distributes student "help card" with phone numbers for local hotlines, etc.
_____	_____	_____	• Urges students to self-refer or refer a friend if they are concerned
_____	_____	_____	• Emphasizes the need to contact an adult if students have concerns about suicidality
_____	_____	_____	• Asks for and respond to students' questions

Table 9.1 *(continued)*

Date	Time	Initials	Responsibility
			15. Postvention coordinator or mental health consultant coordinates individual screenings and keeps a confidential roster of all students referred and screened
_____	_____	_____	• Makes every effort to contact the parents/guardians of each student refereed for screening
_____	_____	_____	• Makes clear to student that interview is voluntary
_____	_____	_____	• Reviews confidentiality policy
_____	_____	_____	• Makes appropriate referral for in or out of school support
_____	_____	_____	• Contacts therapists of students who are in treatment if releases are signed and on file
_____	_____	_____	• Explains where students can go if they have any problems or questions about their loss
_____	_____	_____	• Follows-up with student's parents/guardians and document recommendations
_____	_____	_____	• Follow-up for all students screened should occur on a regular basis by school counselors
			16. Postvention coordinator or principal facilitates follow-up faculty meeting
_____	_____	_____	• Thanks faculty and staff and acknowledges their hard work
_____	_____	_____	• Provides updates on any new developments of the death and/or funeral arrangements
_____	_____	_____	• Reminds staff to refer all media inquiries to the District's designated media spokesperson
_____	_____	_____	• Distributes and reviews the letter that goes home to parents
_____	_____	_____	• Encourages faculty and staff to continue to monitor students
_____	_____	_____	• Explains that students may have a resurgence of feelings after the funeral and in the weeks and months to come
_____	_____	_____	• Reminds faculty and staff that there is no time frame for grieving
_____	_____	_____	• Emphasizes that through natural supports, staff and students will get through this difficult time
			17. Postvention coordinator holds a follow-up meeting for Postvention/Crisis team and building administration
_____	_____	_____	• Reviews all students who were seen
_____	_____	_____	• Identifies plan for the following days, especially the day after the funeral

(continued)

Table 9.1 *(continued)*

Date	Time	Initials	Responsibility
			18. Postvention coordinator or principal holds optional parent meeting
_____	_____	_____	• Reviews school's postvention activities
_____	_____	_____	• Discusses typical child and adolescent responses to sudden death
_____	_____	_____	• Identifies risk factors that indicate a concern
_____	_____	_____	• Reviews symptoms of depressions and suicidal behavior
_____	_____	_____	• Identifies resources available in the community
			19. Postvention coordinator or principal holds meeting with Postvention/Crisis/SAP team and building administration
_____	_____	_____	• Evaluates the postvention
_____	_____	_____	• Plans for anniversary dates and special events
_____	_____	_____	• Reviews student screenings
_____	_____	_____	• Emphasizes that faculty and staff need to stay alert to upcoming events or lessons that may be reminders of the tragedy, e.g., fire safety week, bicycle safety week and literature about suicide, accidents or death
_____	_____	_____	• Makes recommendations for other interventions
_____	_____	_____	• Emphasizes the need to take care of themselves with fluids, rest, exercise, etc.

Source: From *Postvention Standards Manual: A Guide for a School's Response in the Aftermath of a Sudden Death* (5th ed., pp. 80–84), by M. M. Kerr, D. A. Brent, B. McKain, and P. S. McCommons, 2006, Pittsburgh, PA: STAR-Center Outreach. Reprinted with permission.

For instance, the Dylan Blake Foundation, founded by a mother whose son died while playing the choking game, has as its mission awareness and education accessible to parents, schools, law enforcement officials, and children (Dylan Blake Foundation for Adolescent Behaviors, 2006). This is a good example of a situation in which a parent may allow disclosure of information to help prevent future tragedies.

CONTACTING THE VICTIM'S FAMILY

In some cases, the family of the victim is the first to notify the school. If this is not the case, a school administrator should contact the parents of the deceased student and offer to visit the home(s), accompanied by the staff person who knows the family best (Knox & Roberts, 2005). During the communication with the family, the school official should:

- Convey the school's condolences.
- Ask parents about funeral arrangements.

- Find out how the parents would like the school community to participate in the funeral arrangements.
- Reassure the parents that the school will safeguard and return the victim's personal belongings when the family is ready to receive them.
- Let the parents know the school is providing counselors to help students and staff members with their grief.
- Invite parents to share the names of their child's school-age friends and family members not known to the school (e.g., friends and cousins in other schools, teenaged baby-sitters, youth coaches).

SAFEGUARDING THE VICTIM'S BELONGINGS

As soon as the school learns of a death, an administrator should arrange for the safekeeping and subsequent return of the victim's personal belongings to the family. If time allows, the school may invite the family to assist. Remove any articles promptly to prevent personal effects from disappearing or becoming a memorial site for grieving peers. Place the belongings in a safe place and in a suitably respectful container (never a plastic trash bag). Ask students and faculty members to contribute personal items of the victim (e.g., papers, artwork, computer files, awards, trophies, photographs, clothes, projects, newspaper articles, videotapes, poems), so family members might have these last and precious remembrances of their loved one. The coordinator might put aside the student's textbooks, in the event that the school chooses to give them to the family or the family wants to purchase them.

Allowing the deceased's desk to remain in its usual place for a long period can be an unnecessary stressor and can provoke problem behaviors (such as writing comments on the desk or turning it into a shrine to the deceased). Whether adults take on the responsibility alone or share it with students, the aim is to return the classroom to a normal learning environment while minimizing additional stress for those at risk for acute stress disorder or PTSD.

FOLLOWING THE SCHEDULE OF THE DECEASED

A school counselor or other member of the school's postvention team can follow the deceased student or staff member's schedule to provide support to teachers and classes, give everyone a chance to express their feelings, and to answer sensitive questions. In the event that the deceased is a faculty member, the postvention coordinator and principal should decide how to modify the schedule to support that individual's students. For example, a familiar teacher could cover the deceased's schedule if someone is available to take over his or her classes.

GROUP INTERVENTIONS

Schools typically engage in some group sessions as a part of the postvention process. These psychological first-aid activities were described in Chapter 8.

One-Time Educational Support Group

Schools routinely bring together those who were involved in classes, teams, clubs, or friendships with the victim, especially when the victim is a student. An educational support group can provide a supervised and supportive atmosphere where students can express their feelings and reactions to their friend's death.

The group leaders, who should be mental health specialists (e.g., trained school counselors, social workers, or psychologists), provide information on coping skills and grief reactions and help clarify misinformation about the death or suicide. Naturally occurring groups to consider, besides the victim's classmates, might include teammates, students who rode the same bus, lab partners, band members, youth group members, and clubs outside of school (e.g., youth groups and scouts).

For children, we recommend that one-time educational support sessions should not include students who have previously been identified as at risk for psychiatric disorders, drug or alcohol abuse, witnessed the tragedy, or are otherwise seen as highly vulnerable and in need of more personalized attention than the group format can provide. Instead, a mental health professional should screen these individuals at high risk in a one-on-one session, apart from the group.

Before conducting any support group sessions, *the leaders should have training in crisis counseling*. Here are some additional guidelines. First, the goal of these one-time groups is to share information about reactions to the death as a way of helping students understand their feelings and behaviors. These sessions are not intended as therapy. Nevertheless, because of the intensity of emotion often expressed in these support groups, limit each group to 20 students (e.g., those in the deceased's classes or on the same bus), with attention to the selection of group members, as reflected in the safeguards stated earlier. *When dealing with close friends of the victim, small groups of 10 students or fewer are even better*. The leaders should conduct the groups in a private setting to facilitate discussion and guarantee confidentiality. Meetings should last no longer than 50 minutes.

Educational support groups work best when well structured. At the beginning of the session, pass around a sign-in sheet for each student to sign his or her name and home telephone number. Facilitators and students should then introduce themselves. The following issues may be topics for discussion during the session:

- Each student's relationship with the deceased
- Individual reactions to the death and with whom they have shared them
- Misinformation and rumors about the death
- Typical reactions to grief
- Symptoms associated with depression
- What students might expect at the funeral (*Note*: The group leaders may discuss ways of expressing sympathy and condolences to the family survivors; encourage youth to attend the funeral with their parents; discuss appropriate ways for youth to be supportive of each other at the funeral home and during the services; and emphasize the need for adult support and the importance of sharing feelings with family members.)
- Student "help card" resources and how to use them

After the educational support group session, facilitators should meet and review what took place. Consider reactions of individual students and refer any student at risk for suicide or depression for an individual screening. Keep brief notes of the content and process of the group meeting. District policy might also require that you make a follow-up contact with the parents of those students participating in the group.

Although children and adolescents have many of the same reactions to trauma, they are not always able to verbalize their thoughts and feelings in the same way. When children are too young to benefit from an educational support group, using art, puppets, music, or books may help them to open up about their feelings.

Informal Student-Initiated Groups

Whenever possible, student-initiated support groups should include one or two well-liked adults because without adult guidance, student groups may exacerbate the vulnerability of students at risk for suicide, depression, anxiety, and risky behaviors. An unsupervised gathering of adolescents, for example, may use alcohol and other drugs to alleviate their feelings.

INDIVIDUAL SCREENING

General Guidelines

Before you begin any screening activities, be sure you are in compliance with applicable federal, state, and district requirements (e.g., those regulations governing the privacy of student records and informed consent for counseling services). This safeguard is especially important for activities that involve nonschool personnel who gather personal information from students.

Students who should be individually contacted and possibly screened include the following:

- Close friends of the victim
- Any witness of the event
- Students who have experienced a recent loss
- Students who are receiving mental health or drug and alcohol treatment
- Funeral attendees
- Students who identify themselves as needing help

Certain students at particular risk for suicide and/or depression should be screened individually *by a qualified mental health professional or by a school counselor in consultation with a qualified mental health professional* (Poland & McCormick, 1999). The following issues may comprise an individual screening:

- The student's exposure to the suicide, relationship with the deceased, and participation in the funeral
- The student's current and past mental health care, including anytime he or she was in counseling

- Whether the suicide/tragic loss caused any exacerbation of any mental health symptoms
- Any current or past history of suicide for themselves or any family members
- Any symptoms of depression experienced by the student and whether the suicide caused an exacerbation of those symptoms
- Any past or present involvement with the legal or juvenile court system
- Any history of alcohol and/or drug abuse
- Access to firearms (even if in a locked cabinet), alcohol, and other drugs
- Stressors in the student's life
- Any communication about the suicide between the student and the deceased

Despite fears that this method of identification could become unmanageable, it has been our experience that only a finite number of students are at risk. Most students screened during a postvention do not require mental health treatment. However, those students whose severe grief impairs their daily functioning, or those whose histories include the risk factors mentioned earlier are particularly at risk for developing depression or PTSD. These students should be monitored for school attendance, changes in academic performance, and any shifts in behavior.

Prior to the screening, inform students that the interview is voluntary, they do not have to answer any questions they choose not to, and their parents will be contacted afterward. In times following a tragic event, most students in fact *want* their parent, guardian, or emergency contact reached and informed (Crabb, Dreshman, & Tarasevish, 2001). Additionally, explain that information shared by the student is confidential unless there is a risk of the student hurting himself or herself or someone else, any suspicion of abuse to them, or other at-risk behavior. (In this case, the student's parents must be informed of the student's risk, and an appropriate level of support should be provided in the form of referral or transportation to an appropriate place for care.)

Ideally, the person who conducts the screening should be the one who contacts the parent afterward by phone. It helps to have the student present when you call the parent so they can talk with one another as well. If there is no need for follow-up, you can tell the parent, "Your son/daughter is understandably distressed by the death of his/her friend. At this point s/he appears to be experiencing a normal grief reaction." Then review child/adolescent reactions that would be of concern and who to contact if they observe those behaviors. Send a letter containing the same information provided on the telephone.

If you determine the student is at risk for suicide, depression, or another mental health disorder, then take these actions:

- Contact the parents or guardians and facilitate a referral.
- Advise the parents or guardians to remove firearms, alcohol, and other drugs from the student's access.

If a student exhibits serious suicidal ideation (thoughts about suicide), has a suicide plan, or engages in behavior that represents a clear and present danger to self or others, immediately contact the parents or guardians and arrange an emergency evaluation by a qualified mental health professional.

Regardless of their initial status, students screened should always know where they could get help should they have any problems, questions, or concerns about the tragic loss they experienced. Keep accurate records of students screened, for follow-up with parents and for future reference. Each individual screening should be documented on a confidential postvention screening form and recorded on a confidential roster (see the companion website for examples). At the end of each day, the postvention team should meet to review screening results and determine individual follow-up.

Approximately one to two months after the postvention is completed, school staff should review the status of each student screened and determine the need for further intervention. In the unfortunate situation that another tragedy occurs within 60 days, the postvention team should revisit these students as well as attend to the students involved in the current tragedy. Around the anniversary of the tragedy, staff can also touch base with students to see how they are coping.

FUNERAL PLANS

A school representative should speak to the family members who are handling funeral arrangements. Parents are often receptive to the school's input and recommendations (Poland & McCormick, 1999). After speaking with the parents of the deceased, the postvention coordinator should contact the funeral home or religious institution to (1) find out specific funeral arrangements (such as visitation hours, dates, times, interment, etc.), and (2) inform the funeral home director or religious leader about counseling services available for students and the victim's family members as well as a contact person at the school should there be any requests.

POSTVENTION IN OTHER SCHOOLS

Postvention services may extend beyond a classroom, grade, or school building. The tragedy may affect students and adults in other settings; for example, suicidal behavior can be the result of contagion. Feeder schools, where the deceased had friends or relatives, or adjacent school districts may have students affected by the death.

Identify and contact these other sites. A family member or spokesperson can provide information regarding the deceased individual's previous school placements, present and recent participation in community activities, or membership in community organizations. Planning a comprehensive postvention program may involve cooperation among various schools within a district, between districts, and between schools and other community groups. The mental health consultant should contact neighboring mental health providers, if the impact of the suicide extends beyond the school district or local community mental health service area.

COMMUNICATIONS

As Chapter 5 recommends, update the school staff about the postvention efforts regularly and offer them any new information they need to quell rumors or work more effectively. The postvention coordinator or principal can put it in a brief factual memo sent to all staff involved in the postvention. This information can also be shared at the faculty meeting at the end of the day. The same information might be shared with the superintendent, school board, and district spokesperson.

If the school must respond to the media, the spokesperson should prepare a written statement for release to those media representatives who request it. The statement should include a very brief statement (without details about the death of the student) as well as information about the school's postvention policy and program. It may also include an expression of the school's sympathy to the survivors of the deceased. The statement may include references to responsible media reporting in a postvention situation, emphasizing, for example, the positive action the school is taking to help student survivors and providing information about available community resources for troubled students.

Suicide Contagion and the Media

Past research has demonstrated that front-page newspaper reports of suicide can increase the rate of suicide. Similarly, most evidence suggests the magnitude of the increase in suicidal behavior after newspaper coverage is related to how much media coverage the story is given. Suicide contagion is more likely when the suicide is covered on the front page, in large headlines, and is heavily publicized (Gould, 2001). In addition, dramatizations of suicide have resulted in an increased rate of suicide attempts. The effect appears maximized when suicide is presented without information about mental illness and the tragic impact on the family (Gould & Shaffer, 1986); specifically, dramatizations that are followed by imitation rarely portray suicide victims as almost invariably psychiatrically ill.

Schools cannot always prevent media coverage, especially if the particular suicide is sensational. However, the school's preparation, approach, and response in a suicidal crisis can limit the damaging effects of media coverage. After a suicide, take care to emphasize the importance of safeguards against suicide contagion. Casual comments repeated in the media can have serious consequences for the school's recovery from the suicide.

An adversarial relationship with the media can be harmful for all concerned. Communicating clearly the impact of suicide and the need to identify those most in need is an important community service the media can provide.

SUPPORTING THE POSTVENTION TEAM

Team members require their own support during the intense stress of a postvention. Members should have ready access to water and nutritional foods, whenever possible. Team members should take turns dealing with the high-intensity aspects of a postvention.

As described in Chapter 4, carefully planned continuing education refreshers are one of the best ways to support and sustain team members. Advance preparation of a policy and designation of duties can alleviate anxiety and reduce the stress of postvention work. Provide each postvention team member with a crisis kit of essential forms, directories, personal items, maps, and handbooks.

EVALUATION AND FOLLOW-UP

Throughout the postvention, document all services and events to provide a factual representation of the events surrounding the suicide and the school's response. These documents should be handled in the same manner as other confidential information.

At the end of each day during the postvention, or as necessary, the postvention coordinator and the mental health consultant should conduct a debriefing meeting. At this meeting, postvention team members evaluate the delivery of services, review students' screenings, make recommendations for other interventions, and determine the need for further postvention.

Within 6 weeks after the postvention program is completed, team members and local mental health professionals should meet to review student screenings. Close friends of the victim should also be monitored. Some will develop problems that only evolve over time. The staff and students' mutual awareness of this can facilitate access to treatment for those who are having difficulty with grief, depression, or PTSD. Teams should review their services annually and make recommendations for any changes in the school's postvention policy or procedures.

MEMORIALS

Mourning can facilitate the grief process by allowing public recognition of the person's life and a sharing of feelings. In this section, we explore informal student-initiated memorials at school and in the community, as well as formal memorials in these settings. First, we consider the unique considerations for memorials following a suicide.

Memorials Following a Suicide

As we have mentioned throughout this text, suicidal behavior in others is a risk following a suicide. Given this concern, memorials must not glamorize or characterize the victim as a martyr. Because young people are typically highly vulnerable to the actions of their peers, the adults taking care of them have to safeguard them.

However, students, family members, and staff close to an individual who took his or her own life need to express their sadness. As a result, the needs and wishes of the mourners can conflict with the decisions of the school. Consider this case:

> Frankly, we had not even thought about memorials in our school. The school had opened recently, and our climate was one of celebration at the end of the long construction project. An entirely new staff and student body were stunned, then, when Saundra, one of our young teachers, committed suicide three months into the school year.
>
> The following spring, the teacher's family called to meet with me about a memorial they had planned. We met the next day. As Saundra's sister unfurled a landscaper's drawing, her father explained, "As you know, Saundra's entire summer was focused on this new school. She had worked so hard on planning just the right lessons for her new students. In fact she had called each one of them in August to introduce herself. We know that she would

want them to remember her. That's why we have hired a landscaper to create a permanent memorial garden for the side of the school. Having that garden will be such a comfort to us and to her friends and students."

I had been a counselor in another school that experienced a suicide, so I knew that memorials had to be very carefully considered. But that afternoon, I realized for the first time just how painful the situation could be for a family struggling to handle their grief yet find a way to remember their loved one.

Unfortunately, we have no studies of the effects of suicide memorials to guide us (Jones, 2001). Cautiously, many schools adopt a policy of no memorials following suicides, despite the pain this can create for families. To avoid or resolve a potential conflict at a highly emotional time, we suggest that school boards set a policy *in advance* how they will handle all memorials, taking into account the possibility that one or more deaths may be the result of suicide. For example, the district may establish a general memorial scholarship fund for its high school graduates or encourage donations to local charities, including the local chapter of the American Foundation for Suicide Prevention or a local suicide support group. Consider these other suggestions offered by an expert panel convened by the federal suicide prevention center:

> There have been several cases where dedicating public memorials after a suicide has facilitated the suicidal acts of others, usually youth (CDC, 1988). Consequently, dedicating memorials in public settings, such as park benches, flag poles, or trophy cases, soon after the suicide is discouraged. In some situations, however, survivors feel a pressing need for the community to express its grief in a tangible way. Open discussion with proponents about the inherent risks of memorials for youth should help the community find a fitting, yet safe, outlet. These may include personal expressions that can be given to the family to keep privately, such as letters, poetry, recollections captured on videotape, or works of art. (It's best to keep such expressions private; while artistic expression is often therapeutic for those experiencing grief, public performances of poems, plays, or songs may contain messages or create a climate that inadvertently increases thoughts of suicide among vulnerable youth.) Alternatively, suggest that surviving friends honor the deceased by living their lives in concert with community values, such as compassion, generosity, service, honor, and improving quality of life for all community members. Activity-focused memorials might include organizing a day of community service, sponsoring mental health awareness programs, supporting peer counseling programs, or fund-raising for some of the many worthwhile suicide prevention nonprofit organizations. Purchasing library books that address related topics, such as how young people can cope with loss or how to deal with depression and other emotional problems, is another life-affirming way to remember the deceased. (Suicide Prevention Resource Center, 2004)

Student-Initiated Memorials

Students often leave mementos (e.g., banners, letters, poems, balloons, flowers, teddy bears) on or near the victim's locker, desk, grave, or at the accident site. In one case, for example, students painted a large outside wall of the high school to express their grief (Brent, Kerr, Goldstein, Bozigar, Wartella, & Allan, 1989). An Internet search for roadside memorials yields hundreds of sites depicting photographs of such informal tributes.

It is important that students have a means to express their grief and remember their friend; however, the school must also consider the reactions that such visual reminders evoke. Therefore, students can be encouraged to bring cards and other items they would like to share with the family to the main office or other designated location. Remind students that any items left at a locker or desk will be collected carefully throughout the day and shared with the family. A member of the postvention team can review the materials for appropriateness before sharing them with the family.

Community Considerations

In many communities, memorials are an important part of the mourning process. The norms in the community will influence what will occur in any memorial or service. However, community norms, laws, and policies also must be honored. After the Columbine High School shootings, for instance, the school district became involved in a legal dispute over memorial tiles the students had painted. Ultimately, the court banned tiles that depicted the date of the event as well as religious references (Dowling-Sender, 2003).

Any community memorial should take into consideration how past losses were handled. The public has a natural tendency to compare memorials, which can prove painful for survivors. In planning a service or permanent memorial, consider four concepts: proportion, taste, outlook, and family wishes. The memorial should be in *proportion* to past activities and with consideration of the amount of time and involvement from the school and community at large.

Schools must always consider what they have done historically in similar situations (Poland & McCormick, 1999). For example, a memorial park should be smaller than a playground; a graduation ceremony should not be remembered for a eulogy delivered for a deceased graduate. Second, the memorial should be in good taste, with considerations given to how the memorial will be viewed by future persons who experience it. Avoid fads and trends that may not withstand the test of time. Third, the theme of looking to the future with a sense of *hopefulness* is an important element in any memorial service, writing, or activity. Fourth, the surviving family's wishes and preferences should be honored whenever possible within the policies of the school. Finally, before any student attends a memorial service during school hours, parental permission should be obtained. The student then has the choice whether to attend the memorial service or not.

Yearbook Memorials

It is important to help adolescents and younger students understand that the yearbook is a celebration of memories that will remain in their possession for many years to come. The yearbook represents a collection of many different persons' memories, recollections, contributions, writings, and photographs. Therefore, a guiding concept is to avoid overwhelming the primary purpose of the yearbook, a celebration and remembrance of mostly happy times. In other words, do not allow students to turn the entire yearbook experience into a memorial. To do this would be to deny many students and their families the pleasure that a yearbook offers.

The approval of the deceased student/faculty member's surviving family is crucial to the process. Prior to designing any memorial in the yearbook, the yearbook staff, along with their faculty adviser, should meet with the family of the deceased to determine their wishes, preferences, concerns, and feelings about a memorial. This can be accomplished through a scheduled meeting at the family's home or at school. Such a meeting provides the school's mental health specialist with an opportunity to share concerns about suicide contagion, asking for the parents' support.

The proportion of the memorial to the entire yearbook is important to keep in balance. For example, the memorial should not overwhelm or dominate the senior class section of the book.

The content and visual qualities of the memorial are important. Adequate space can be given to a photograph or two but without reference to the details of the death. Avoid dramatic colors and designs because they detract from the overall goal of a yearbook. Consider including a photograph of the deceased, even if the photograph is supplied by the family or from a previous school year. This may be less dramatic than a blank or darkened space.

Keep in mind that the yearbook memorial is but one way in which students and faculty may remember and honor their friend. The yearbook staff might want to produce a separate memory book with pictures, anecdotes, stories, and poems about the deceased. The memory book could be presented to the victim's family. Creating such a project may relieve some of the tension regarding decisions about what is and what is not included in the yearbook itself.

Let's reflect...

As we conclude this discussion of memorials, we turn to the importance of respecting cultural norms in honoring those who have died. Consider this narrative by a teacher who learned about another culture while caring for a grieving child.

Within my fifth-grade class, I teach my grade level's English as a Second Language (ESL) population. Many are refugees fortunate enough to escape from places that are in the center of political upheaval, corruption, violence, and civil war. One of my students, a refugee from Liberia, has lived in Guinea and Sierra Leone, all coastal West African nations. After Ameena had been in my class for a little over three months, she came to me and asked, "Mr. Blaiko, have you ever been to a funeral?"

As I could see that Ameena was beginning to get upset, I brought her out into the hallway to inquire if there was anything behind this question or if she was just curious about a new word she had heard, which was often the case. She instantly erupted into tears, so much so that I had to catch her before she collapsed to the ground. She had a difficult time composing herself, but I was able to determine that her father was badly injured, in the hospital, and may have passed away.

After the school day was over, I called Ameena's home and left a message saying that she had talked with me and if there was anything the school or I could do to help, just to let us know.

To my amazement, Ameena was in school the next day. As my students filed in and began their morning exercise, I pulled her aside and asked her how she was and how her father was. She said, very matter-of-factly, "Oh, he died." I was stunned, grabbed her hand, and expressed how sorry I was. She nodded her head and asked me a question about the morning exercise. Again, I was surprised. I asked her, "Would you like to talk to me or anyone else about things?"

She said, "No. I just want to stay in class."

I said, "OK," answered her question about the morning exercise, and watched as she walked to her seat.

I sat down and started to write an e-mail to my principal, social worker, and her ESL teacher. I explained the news of her father's death, the morning interaction I had had with her, and her request not to talk about it with me or anyone else.

Ameena went through the entire day as she would any other day. I spoke with the ESL teacher midafternoon and she told me that her entire 90-minute session (small group) was spent talking about and around death, funerals, and what happens afterward. Ameena felt very comfortable with this small-group setting of her African immigrant peers as opposed to her larger homeroom with me, understandably so.

During my planning period, I called home again. This time Ameena's mother answered. I went on to express my condolences and told her there are many people in our school who love and care for her daughter very much and we would help Ameena through this difficult time. She thanked me and hung up the phone. I felt absolutely terrible and wished there was something more that I could do.

I went to my principal after school to talk about some ways our school could help. We agreed to fund-raise among the staff and use the money to buy a gift card to the grocery store in walking distance of the family's home. We also contacted the local center for grieving children for general information. Nothing I learned from them prepared me for seeing my student in school yet again the next day. Ameena pulled me aside to ask if I thought she should go to her father's funeral. I told her that even though I thought it would be very difficult, she might regret it later if she did not attend. She nodded her head as a sign of her understanding and went to her seat. Once again, she went through the day as she would any other day.

I searched for the obituary and read there was to be a single-night viewing at a local church. I forwarded this information to our principals and to teachers who knew Ameena.

My colleagues and I arranged a meeting place and arrived at the church together. I felt very uneasy stepping into the personal life of one of my students, certainly out of my comfort zone, but I wanted to support my student. When we walked in, we were welcomed with embraces. Dressed in vibrant and colorful clothing of their native country, many people gathered in the front of the church. I took a seat near the back to listen to the pastors and the beautiful music.

After a few minutes, the entire congregation was asked to join in a traditional song and dance in the front of the church. I was reluctant because I was not familiar with this custom, but I was embraced by another family member and strongly encouraged to come to the front. For the better part of an hour we sang, chanted, and danced in celebration of my student's father's life. Upon the completion of the dance, my student came up to me with a tear-stained face and thanked me for coming with a lengthy hug. It was an extraordinary experience for me, something I will never forget.

In your own community, you will encounter different traditions regarding death. Perhaps you could invite members of organizations (e.g., churches, ethnic social clubs, neighborhood groups) to share their traditions with your crisis team. Employees who live in the community may be a valuable source of information as well.

GRADUATION ACTIVITIES AFTER A DEATH

Commemorations at the end of the school year can be especially painful for the victim's loved ones. If a high school senior has died, try to make private arrangements with the family of the deceased to meet them at a place of their choice (usually their home) and to present them with their child's diploma. This should be scheduled near the day of graduation because they will be feeling left out of that day. The principal, superintendent, or some authority from the school should go, accompanied by someone who knows the family. If there are any awards banquets or other occasions where the student would have been recognized, then the same idea is helpful. Do not designate an empty chair at the ceremony because the visual may trigger strong reactions from other students and attendees.

At the graduation ceremony, a word of recognition about the tragedy is helpful, especially if a statement that indicates the school has recently reached out to the parents/family by visiting them and presenting the diploma can follow it. This kind of statement seems to put other parents and students at ease and shows compassion. The superintendent or principal may want to mention a memorial fund or other memorial that the school is arranging.

Deal with the tragedies at the beginning of the ceremony, so you can say what you have done and then move on to the happy evening that is well deserved by students and their families. Do not be surprised if students mention the tragedies in their remarks. This is often their choice, and students handle it appropriately, in our experience.

Check with the victims' families to see if they have any particular wishes you may be able to honor—developing a memory book of photos for them, donating a book to the library in the victim's name, and so on. Do not leave the victims' names off the list of graduates.

The same concepts apply to situations in which a younger student has died. That student should be recognized at any elementary or middle school graduation activities or remembered at commemorative activities, as appropriate.

ANNIVERSARY DATES

Student and staff may revisit grief feelings on or near the anniversary date of a tragic loss. This can be a normal remembering or it may be of more intensity, including unresolved grief or a delayed grief reaction. Faculty and staff, if reminded of the anniversary, can be prepared to monitor and support students at that time. Adults are not immune to this. Depending on their own personal history, various staff members may also revisit the loss. The postvention team may consider a follow-up program on the anniversary date. Be aware that similar responses may occur on special occasions like the victim's birthday. Other potentially difficult dates include the first holidays, games, recognition dinners, proms, and graduation without the victim.

SUMMARY

Postvention following a death is a complex set of services that begin immediately but may extend to a lesser degree across years as the school revisits anniversaries and special commemorations. Immediate attention focuses on supporting the school community, managing internal and external communications, identifying and screening those at elevated risk, and reducing the possibility of suicide contagion. Follow-up actions, facilitated by accurate record keeping, include contacts with the family and friends of the deceased and monitoring of those at risk for suicidal behavior, anxiety, and depression. Memorials require special consideration and may be designed in the months that follow the death.

CASE STUDY CONCLUSION

The following morning before the faculty meeting, I contacted the local police, who verified that Jerell's death was self-inflicted. Anne, Jerell's mother, asked them to share the notes Jerell left for his mother and sister. In the notes, he explained he simply could not stand the pain and humiliation any longer. He feared he had let his team down and that his father's outbursts would jeopardize his mother's job.

With tears in my eyes, I faced the faculty gathered that Saturday and shared only the facts about Jerell's death. I did not share the contents of the notes. As members of the crisis team began to work on lists of those likely to be affected, classroom announcements, parent letters, and a short press statement, calls began coming in to the school. Jerell's teammates had gotten word of his death and began sending instant messages to their friends. Parents were frantic and calling for advice.

We made a decision to open the school for students and staffed the counseling center and the cafeteria, where we knew students would congregate. Parents volunteered to serve coffee and doughnuts, and all of the basketball coaches set up a place in the locker rooms to meet with the team and a school psychologist who specializes in grief counseling. We asked students to sign in when they arrived, and I was surprised how many West High students also showed up. I put in a call to their principal, who offered to come over with a few of her counselors.

By early afternoon, the news had reached the local radio and television stations. Thankfully, we had decent relationships with them, so they accepted only a short statement. The local newspaper editor agreed to withhold the cause of death and offered to run a separate article in a couple of weeks on how to identify teen depression. The local television station had planned a segment on irate parents in sports but agreed to postpone it.

We opened the school again on Sunday and even more students came. On Monday and Tuesday, we checked on any student who was referred and did about 40 screenings. Eight kids needed psychiatric evaluations and two—those in whom Jerell had confided his plans—are still in treatment.

Two weeks later, Anne returned to work, only to find that the high school brought back too many painful reminders of her son. We made arrangements for her to transfer to the middle school for the remainder of the year and set up counseling through our employee assistance program for her and her husband. Anne later told me that her husband finally acknowledged his own depression in one of their sessions. The staff decided to donate our "Dress Down Friday" fund to Compassionate Friends, a support group for parents who have lost a child.

Three months later, on the night of the senior prom, a few of Anne's coworkers spent some time with her and her husband. The last weeks of school were especially hard on everyone because Jerell was on everyone's mind. The sports banquet had a moment of silence and two coaches met with the family beforehand to share the program and Jerell's varsity letter. We assigned an adult to meet with every one of the students we had identified as either at risk or especially close to Jerell. They touched base throughout the last week of school and gave students their e-mail addresses so they could stay in touch over the summer.

DISCUSSION AND APPLICATION IDEAS

1. Can you describe the process and procedures for conducting postventions after a suicide?
2. Discuss issues that should be considered when identifying a school's particular needs after a tragedy.
3. How would your school screen students who are at risk for suicidal behaviors?
4. Practice postvention procedures by using news accounts or scenarios you create. Develop hypothetical postvention plans, including media statements, screening procedures, and parent letters.

REFERENCES

Besançon, F. (2003). *Evaluating postventive actions after suicides. Communication par affiche au XXII World Congress of the International Association for Suicide Prevention (IASP), Stockholm, 10-14 septembre 2003.* Stockholm Convention Bureau édition. Retrieved October 17, 2007, from http://perso.orange.fr/sante-infofb/english_suicide_postvention.htm

Brent, D. A., Kerr, M. M., Goldstein, C., Bozigar, J. A., Wartella, M., & Allan, M. J. (1989). An outbreak of suicide and suicidal behavior in a high school. *Journal of the American Academy of Child and Adolescent Psychiatry, 28,* 918-924.

Brent, D. A., Perper, J. A., Moritz, G., Baugher, M., & Allman, C. (1993). Suicide in adolescents with no apparent psychopathology. *Journal of the American Academy of Child and Adolescent Psychiatry, 257,* 494-500.

Callahan, J. (1996). Negative effects of a school suicide postvention program: A case example. *Crisis, 17* (3), 108-115.

Commission on Adolescent Suicide Prevention. (2005). Youth suicide. In D. L. Evans, E. B. Foa, R. E. Gur, H. Hendin, C. P. O'Brien, M. Seligman, & B. T. Walsh (Eds.), *Treating and preventing adolescent mental health disorders: What we know and what we don't know* (pp. 434-443). New York: Oxford University Press.

Crabb, C. I., Dreshman, J. L, & Tarasevish, S. (2001). *Caring in times of crisis.* Columbia, SC: YouthLight.

Dowling-Sender, B. (2003). The sad case of the Columbine tiles. *American School Board Journal, 190* (1), 41-42.

Dylan Blake Foundation for Adolescent Behaviors. (2006). Retrieved October 17, 2007, from http://www.dylan-the-boy-blake.com/index.html

Gould, M. S. (2001). Suicide and the media. *Annals of the New York Academy of Sciences, 932,* 200-224.

Gould, M. S., Jamieson, P., & Romer, D. (2003). Media contagion and suicide among the young. *American Behavioral Scientist, 46,* 1269-1284.

Gould, M. S., & Shaffer, D. (1986). The impact of suicide in television movies: Evidence of imitation. *New England Journal of Medicine, 315,* 690-694.

Jones, R. (2001). Suicide watch. *American School Board Journal*. Retrieved July 7, 2007, from http://www.asbj.com/2001/05/0501coverstory.html

Kerr, M. M., Brent, D. A., McKain, B., & McCommons, P. S. (2006). *Postvention standards manual: A guide for a school's response in the aftermath of a sudden death* (5th ed.). Pittsburgh, PA: University of Pittsburgh, Services for Teens at Risk (STAR-Center).

Knox, K. S., & Roberts, A. R. (2005). Crisis intervention and crisis team models in schools. *Children & Schools, 27* (2), 93–100.

O'Carroll, P. W., Mercy, J. A., & Steward, J. A. (1988). *CDC recommendations for community planning for the prevention and containment of suicide clusters*. Epidemiology Program Office, MMWR. Atlanta, GA: Centers for Disease Control, Public Health Service, U.S. Department of Health and Human Services.

Poland, S., & McCormick, J. S. (1999). *Coping with crisis: Lessons learned*. Colorado Springs: Sopris West.

Shneidman, E. S. (1981). The psychological autopsy. *Suicide and Life-Threatening Behavior, 11* (4), 325–340.

Suicide Prevention Resource Center. (2004). *After a suicide: Recommendations for religious services and other public memorial observances*. Newton, MA: Education Development Center.

CHAPTER 10

RECOVERY: SUPPORTING SCHOOL CRISIS RESPONDERS

CASE STUDY

As the director of a crisis response center, I pulled into the driveway, emotionally drained from meeting with a postvention team after the accidental death of a child. My husband met me in the driveway.

"There has been a plane crash, a bad one. You'd better see the news," he advised.

Stunned, I dashed to the television, where reporters were describing a fiery crash site. Suddenly, I realized they were standing only a few miles from the school I had left that afternoon. Then our phone rang.

"The county is calling out the community mental health disaster team. They want you to report to the airport."

I climbed back into my car, still shocked by the news and feeling unsure of myself. The reporter's words echoed in my head: "This is a disaster … a disaster."

INTRODUCTION

Tragedies in schools require us to be present during hours of chaos, fear, and despair. When crisis teams respond to a serious accident, death, or disaster, they may be reminded of the expression, "too much, too little, too late." After all, the tragedy can be overwhelming, *too much* even for veteran responders. One's efforts may seem *too little* in the face of death or victimization and *too late* to be of real help. On one hand, responders often wish they could have done more or responded sooner. On the other hand, frequent responders may resent being called out so often. Nevertheless, school and community crisis responders often remark that they are transformed by the work and the many gifts it offers. These challenges and rewards are the subject of this final chapter. In the next section, we review some of the general changes that take place following a critical incident, changes that affect the way we work and interact with one another.

RISK FACTORS FOR BURNOUT

Maslach and Leiter (1997) identified six risk factors for **burnout**, which they defined as the dislocation between who people are and what they have to do. The risk factors are:

1. Work overload
2. Insufficient rewards
3. Sense of unfairness
4. Lack of control
5. Loss of community
6. Values conflict

Let's examine how these risk factors become more pronounced during school crises.

First, common to all crises is the *additional workload* thrust suddenly on school personnel, including office staff, teachers, administrators, and members of the crisis team. The critical incident commands the attention and time of staff members, who must return to their normal overdue deadlines. School crisis responders, already drained emotionally and tired from the day's work, often find themselves besieged by telephone calls and e-mails from those in other schools eager to gain information. As one counselor observed, "I go to another school to help them in a crisis. Then, I return to my own school, where no one is sympathetic. Everything I left on my desk is there ... and more. Finally, I get home and the phone rings off the hook with people wanting to know what is going on."

These effects are not limited to those on a crisis team. For example, office staff may be racing against deadlines to produce parent letters, and maintenance workers are called on to stay longer hours or take on additional roles. Naturally, these additional obligations are easy to face when one is fairly compensated. Conversations with union officials may identify ways to grant "compensatory time" or to otherwise make such assignments fairer. Such arrangements can protect team members from the risk factor, *insufficient rewards.*

If they have been called out several times or for a prolonged assignment, crisis responders may begin to see their duties as *unfair.* They may feel emotionally drained and in need of relief. Yet many would not feel comfortable acknowledging these feelings openly. After all, they are trying to aid those whose suffering is far worse. Here are some comments from two veteran crisis responders gathered to debrief after a series of critical incidents, including a plane crash:

> "We have a saying in our office: 'I'm glad you called. I wish you hadn't.' Don't get me wrong. I value this work and would never change my decision. But sometimes, it feels unfair, like you are on call constantly. I ask myself, 'Why me?' Then I feel guilty thinking about what these poor survivors have been through."

> "What I find hard is that no one else can really understand what it's like. Let's face it: You don't want to burden your family and friends with the details of a terrible tragedy. But you begin to feel that no one understands what you are dealing with. Listen to this one. Last night as soon as I got home, my husband asked me if corn was in season yet. I wanted to scream. Who cares about corn after all these people were killed?"

Disruptions in work schedule and space exacerbate a *loss of control*, as school personnel find themselves sharing space and extending their work hours to accommodate the needs of students and outside support personnel. The stress of making these accommodations can contribute to conflict. "For weeks after the incident, I commuted an extra hour, shared an office with three other crisis workers, and virtually abandoned my family. When I asked a secretary if I could use her phone, she snapped at me. I almost lost it," complained a school social worker.

A *loss of community* can result when working under extreme stress with unfamiliar people replaces the normal collegial community of crisis responders. "Crises require teamwork, but you've never seen some of these people before," mused a veteran responder. Summoned to a critical incident, individuals with different backgrounds, training, experience, and personal styles must make and follow decisions together rapidly. Misunderstandings and conflict are common. To minimize these conflicts, we rely on well-rehearsed protocols, and we try to get to know one another in advance, as explained in Chapter 3. Compounding the stress, school staff may come to resent the presence of outside responders. As a psychiatric nurse responder offered, "You go to help them. After a week or two they don't thank you anymore. It's like they forget why you came and begin to get mad about your intrusion. That's when you know it's time to leave. It's just not fair."

In summary, a crisis creates a work overload, which in turn may generate a feeling of unfairness or loss of control. When others don't share the gravity of the situation, the crisis responder may perceive that they devalue the work, leading to a conflict in values or a sense of insufficient recognition. Faced temporarily with new colleagues, one may experience a loss of community.

Let's reflect...

As you recall the conversations you've had with others from your crisis team or colleagues who work with individuals in crisis, can you detect in their words any of the risk factors for burnout?

We would not expect burnout from those responding to an occasional short-term crisis, but those who are on a school or district crisis team may be responding to many more crises, thereby becoming at greater risk for burnout. Even those not providing direct care to those traumatized, therefore, should be aware of the risk factors for burnout. To help school personnel understand burnout and its risk factors, a useful video, *Working with Stress*, is available free of charge from the National Institute for Occupational Safety and Health (2002).

Let's turn now to the particular stresses experienced by those supporting trauma victims: **caring burnout, meaning burnout,** and **compassion fatigue,** or **secondary stress disorder**.

BURNOUT AND COMPASSION FATIGUE

Skovholt (2001) differentiated between *meaning burnout* and *caring burnout. Meaning burnout,* he offered, occurs when one's work no longer holds the "psychic income" it once did. For example, a frequent crisis responder might comment that she no longer feels the connection and importance of her work as she once did. As Skovholt explained, meaning burnout can occur when individuals no longer have the same needs as they once did. One responder discovered that her volunteer work at an animal shelter was more fulfilling and less stressful than being on call for postventions year after year. This realization was compounded by new district policies that prohibited her from working with trauma victims for a long term, rendering her work ineffective.

Caring burnout, in contrast, refers to the emotional exhaustion, depersonalization, and lack of personal accomplishment that can drain the energy of crisis responders over time.

Skovholt (2001) refers to this as "disengagement of the self from the caring cycle of empathic attachment ⟶ active involvement ⟶ felt separation" that characterize the cycle of helping professionals (p. 113).

Others have described work-related psychological reactions of therapists and trauma workers as *compassion fatigue (CF)* or *secondary traumatic stress disorder (STS)*, nearly identical to PTSD, except it affects those taking care of the direct victims of trauma (Figley, 1995). Left unchecked, secondary traumatic stress disorder may occasionally lead to PTSD. More common, but nevertheless debilitating, are stress-related reactions (Auger, Seymour, & Roberts, 2004). Ochberg (n.d.) describes it this way:

> We have not been directly exposed to the trauma scene, but we hear the story told with such intensity, or we hear similar stories so often, or we have the gift and curse of extreme empathy and we suffer. We feel the feelings of our clients. We experience their fears. We dream their dreams. Eventually, we lose a certain spark of optimism, humor and hope. We tire. We aren't sick, but we aren't ourselves. (p. 1)

A third term you may hear is *vicarious traumatization*, the psychological response to indirect exposure to trauma though the stories of those you aid (McCann & Pearlman, 1990). Unlike typical workplace burnout, compassion fatigue and secondary stress disorder are not gradual but "usually rapid in onset and associated with a particular event" (Stamm, 2005, p. 5).

Understanding compassion fatigue is essential to preventing it from overtaking you and impairing your work. Table 10.1 lists the symptoms of compassion fatigue.

We encourage you to view the video, *When Helping Hurts: Sustaining Trauma Workers* (2006), produced and directed by Joyce Boaz, executive director of Gift from Within, a training and support organization for trauma workers (www.giftfromwithin.org). Crisis teams can discuss this short film as a training activity.

In the next section, you'll learn about other steps to protect yourself and your colleagues from compassion fatigue and burnout.

SUPPORTING CRISIS RESPONDERS

To safeguard team members from burnout and compassion fatigue, we must pay attention to the balance between caring for ourselves and caring for others (Skovholt, 2001). Those in charge of crisis teams should organize ongoing supports for their members, as illustrated throughout this book. These supports should be introduced during crisis team orientation and training and before a crisis, so the crisis team members are able to access them without delay or reluctance. For example, the employee assistance program may be involved in crisis team training, to reduce the stigma associated with seeking help.

Consider the model of crisis team support based on Maslow's hierarchy in Figure 10.1.

First, we must address the basic survival needs of crisis responders. As we explained in Chapter 3, the crisis response kit provides personally sustaining items such as food, water, a blanket, a handheld fan, and medication.

Second, solid planning and preparation equips crisis responders to feel secure when facing the chaos of a critical incident. Team members not only need to feel physically safe,

Table 10.1
Examples of Compassion Fatigue and Burnout Symptoms

Cognitive	Emotional	Behavioral	Spiritual	Personal Relationships	Physical/ Somatic	Work Performance
Lowered concentration	Powerlessness	Impatient	Questioning the meaning of life	Withdrawal	Shock	Low morale
Decreased self-esteem	Anxiety	Irritable	Loss of purpose	Decreased interest in intimacy or sex	Sweating	Low motivation
Apathy	Guilt	Withdrawn	Lack of self-satisfaction	Mistrust	Rapid heartbeat	Avoiding tasks
Rigidity	Anger/rage	Moody	Pervasive hopelessness	Isolation from others	Breathing difficulties	Obsession about details
Disorientation	Survivor guilt	Regression	Anger at God	Overprotection as a parent	Aches and pains	Apathy
Perfectionism	Shutdown	Sleep disturbance	Questioning of prior religious beliefs	Projection of anger or blame	Dizziness	Negativity
Minimization	Numbness	Nightmares	Loss of faith in a higher power	Intolerance	Increased number and intensity of medical maladies	Lack of appreciation
Preoccupation with trauma	Fear	Appetite changes	Greater skepticism about religion	Loneliness	Other somatic complaints	Detachment
Thoughts of self-harm or harm to others	Helplessness	Hypervigilance		Increased interpersonal conflicts	Impaired immune system	Poor work skills and communication
	Sadness	Elevated startle response				Staff conflicts
	Depression	Accident proneness				Absenteeism
	Emotional roller coaster	Losing things				Exhaustion
	Depleted					
	Overly sensitive					Irritability
						Withdrawal from colleagues

Source: From *Treating Compassion Fatigue* (p. 7), by C. R. Figley, 2002, New York: Brunner-Routledge. Reprinted with permission of the author.

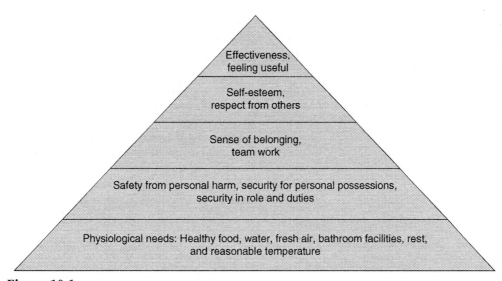

Figure 10.1
Hierarchy of Need of Crisis Responders, Based on Maslow's Model.
Source: Based *on Lifespan Development* (2nd ed.), by H. Bee, 1998, Boston, MA: Pearson/Allyn and Bacon.

but they need to be relieved of concerns about the security of their personal possessions, as illustrated in this example:

> We are in an urban school district with regional crisis teams who must drive in traffic and find parking spaces when they arrive at a school. In our first dry-runs years ago, we discovered a major cause of delay in responding: no parking spaces at the schools. That's when we instituted a system whereby responders would leave a placard on their dashboard and deposit their car keys in labeled envelopes with someone in the front office. This setup allowed them to park anywhere without fear of being towed. Now, we keep those envelopes and placards in our crisis kits. It was such a small thing, but it made a big difference.

Good crisis plans enhance our feelings of security because they increase our sense of control.

Third, crisis team refresher training builds a sense of belonging and community, as does learning about your own reactions to stress while getting to know your fellow responders (see the exercises in Chapter 3). Coming together after an incident improves a response and enhances teamwork for the next response. Unfortunately, this step often is dismissed in the hurried pace of school district life. Yet examining and evaluating our responses is essential if we are to build an empirically documented methodology for our work. This growth as professionals leads us to the next stage, producing self-esteem and respect from others.

Finally, knowing what to do enhances a responder's sense of effectiveness, as seen at the top of the hierarchy. School crisis responders engaged actively in crisis prevention and response evaluation (as outlined in Chapters 7 through 9) can reduce the guilt that contributes to ineffectiveness or burnout. As we become effective, we can mentor others, deriving satisfaction from our role as a mentor. Taken together, these professional practices

Table 10.2
Guidelines for Burnout Prevention Using VICTORY Mnemonic Device

VICTORY Guideline	Examples
Vary your routines for relief.	• "Routine has pluses—predictability, reliability and consistency. Habits can also be mind-numbing, however. Avoid getting into a rut. Recharge by altering habits occasionally. Vary the commute to work. Breathe fresh life into your daily habits." (Quinley, 2000)
Invite your colleagues for reward and recognition.	• Rebuild your sense of community through rituals and celebrations. • Seek the advice of others when you can't reach a kid or family. • Organize a "lesson study" or exchange helpful ideas, materials, and tips. • Take time at the beginning of your meetings to recognize one another. • Be a little silly!
Close those open energy circles (unfinished tasks) for results and relief.	• Be realistic about the time you have. • Pace yourself and your family by planning ahead for the hectic times. • Make lists! • Remember that your results may be in the distant future not today.
Tackle one of the six workplace risk factors with your colleagues for results, rewards, and recognition.	• Make burnout prevention a standing item on your agendas! • Remember that the process is more important than a "happy ending." The process reengages you and renews your support system at work.
Open up to your support system for relief, reward, and recognition.	• Spend time with your family and friends. Ask for help during hectic periods. • Resist the urge to blend work and home. • Find a professional listener! • Renew your spiritual supports. • Find the recognition you need in nonwork activities.
Recharge your batteries for relief, results, and recognition.	• Exercise! • Find recreation—a hobby. • Learn something new. • Ask colleagues about their life outside of work. • Sleep. • Drink water. • Use relaxation strategies. • Respect your personal limits. • Laugh!
You are not your job.	• Say "yes" less often. • Set noncareer goals. Write two or three nonprofessional goals or desires on a 3 × 5 card, carry it at all times, and look at it at least once a day.

protect us. Skovhold (2001) charges us to create a "professional greenhouse" at work, based on the protective factors cited by Maslach and Leiter (1997): leadership that pays attention to the well-being of the individuals and the team, a sense of community among peers, mentoring and being mentored, and having fun.

Let's reflect...

> If your district has a crisis team, can you identify ways in which the team is supported in its basic survival needs as well as its higher-order needs such as security and community? How could these supports be strengthened?

Personally, each of us must discover how to renew *ourselves* during and after a school crisis. Table 10.2 displays some suggestions taken from the literature on burnout and compassion fatigue. To help you remember these coping strategies, we use the acronym VICTORY. We use this term because (in the words of an unidentified astronaut after the *Challenger* shuttle accident), "Risk gives victory its meaning."

THE PARADOXICAL REWARDS OF CRISIS RESPONDING

Although risky, crisis responding rewards us. **Compassion satisfaction** is a term that describes this state of being able to work well and feel positively about our efforts (Stamm, 2005). Being present during a school's dark and confused hours can be transformational. Setting aside petty concerns for riveting moments of human connection, we recalibrate our own life's priorities. Initially alone in our fears, we find courage in the strength of survivors. Confronted with our own vulnerability and immortality, we search ourselves and discover unexpected abilities. In the words of Thoreau, "Not until we are lost do we begin to understand ourselves."

SUMMARY

Tragedies in schools require us to be present during hours of chaos, fear, and despair. Vulnerable school crisis responders must balance their needs with those of the school community in crisis. Work overload, loss of control, overwhelming and seemingly unfair demands, and insufficient rewards and relief foreshadow burnout and compassion fatigue. Fortunately, we can protect ourselves by engaging in thoughtful planning and preparation. We can ensure a balance when we pace ourselves, enjoy recreation, spend time with loved ones, and discover the rewards of rediscovering ourselves.

CASE STUDY CONCLUSION

To conclude our case study we share an article describing the reactions of responders to the crash of Flight 427, which fell from the sky in the early evening of September 8, 1994, taking with it all 132 passengers and crew.

The crash deeply affected many schools as they discovered that students, parents, and community members had perished. Moreover, students playing soccer outdoors on a school field and nearby community members witnessed the accident. Airline employees, many of whom lived only a few miles from the crash site and whose children attended local schools, were distraught and troubled by accusations of airline negligence.

Remarkably, surviving friends and family members found meaning in this tragedy by forming the Air Disaster Support League. This organization changed forever the way families are supported following an air disaster.

As you read this article, reflect on the symptoms of burnout and compassion fatigue. Then try to identify the hierarchy of supports offered to the responders.

Pitt Volunteers Contribute in Aftermath of Crash

Within minutes of the first reports of last Thursday's crash of USAir Flight 427 in Hopewell, University of Pittsburgh Medical Center (UPMC) faculty, staff and students began mobilizing to help comfort the living and identify the dead. Presbyterian-University Hospital emergency staff stood ready to begin treating an expected 60–70 injured survivors, only to learn soon after the crash that all 132 passengers had been killed...

Since Thursday night, Pitt psychiatrists, psychologists, radiologists, pathologists, social workers, dentists and other professionals and students—many of them volunteers, and most of them working unusually demanding shifts—have been at the crash sight, at Greater Pittsburgh International Airport, and at schools, hotels and other places where relatives and friends of victims are to be found.

A comprehensive list of Pitt personnel and students who have helped in the crash's aftermath is impossible to compile—partly because no one knows how many have served through disaster relief agencies such as the Salvation Army, and partly because some of the help isn't easily recognized as being crash-related.

Mary Margaret Kerr, director of school and community outreach for Western Psychiatric Institute and Clinic (WPIC), cited this example of unsung heroism: Weeks ago, staff from WPIC's Services for Teens at Risk (STAR) program had scheduled a training session at the Pitt Club for Sept. 9, the day after the crash. They had planned to discuss techniques of "postvention," or helping people to cope with tragedies. Knowing they would now be getting plenty of real-life experience in such counseling, the staff went ahead and met at the club with the idea that they would assign teams of counselors from there to travel throughout Allegheny County as needed.

To the STAR staff's surprise, Pitt Club personnel encouraged them to set up a dispatching center in club offices, provided telephones, and prepared box lunches in place of the scheduled sit-down meal. "For some of us, that was the only food we saw for the next 24 hours," Kerr said. "That kind of nurturance for people who are going out into very stressful work situations often goes unrecognized because people tend to focus on the relief workers, but what the Pitt Club people did for us also deserves recognition." Kerr said that some 20 STAR professionals have been working at various locations, including the airport and several public schools, to console victims' surviving family members and friends as well as distraught USAir employees.

Kerr said she began one day with a 7:30 A.M. visit to a public school and ended the day with an evening counseling session with the Upper St. Clair hockey team, whose members were mourning a teammate killed in the crash.

"Our task is to try to offer the survivors different ways to express their feelings," Kerr said. "Some of those ways are talking and listening. For younger children, who don't have the words for something like this, it may involve drawing or playing or using puppets to express themselves." Often, she said, parents and teachers ask STAR staff what to tell a child whose parent was killed in the crash. "More than telling them anything, we've found it's better to listen for what it is they need to say and ask," Kerr said. "With the children, the questions are often things like, When is Daddy coming back? With older survivors, the questions can be highly technical and related to the crash itself, or they can be comments about life after death. There's really a wide range, and it's been our experience that both adults and children are most comforted when they can take the lead." Kerr advised Pitt employees and students who feel untouched by the disaster to be patient with others on campus. "People who you're working with may have known someone on the flight, but they're not talking about it," she said. "The secretary who's typing your course syllabus may have lost a friend in that accident or may have stayed up all night with a child who's having nightmares." Nightmares about Flight 427 haven't been limited to children. Workers at the crash site have suffered a wide range of emotional and physical trauma, said Ed Marasco, clinical administrator of UPMC's Critical Incident Stress Debriefing (CISD) program...

"It's just total, almost unbelievable devastation," he said, noting that some Vietnam veterans volunteering at the site told him the Flight 427 carnage was more horrific than anything they had ever seen. "At the most basic level, we're looking for signs of fatigue in the relief workers," said Marasco. "They're wearing suits designed to keep them from being exposed to potential biohazards, and those suits get pretty hot. The terrain itself is rough. One of the things the CISD team does is encourage the rescue workers to make sure they get enough rest and enough to eat and drink. Frequently, people get focused on getting the job done and they forget to take care of their basic needs."... As for emotional needs, CISD staff talk with the workers before and after their shifts, trying to prepare them for the stresses they'll be encountering and listening as they recount their experiences. When debriefers see signs that particular relief workers aren't coping well (vomiting is one unsubtle sign; vacant facial expressions are another), they recommend that those workers be reassigned to less grisly jobs.

"What makes this (recovery) effort so hard for the relief workers is that there were no survivors," he pointed out. "The first firefighters and police who went out to the scene did so with the full expectation they were going to have the opportunity to do some good in a bad situation—only to realize very quickly that nobody survived the crash. That's very demoralizing for the rescue crews." Marasco recalled a recent airplane crash that only one little girl survived. "Even though she was the only survivor, she was a ray of hope for the emergency workers. With this crash, there's nothing." (From "Pitt Volunteers Contribute in Aftermath of Crash," by B. Steele, 1994, *University Times, 27* (2), Pittsburgh, PA: University of Pittsburgh. Reprinted in part with permission.)

DISCUSSION AND APPLICATION IDEAS

1. In your own words, give examples of *meaning burnout, caring burnout, vicarious traumatization,* and *secondary traumatic stress.*
2. How does the following summary of burnout align with the six risk factors (work overload, lack of control, sense of unfairness, insufficient rewards, values conflict, and loss of community) identified by Maslach and Leiter (1997): "If no matter what you say or what you do, Results, Rewards, Recognition and Relief are not forthcoming, and you can't [say] "no" or won't let go... trouble awaits" (Gorkin, n.d.).
3. Consider these stories from the field. As you read them, see if you can identify the six risk factors for burnout.

    *   "As a school counselor, I felt trapped. No matter how hard I worked, it was like nobody noticed. I never saw my principal unless there was a problem. Look, I didn't go into this for the money. But, hey, even I need to feel I am accomplishing something. The lines between work and home were nonexistent. I dealt with teenagers at work and then went home and did the same thing. The only way I could unwind was with a few drinks. Then I woke up tired in the morning and started the cycle all over again."

    *   "I had been so enthusiastic at the beginning of the year. I had such high hopes. But after six thankless months of teaching teenagers with behavioral problems in the high school and then volunteering for the crisis team, I was completely spent. I skipped lunch, rarely stopped to drink even a glass of water, and stayed late nearly every day. My friends never saw me, and I didn't have time to make friends at school. When an angry parent accused me of not helping her kid after a friend died in a car accident, I lost it—and nearly lost my job."

4. What would you say to a team member who showed signs of burnout or compassion fatigue?
5. Can you rewrite your story from the field? What steps can you take to do the following:
   - Build community at work?
   - Explore something new outside work?
   - Close those circles and enjoy that energy?
   - Take better care of your health?

REFERENCES

Auger, R. W., Seymour, J. W., & Roberts, W. B. (2004). Responding to terror: The impact of September 11 on K–12 schools and schools' responses. *Professional School Counseling, 7* (4), 222–231.

Figley, C. R. (1995). Compassion fatigue: Toward a new understanding of the costs of caring. In B. H. Stamm (Ed.), *Secondary traumatic stress: Self-care issues for clinicians, researchers, and educators* (pp. 3–28). Lutherville, MD: Sidran Press.

Gift from Within. (2006). *When helping hurts: Sustaining trauma workers* (Video). Available at http://www.giftfromwithin.org/

Gorkin, M. (n.d.). *The four stages of burnout.* Retrieved December 22, 2006, from http://www.stressdoc. com/4stages.htm

Maslach, C., & Leiter, M. (1997). *The truth about burnout: How organizations cause personal stress and what to do about it.* San Francisco, CA: Jossey-Bass.

McCann, I. L., & Pearlman, L. A. (1990). Vicarious traumatization: A framework for understanding the psychological effects of working with victims. *Journal of Traumatic Stress, 3,* 131–149.

National Institute for Occupational Safety and Health. (2002). *Working with stress* (DHHS [NIOSH] Publication No. 2003-114d). Atlanta, GA: Author.

Ochberg, F. (n.d.). *When helping hurts.* Retrieved October 16, 2007, from http://www.giftfromwithin. org/helping.html/

Quinley, K. M. (2000, April 1). Battling the burnout. *Risk and Insurance.*

Skovholt, T. M. (2001). *The resilient practitioner: Burnout prevention and self-care strategies.* Boston, MA: Allyn & Bacon.

Stamm, B. H. (2005). *The professional quality of life scale: Compassion satisfaction, burnout & compassion fatigue/secondary trauma scales.* Institute of Rural Health, Idaho State University. Retrieved October 16, 2007, from http://www.isu.edu/~bhstamm

Steele, B. (1994, September, 15). Pitt volunteers contribute in aftermath of crash. *University of Pittsburgh University Times, 27* (2), 1, 4.

NAME INDEX